EDITED BY LEONARD HOLLIS

The
Rose
Annual
1969

THE ROYAL NATIONAL
ROSE SOCIETY

Copyright © 1969 Leonard Hollis
Published by
THE ROYAL NATIONAL ROSE SOCIETY
Bone Hill, Chiswell Green Lane, St Albans, Hertfordshire
Telephone: St Albans 50461. *Telegrams:* Natiorose, St Albans
Printed and bound in England by
Hazell Watson and Viney Limited
Aylesbury, Buckinghamshire
Illustrations printed by
Clarke & Sherwell Limited
Northampton

'MOLLY McGREDY' (floribunda—H.T. type)
'Paddy McGredy' × (*'Mme Léon Cuny'* × *'Columbine'*)
Raised by S. McGredy IV, N. Ireland.
PRESIDENT'S INTERNATIONAL TROPHY AND GOLD MEDAL 1968
See page 183

Contents

CONTENTS
5

THE ROYAL NATIONAL ROSE SOCIETY

(founded 7th December, 1876)

COMMITTEES FOR 1969

PRESIDENTS OF THE
ROYAL NATIONAL ROSE SOCIETY

1877–1904 The Very Rev. DEAN HOLE, v.m.h.

1905–06 CHARLES E. SHEA
1907–08 E. B. LINDSELL
1909–10 Rev. F. PAGE-ROBERTS
1911–12 Rev. J. H. PEMBERTON
1913–14 CHARLES E. SHEA
1915–16 EDWARD MAWLEY, v.m.h.
1917–18 Sir EDWARD HOLLAND
1919–20 H. R. DARLINGTON, v.m.h.
1921–22 Sir EDWARD HOLLAND
1923–24 SYDNEY F. JACKSON
1925–26 C. C. WILLIAMSON
1927–28 H. R. DARLINGTON, v.m.h.
1929–30 ARTHUR JOHNSON
1931–32 HERBERT OPPENHEIMER
1933–34 Dr. A. H. WILLIAMS
1935–36 Major A. D. G. SHELLEY, r.e.
1937–38 HERBERT OPPENHEIMER
1939–40 JOHN N. HART, c.b.e.

1941–42 CHARLES H. RIGG
1943–44 HERBERT OPPENHEIMER
1945–46 A. NORMAN ROGERS
1947–48 A. E. GRIFFITH
1949–50 E. J. BALDWIN, o.b.e.
1951–52 D. L. FLEXMAN
1953–54 WILLIAM E. MOORE
1955–56 OLIVER MEE, o.b.e.
1957–58 A. NORMAN
1959–60 F. FAIRBROTHER, m.sc., f.r.i.c.
1961–62 E. ROYALTON KISCH, m.c.
1963–64 Maj.-Gen. R. F. B. NAYLOR, c.b.,
          c.b.e., d.s.o., m.c.
1965–66 F. A. GIBSON
1967–68 Maj.-Gen. R. F. B. NAYLOR, c.b.,
          c.b.e., d.s.o., m.c.
1969   JOHN CLARKE

THE QUEEN MARY COMMEMORATION
MEDAL AWARDS

1957 ALEX. DICKSON & SONS
1957 SAMUEL McGREDY & SON
1957 E. B. Le GRICE
1957 HERBERT ROBINSON, m.b.e.

1957 OLIVER MEE, o.b.e.
1957 A. NORMAN
1964 BERTRAM PARK, o.b.e., v.m.h.

THE DEAN HOLE MEDAL AWARDS

1904 The Very Rev. DEAN HOLE, v.m.h.
1906 CHARLES E. SHEA
1908 E. B. LINDSELL
1910 Rev. F. PAGE-ROBERTS
1912 Rev. J. H. PEMBERTON
1912 GEORGE DICKSON, v.m.h.
1916 EDWARD MAWLEY, v.m.h.
1918 Sir EDWARD HOLLAND
1919 GEORGE PAUL
1920 H. R. DARLINGTON, v.m.h.
1921 SAMUEL McGREDY
1923 Miss E. WILLMOTT, f.l.s.
1924 SYDNEY F. JACKSON
1925 COURTNEY PAGE
1926 C. C. WILLIAMSON
1930 ARTHUR JOHNSON
1930 Dr J. CAMPBELL HALL
1930 WILLIAM E. NICKERSON
1932 HERBERT OPPENHEIMER
1934 Dr A. H. WILLIAMS
1935 WALTER EASLEA
1936 Major A. D. G. SHELLEY, r.e.
1936 ALISTER CLARK
1940 JOHN N. HART, c.b.e.
1942 CHARLES H. RIGG
1942 Dr HORACE J. McFARLAND
1945 Dr H. V. TAYLOR, c.b.e.
1946 A. NORMAN ROGERS

1948 A. E. GRIFFITH
1948 WILLIAM E. MOORE
1948 Dr G. E. DEACON
1950 E. J. BALDWIN, o.b.e.
1950 JOHN RAMSBOTTOM, o.b.e., m.a.,
        Dr.sc.
1951 F. S. HARVEY-CANT, m.b.e.
1952 BERTRAM PARK, o.b.e., v.m.h.,
        Mérite Agri.
1952 D. L. FLEXMAN
1952 Dr A. S. THOMAS, o.b.e., v.m.a.
1954 W. E. HARKNESS
1956 OLIVER MEE, o.b.e.
1958 A. NORMAN
1959 W. J. W. SANDAY
1960 F. FAIRBROTHER, m.sc., f.r.i.c.
1962 H. G. CLACY
1963 E. ROYALTON KISCH, m.c.
1964 G. D. BURCH
1965 Maj.-Gen. R. F. B. NAYLOR, c.b.,
        c.b.e., d.s.o., m.c.
1965 H. EDLAND
1965 E. BAINES
1966 EDGAR M. ALLEN, c.m.g.
1967 F. A. GIBSON
1967 ALEX. DICKSON
1967 W. KORDES

8

Arrangements 1969

Amateur Spring Competition *29th and 30th April*

The Amateur Spring Competition for roses under glass is to be held in conjunction with the Flower Show at the Royal Horticultural Society's Halls, Westminster. By courtesy of the Royal Horticultural Society, members will be admitted to both Halls on presentation of their Membership Certificates. Payment for accompanying visitors may be made at the turnstile.

Summer Show *27th and 28th June*

The Summer Show is to be held at the Alexandra Palace, London, N.22 and will occupy the Great Hall and Palm Court for both days.

Northern Show *18th and 19th July*

The Northern Show is to be held in conjunction with the Roundhay (Leeds) Horticultural Society at Roundhay Park, Leeds. Members will be admitted on presentation of their Certificate of Membership. Holders of the Guinea certificate may be accompanied by one other person. Members should note that the Show is to be held on Friday and Saturday and not on Tuesday and Wednesday as in the past.

Autumn Show *12th and 13th September*

The Autumn Show is to be held in the Royal Horticultural Society's Halls, Westminster, and will occupy both New and Old Halls for the two days.

Schedules for these Shows are available on request to The Secretary, The Royal National Rose Society, Chiswell Green Lane, St. Albans.

Admission Tickets

One-Guinea Subscribers will receive a Certificate of Membership, which will admit the holder to all the Shows listed thereon, five transferable tickets for the Summer Show and three transferable tickets for the Autumn Show.

Half-Guinea Subscribers will receive a Certificate of Membership, which will admit the holder to all the Shows listed thereon, one transferable ticket for the Summer Show and one transferable ticket for the Autumn Show.

Prices of admission to the Public will be:

Summer Show 27 June Noon to 5 p.m. 10s., 5 p.m. to 8 p.m. 5s.
28 June 10 a.m. to 5 p.m. 5s.

Autumn Show 12 September 11 a.m. to 7 p.m. 5s.
13 September 10 a.m. to 5 p.m. 2s. 6d.

Members may purchase additional tickets for the Summer and Autumn Shows at half price. Applications accompanied by remittances must be received at the Society's Office not less than three days before the respective show.

Northern Show 18 July 11 a.m. to 3 p.m. 12s. 6d., 3 p.m. to 6 p.m. 7s. 6d. After 6 p.m. 5s.
19 July 9 a.m. to 4 p.m. 5s., after 4 p.m. 3s. 6d.

No price reductions for adults are granted at the Northern Show, but children under fourteen years of age will be admitted for 2s. 6d.

R.N.R.S. Classes at Provincial Shows and Admission Arrangements

By the courtesy of the organizers of the following Shows, members of the Royal National Rose Society are offered special concessions in respect of exhibiting and free admission which the Council acknowledges with thanks. Unless indicated by an asterisk both concessions will apply. Details of the Shows offering free admission to R.N.R.S. members are given on the Membership Certificate:

Alderley Edge and Wilmslow Horticultural and Rose Society's Show on 12 July

Ashington Rose Society's Show on 2 August.

Berwick-upon-Tweed and District Rose Society's Show on 27 July.

★*Bexleyheath & District Rose Society's Show* on 21 June. (No R.N.R.S. classes.)

Bramhall, Cheadle Hulme and Woodford Agricultural and Horticultural Society's Show on 16 August.

Bristol and District Group of R.N.R.S. Members' Show on 2 July.

Bryndorion (Swansea) and District Rose Society's Show on 28 June.

★*Caledonian (Royal) Horticultural Society's Show* at the Waverley Market, Edinburgh on 17 and 18 September (12 noon to 10 p.m. and 10 a.m. to 9 p.m.) J. Turnbull, 44 Melville Street, Edinburgh, 3. (No free admission to Show, but R.N.R.S. Classes exempt from entry fee.)

Cardiff and District Group of R.N.R.S. Members' Show on 28 June.

Clontarf Horticultural Society's Show on 28 June.

Colchester Rose and Horticultural Society's Show on 5 July.

Congleton & District Horticultural Society's Show on 12 July and 30 August.

Eastleigh and District Rose, Carnation and Sweet Pea Society's Show on 5 July.

Formby Horticultural and Agricultural Society's Show on 12 July.

Franche (Kidderminster) and District Rose Society's Show on 21 June.

Glamorgan (Vale of) Agricultural Society's Show on 20 August.

Heart of England Summer Show on 19 and 20 July.

Hereford and West of England Rose Society's Show on 5 July.

★*Hitchin Horticultural Society's Show* on 5 July. (No R.N.R.S. classes.)

Ipswich and East of England Horticultural Society's Show on 12 July.

Isle of Wight Rose, Carnation and Sweet Pea Association's Show on 28 June.

Lakeland Rose Show on 4 and 5 July.

Leicester and Leicestershire Rose Society's Show on 26 and 27 July.

Manx Rose Society's Show on 12 and 13 July.

North of England Rose, Carnation and Sweet Pea Society's Show on 15 and 16 August.

Nottingham Rose Society's Show on 12 and 13 July.

Reading Horticultural Federation's Show on 22 and 23 August.

Scottish National Sweet Pea, Rose and Carnation Society's Show on 7 and 8 August.

Southampton (Royal) Horticultural Society's Show on 11 and 12 July.

★*Southport Flower Show* in Victoria Park, Southport on 27, 28 and 29 August (10 a.m. to 9 p.m., 9 a.m. to 9 p.m. and 9 a.m. to 6 p.m.) Colonel J. S. Rees, Flower Show Department, Lord Street, Southport, Lancs. (R.N.R.S. Classes but *not* free admission.)

West Cumberland Rose Society's Show on 12 July.

West Midlands Rose Society's Show on 4 and 6 July.

Please note that the Certificate of Membership does not admit to the Southport Flower Show, The Royal Caledonian Horticultural Society's Show or any other Show not listed.

Display Gardens

Members and their friends are cordially invited to visit the displays of rose varieties that have received awards provided at:

Cardiff—Roath Park
Edinburgh—Saughton Park
*Harrogate—Northern Horticultural Society's Gardens, Harlow Car.
Southport—Botanic Gardens.
Taunton—Vivary Park.

* At Harlow Car the rose displays occupy a small portion of the ground only and it is hoped that visitors will each be willing to contribute a donation of two shillings towards general upkeep.

International Conference – 1971

The First World Convention of National Rose Societies will be held in Hamilton, New Zealand, 1–6 November, 1971. If sufficient members are interested it is hoped to arrange a charter party. The tour will last approximately 19 days allowing 14 days in New Zealand. A full itinerary for the whole period could be organized, or members may prefer to make their own arrangements. Preliminary enquiries indicate that, provided 150 members participate, the return fare would be approximately £320.

Those members who attended the London Conference in 1968 will recall the unbounded enthusiasm and friendliness of the New Zealand contingent. We can be assured of a warm and hospitable welcome from our hosts, and an interesting and enjoyable tour of their beautiful country.

Undoubtedly many will wish to take advantage of this opportunity to visit New Zealand, but until definite interest is shown no further action can be taken. Application for a preliminary booking form must be made to the Secretary before 30 June, 1969.

Lecture Aids

It is regretted that no lecture equipment may be borrowed for private viewing.

Film
"Focus on the Rose" is the title of the new 16-mm. colour film with sound track. It is loaded on two spools and runs for 1 hour 17 minutes. Every aspect of rose cultivation is covered and also included are beautiful views of the Society's Garden at St Albans and shots of the Summer Show at Alexandra Palace, London.

It is available for hire by members and Affiliated Societies for lecture purposes subject to the following conditions:

1. Borrowers shall pay a hire charge of £3 at the time of booking. The fee includes outward carriage.

2. The booking form and indemnity must be signed before any reservation is made.

3. A first-class sound projector and experienced operator must be employed for the screening.

4. A spare take-up spool and can will be provided, and these must be returned with the film.

5. The film must not be re-wound after screening.

6. Any damage must be reported on the "Damage Report" accompanying the film. Under no circumstances should any attempt be made to repair a break.
The film must not be screened on a silent projector.
A charge of £1 per day will be made for each day the film is retained after the day following the screening.

Slides
There are sets of slides available covering:
  General cultivation
  Bed preparation and planting
  Varieties with historical connections
  Modern varieties
  The Evolution of the Rose – a set prepared by Gordon Rowley of Reading University.

Film Strip
This is in two parts:
  Preparation of the soil and planting – 36 frames
  Rose pruning – 37 frames
Full details of all equipment and booking form may be obtained from the Secretary.

Library
The library at St Albans contains a comprehensive collection of books on rose growing and is open to members during office hours (Monday to Friday, 9 a.m. to 5 p.m.) Alternatively, books (not more than two at one time) will be despatched by post, subject to postage being paid by the borrower. A list of books available will be sent on application.

Extra Copies of Publications
Members may purchase copies post free of *The Rose Annual* for 1969, price 8s. 6d.; the handbooks *Roses: A Selected List of Varieties*, price 5s., and *Roses: The Cultivation of the Rose*, price 5s., on application to the Secretary.

Society Tie
The Society tie, made in good quality terylene and bearing a single motif of the Tudor rose on a plain background, is available at 15s. 6d. each, three for 45s. Choice of maroon, navy blue, rifle green, medium grey, dark brown, moss green or bronze background.

Badges
A membership Badge is available. Price 6s. each for Stud or Brooch fitting.

Views of Gardens
Postcard views of the gardens, price 6d. each may be purchased from the office.

The American Rose Society
An arrangement has been made whereby members resident in Great Britain may join the American Rose Society by remitting their subscriptions of £3 7s. 6d. to The Secretary, The Royal National Rose Society, Chiswell Green Lane, St. Albans, Herts.

Subscriptions and Resignations
Members are reminded that subscriptions are due and payable on 1 January each year. Any member wishing to resign must give notice to the Secretary on or before 1 February, after which date the member will be liable for the subscription for the current year.

It was unanimously confirmed at the Annual General Meeting that the minimum annual subscription be increased to £1. The revised rate will apply to all new members enrolled after 1 February, 1969 and to all existing members from 1 January, 1970.

Admission Tickets for 1970 Shows (Advance Notice)
The number of tickets to be issued to all members for the Summer and Autumn Shows for 1970 onwards will be:
  2 transferable tickets for the Summer Show
  2 transferable tickets for the Autumn Show.
The Certificate of Membership will admit the holder to the above shows and the holder and one friend to the gardens at Bone Hill.

The Society's Gardens

The Society's Gardens at St Albans are provided for the enjoyment of members and their friends. They are divided into two sections, the Trial Ground and Display Garden.

THE TRIAL GROUND is for new seedlings where some 750 varieties may be seen undergoing trials. Varieties are submitted before being introduced into commerce and for this reason the majority will be under number. Adjudication is carried out by the New Seedling Judging Committee and varieties are eligible for the Society's Gold Medal, Certificate of Merit and Trial Ground Certificate awards. The President's International Trophy is awarded annually to the best seedling and the Henry Edland Memorial Medal to the most fragrant variety on trial.

THE DISPLAY GARDEN occupies approximately six acres of the ground and in this section more than 450 named varieties will be found.

How to Get to the Gardens

The Gardens are situated approximately four miles from St Albans Station and are off the main Watford Road (A412). Visitors using public transport may travel by the following routes:

British Railways to St Albans City Station—London terminus St Pancras or Underground (Bakerloo Line) to Watford, and thence by No. 321 bus which runs between Watford Junction and St Peter's Street, St Albans.

Green Line coach No. 712 Luton—London (Victoria)—Dorking. No. 724 Romford—St Albans—High Wycombe. Also routes 713 Dorking—London (Victoria)—Dunstable and 714 Dorking—London (Hyde Park Corner)—Luton to St Albans centre and thence by bus No. 321 or 361.

The fare stage at which to alight from bus or coach is The Three Hammers Inn, Chiswell Green. The gardens are half a mile along Chiswell Green Lane which is adjacent to the inn.

Visiting Arrangements for 1969

The Gardens will be open from Saturday, 14 June to Saturday, 27 September, at the following times:

Monday to Friday	9 a.m. to 5 p.m.
Saturday	9 a.m. to 6 p.m.
Sunday	2 p.m. to 6 p.m.

The Gardens will be closed on Monday, 1 September. Members wishing to see the Gardens before 14 June may do so from Monday to Friday only.

Terms of Admission

(Membership Certificates to be shown at turnstiles)

One-Guinea Membership Certificate will admit the holder and two guests free of charge and three additional persons on payment.

Half-Guinea Membership Certificate will admit the holder free of charge and five additional persons on payment.

Affiliated Society Certificate will admit two persons free of charge and five additional persons on payment.

Affiliated Societies may arrange for a party to visit the Gardens each year. Applications must be made in writing to the Secretary at least fourteen days beforehand, stating the number in the party and the proposed date and time of the visit. Holders of Certificates and accompanying guests as specified above will be admitted free of charge. Members of the party not covered by such certificates will be admitted on payment.

Price of admission to persons accompanied by a member or in the party of an affiliated society, but not covered by certificate, is 2s. each.

The Gardens are not open to the public.

Refreshments

There is no restaurant within the Gardens. A Visitors' Lounge is provided where cups of tea and biscuits may be obtained from 1 p.m. on Saturdays and on Sundays. Soft drinks are available at all times.

Picnics are not allowed in any part of the Gardens.

The Three Hammers Inn, Watford Road (half a mile from the Gardens) provides luncheons from Monday to Saturday.

Car Park

A car park is provided but the Council accepts no responsibility for loss or damage to property or vehicles.

It is regretted that coaches cannot be accommodated in the car park or Grounds.

Disabled or Invalid Members

Two wheel chairs (not self-propelled) are available for the convenience of disabled members. Visitors desirous of using these should apply in advance.

Guides

An alphabetical list of varieties, giving their location in the Display Garden, may be obtained at the turnstile.

Photography

Amateur photographers may use cameras in the Gardens but photographs or transparencies must not be used commercially. Professional photographers must obtain written authority from the Secretary.

General Regulations

Dogs must be kept on a leash at all times.

Entry and exit shall be through the respective turnstiles.

Rose blooms, buds, trees or parts of trees must not in any circumstances be cut, removed or taken from the Grounds.

'DUKE OF WINDSOR' (H.T.)
'Prima Ballerina' × *unnamed seedling*
Raised by M. Tantau, Germany
HENRY EDLAND MEMORIAL MEDAL AND CERTIFICATE OF MERIT 1968
See page 184

'COPPER POT' (floribunda)
Seedling × *'Spek's Yellow'*
Raised by Alex. Dickson & Sons Ltd, N. Ireland
TRIAL GROUND CERTIFICATE 1968
See page 184

Report of the Council

For the year ended 31st December 1968

Membership

The nett increase in membership, although slightly below that of 1967, remains gratifying.

During 1968 15,000 new members were enrolled, and after the customary deductions due to deaths, resignations and lapsed subscriptions the total membership is 118,450.

Council thanks everyone and especially the Rose trade, who have contributed to this satisfactory outcome of a difficult year.

Attention is drawn to the high cost of sending reminders to members who do not renew their subscriptions promptly. Several thousand have to be sent as many as five times, thus incurring an extra heavy postage bill.

Finance

Much thought has been given to the many problems stemming from the ever increasing costs. At the Annual General Meeting an amendment to rule 4 providing for a single tier subscription of £1 per annum will be presented, which it is hoped will be accepted by all members as a reasonable solution.

Conference

The outstanding event of the year was the International Rose Conference held in London, the theme of which was The Modern Development of the Rose. Speakers came from many parts of the world and visitors attended from fifteen countries, including large parties from America and New Zealand.

With the gracious permission of Her Majesty the Queen an afternoon Reception was held in St James's Palace for delegates from overseas which our Royal Patron Her Majesty Queen Elizabeth The Queen Mother honoured with her presence. This proved a memorable occasion for all those privileged to attend.

Publications

The Rose Annual was published in March and the Hon. Editor is to be congratulated on the high standard of production maintained.

A new edition of "Roses: The Cultivation of the Rose" is in course of preparation and should be available in July for members requiring a copy.

The Trial Ground and Display Garden

Over 250 varieties were received for trial and planted in the new trial area. The New Seedling Judging Committee inspected the trees throughout the season and awards were made at the end of September. The President's Trophy and a Gold Medal were awarded to S. McGredy & Son Ltd, for 'Molly McGredy' and the Henry Edland Memorial Medal and a Certificate of Merit to M. Tantau for the variety 'Duke of Windsor'.

There are now 182 varieties in the collection maintained for Plant Variety Rights. The alterations in the Display Garden commenced last year have been completed. The pergola and pond have been much admired by many visitors.

Further developments of the overall plans are continuing.

Shows

The Amateur Spring Competition was held at the Royal Horticultural Society's Hall on 30 April and 1 May.

Torrential rain on the first day of the Summer Show at Alexandra Palace reduced considerably the attendance. Trade and amateur exhibits were of a high standard. The special exhibit staged by eight affiliated societies, each using roses raised in a particular country, proved a popular centrepiece. The exhibit of the Genus Rosa ably staged by Mr & Mrs F. Fairbrother and Mr & Mrs E. F. Allen attracted much attention, and deservedly earned great commendation.

The Northern Show was held in co-operation with the Roundhay (Leeds) Horticultural Society. Although the exhibits were very good the incessant rain preceding and during the Show had a serious effect on the attendance.

By the time of the Autumn Show at Westminster the weather had temporarily improved and this was reflected in the quality of exhibits and attendance.

The National Championship was won by Mr L. Poole of Cardiff. This was the first occasion on which points secured at all three Shows contributed to the final result.

Research

The Council has extended its contribution to research by granting £250 per annum for a period of three years to Bangor University to assist their work on rose seed germination and dormancy.

Provincial Display Gardens

Additional displays have been planted at Southport and Taunton.

There are now five such display gardens—at Cardiff, Edinburgh, Harrogate, Southport and Taunton. Here are to be seen varieties which have received awards at Bone Hill growing under local conditions—and is a service much appreciated. The Council is grateful to the Public Parks concerned and the Northern Horticultural Society for maintaining them so well.

It is the ambition of Council to give consideration to further extension of this scheme.

Bureaux, Library and Lecturing Material

Bureaux were staged at Chelsea, Southport, the Northern and London Shows. Local groups and affiliated societies have displayed publicity exhibits and provided facilities for the registration of new members. The Council is grateful to all who have helped in this way.

The premiere of the new 16 mm. colour film "Focus on the Rose" took place at the Hilton Hotel during the Conference. Bookings for the film and also for slides are heavy and applications should be submitted at least two months before the date required.

The library service is in constant use. Borrowers are reminded that they must pay postage in both directions.

Federation of National Rose Societies

The formation of a Federation of National Rose Societies was proposed at a meeting of representatives from overseas societies attending the 4th International Rose Conference. The aims of the Federation will be:

To co-ordinate any activities of an international character which have as their object the development and knowledge of the Rose. To disseminate information of a scientific or cultural nature. To regulate and standardise as far as may be possible in the light of differing national needs such matters as classification and nomenclature and to co-operate in all matters pertaining to Conferences and other International meetings or Assemblies.

Membership will be open to all recognised National Rose Societies.

The Council has agreed to participate and has accepted responsibility for the Secretariat for the first three years. The next Conference will be held in New Zealand during November 1971.

Hon. Vice-President

D. S. Butcher, President of the National Rose Society of New Zealand and leader of the New Zealand party attending the Conference, was elected Hon. Vice-President of the Society in recognition of the work he is doing on behalf of the rose in New Zealand.

Dean Hole Medal

The Dean Hole Medal awarded last year to Mr Alex Dickson was presented to him by the President at the Banquet that terminated the Conference. Herr Wilhelm Kordes was unfortunately unable, due to ill health, to be present to receive the medal awarded to him; it was presented in his absence to his son Herr Reimer Kordes.

Obituary

It is with deep regret Council announces the deaths during the year of Herbert Oppenheimer, D.H.M. and of William C. Thorn. Mr Oppenheimer was president in 1931–32, 1937–38 and 1943–44, an outstanding record. He was the leading exhibitor at the Spring Shows in pre-war years and wrote many articles for the Rose Annual on growing roses under glass. Mr Thorn, a Vice-President, was a most energetic member of the Editorial Board and Exhibitions Committee until his death. His vast experience and knowledge were always freely given to the Society. His last great work was as Chairman of the committee responsible for the production of the new film "Focus on the Rose".

Conclusion

In conclusion the Council desires to express its thanks to all Committee members, the Hon. Editor, the Secretary and staff at Bone Hill for their work during the year.

By order of Council,

R. F. B. NAYLOR

BALANCE SHEET, 30th SEPTEMBER, 1968

Liabilities

1967 £		£	£
	SURPLUS		
77,375	Balance 1st October 1967 ..	77,375	
	Add Excess of Revenue over Expenditure for the year ended 30th September, 1968 ..	526	
			77,901
	SPECIAL FUNDS		
	P. P. Gaskill Prize Fund ..	100	
	L. Hewlett Prize Fund ..	100	
	A. E. Griffith Memorial Fund ..	100	
	Gilbert Burch Memorial Fund ..	100	
400			400
	RESERVE FOR DEVELOPMENT—TRIAL GROUND DISPLAY GARDEN AND PROPERTIES		
	Balance 1st October, 1967 ..	16,000	
	Add Charge against Revenue Account ..	4,870	
		20,870	
	Less Expenditure during year ..	5,870	
16,000			15,000
	RESERVE FOR NEW EDITIONS OF PUBLICATIONS FILM AND CONFERENCE		
	Balance 1st October, 1967 ..	13,000	
	Add Charge against Revenue Account ..	5,594	
		18,594	
	Less Expenditure during year on Film and Conference (net) ..	5,594	
13,000			13,000
	RESERVE FOR PENSIONS		
12,000	Balance I October 1967 ..	12,000	12,000
	CURRENT LIABILITIES		
7,793	Sundry Creditors ..	5,594	
22,819	Subscriptions received in advance and one quarter of 1968 subscriptions (excluding Life Members)	23,485	
			29,079
149,387			147,380

Assets

1967 £		£	£
	FIXED ASSETS		
37,000	Freehold Properties ..		37,000
	Alterations to Bone Hill:		
	Balance I October 1967..	2,250	
2,250	Less Amount written off ..	2,250	—
	Office Equipment, etc.		
	Balance I October 1967..	2,600	
	Additions during the year	338	
		2,938	
	Less Amount written off	538	
2,600			2,400
	Motor Vehicles, Mower and Equipment:		
	Balance I October 1967..	1,200	
	Additions during the year	915	
		2,115	
	Less Amount written off	515	
1,600			1,600
1,650	Library at Professional Valuation (1967) ..		1,650
	INVESTMENTS AT COST		
44,700			42,650
89,931	(Market Value 30 September 1968 (£82,214) ..		74,431
(89,048)			
	CURRENT ASSETS		
2,266	Stock of Publications, Badges, etc. as valued by the Secretary ..	2,710	
1,485	Sundry Debtors for Advertisement, etc. ..	1,083	
8,913	Cash at Bankers on Deposit and Current Account and in Hand ..	23,826	
2,092	Income Tax Recoverable ..	2,680	
			30,299
149,387			147,380

18

REVENUE ACCOUNT FOR THE YEAR ENDED 30th SEPTEMBER, 1968

Expenditure

1966/67 £	£	£	£	Particulars
				PUBLICATIONS
29,351		25,306		Expenditure
499	434			Less Sales
3,728	3,636	4,070		Advertising Revenue
25,124			21,236	
				SHOWS
4,249	3,639			Prize Monies, Medals and Plate
3,820	4,842			Expenses
8,069		8,481		
762		709		Less Proceeds
7,307			7,772	
5,999			8,519	**TRIAL GROUND AND DISPLAY GARDEN**
				ADMINISTRATION
11,766	12,195			Salaries and Assistance, Superannuation Contributions & Supplementary Pensions
1,104	1,323			Rates, Lighting, Heating, etc.
3,515	3,721			Printing and Stationery
9,562	7,985			Postages
1,907	1,337			General Expenses, Telephone, Hire of Rooms, etc.
478	472			Repairs and Renewals—office and premises
250	300			Auditors' Fee
776	785			Bank Charges
29,358			28,118	
4,148			3,772	ADVERTISING AND PUBLICITY
386			497	PRESENTATION ROSES INCLUDING PROVINCIAL DISPLAYS
—			1,050	GRANTS TO UNIVERSITIES FOR RESEARCH
888			5,594	RESERVE FOR NEW EDITIONS OF PUBLICATIONS, FILM AND CONFERENCE
2,914			2,250	ALTERATIONS TO BONE HILL—Amount written off
—			4,870	RESERVE FOR DEVELOPMENT—TRIAL GROUND, DISPLAY GARDENS AND PROPERTIES
472			515	MOTOR VEHICLES, MOWER AND EQUIPMENT—Amount written off
584			538	OFFICE EQUIPMENT—Amount written off
77,090			84,731	
5,232			526	BALANCE—Excess of Revenue over Expenditure for the year
82,322			85,257	

Income

1966/67 £	£	£	Particulars
			SUBSCRIPTIONS AND AFFILIATION FEES
75,080	77,593		Subscriptions
967	1,025		Affiliation Fees
76,047		78,618	
6,275		6,639	**INCOME FROM INVESTMENTS, ETC.** — Gross
82,322		85,257	

The President's Page

In writing these few words to you as President of the Society I do so conscious of the high honour which has been bestowed upon me by election to this office, and it will be my endeavour to serve the Society in every way possible during the next two years.

This will be a year of transition from the financial point of view in that, for the first time in this Century, the subscriptions will be based on the single figure of £1 for all new members, and this will also apply to existing members as from 1 January 1970. It is my sincere hope and belief that the majority of our members will accept this change as a reasonable and fair solution to the problems with which the Society has been faced, and in an increasing degree, for some years.

The highlight of last year was undoubtedly the International Rose Conference.

Looking to the future there is much work to be done to continue the progress which has been such an outstanding feature of our activities for many years.

It is hoped to complete the work already begun on the question of colour.

The development and planning of Bone Hill continues, and further progress will be seen by all visitors. This—our headquarters—should be visited by many more members—it is fast becoming one of the finest rose gardens in the country.

Some closer co-operation with our Affiliated Societies will take place, and consideration will be given to the establishment of additional Display Gardens in the Provinces.

I welcome especially all our new members and hope that they derive lasting pleasure and profit, and make many friends by their association with us.

All in all I look forward to the future with great confidence, and I wish all our members good weather and good rose growing.

J. CLARKE

John Clarke
President 1969 – 70

Feeding Roses for Garden Display

R. L. PALLETT

A year ago, for the 1968 Annual, I put together a few ideas on the subject of mulching roses. This year I am trying to give my views, arising from my own and other peoples' experience, on feeding roses. I am not addressing my remarks to the many successful exhibitors among us but rather to the far greater number of our members who grow roses for their own delight, for cutting for the house and for garden display for all who see them to enjoy.

Some forty-five years ago, when I first had a garden of my own, the motor car, although it had already "arrived", still shared the roads with a good many horsedrawn vehicles. As an ardent beginner, I kept a fire shovel handy and a few excursions into the road at the right moment produced enough manure to provide a regular feed for my half dozen roses. At that time rivalry was not confined to the showing of the rose. It was also displayed in the speed at which the shovel was produced and the precious deposits collected before one's neighbour took similar action.

Dean Hole, of blessed memory, writing in 1896 in his "classic" *A Book About Roses*, says that "in a heap of farmyard manure was to be found the mine of gold medals and silver cups for the grower of prize roses."

How true, but how the position has changed! Few, now, can obtain stable manure in quantity and at reasonable prices. Cow and farmyard manure is still obtainable in dairy farming country districts, but cost of transport and facilities for storing make it a difficult commodity to use in towns and built-up areas. Where it is obtainable I am quite satisfied that very little more food is required by roses which are regularly mulched with it. A friend, now in his eighties, still a keen rosarian, who grows grand roses for display and cutting, tells me that for nearly forty years his garden has received an annual dressing of animal manure and nothing else whatever.

The fact is, however, that most gardeners now have to manage without this valuable commodity. What, then, is to be done by way of supplying the roses with their basic needs and that little extra which enables them to give the magnificent and prolonged display of which they, surely more than any other flower, are capable.

We read—*ad nauseam*—that the essential minerals required for plant life are N., P. and K.—Nitrogen, Phosphate and Potash, plus a number, about ten, of trace elements. Before enlarging on these chemical essentials it must be stressed that another essential, the physical condition of the soil must be attended to before any real benefit from fertilisers can be obtained. This article is not concerned with the preparation of rose beds and it is assumed that this most important work was done thoroughly and that when the roses were planted the soil had a good humus content. The humus holds moisture in the soil and it must be remembered that the salts taken up by the roots must be in solution. This humus then not only holds the fertilisers which are applied but checks the leaching of them by rain which, particularly on a light soil, can be very rapid, carrying away the food so expensively applied at the surface, beyond the reach of the ever hungry roots.

Having read, for many years, everything on the subject of roses that has come my way, I realise that, to the inexperienced amateur, the formulae for feeding roses can indeed be bewildering.

They all, of course, include chemicals supplying Nitrogen, Phosphate and Potash. The proportions of each chemical, measured by weight, vary very slightly; so too do the chemicals used. To name the more common of these, Ammonium Sulphate (Sulphate of Ammonia) provides nitrogen, Super-phosphate supplies phosphate, Sulphate of Potash gives potash, Magnesium Sulphate (Epsom Salts) gives Magnesium, Iron Sulphate provides iron and Calcium Sulphate gives calcium.

These chemicals, known as "inorganic", form the basis of all fertilisers and become immediately available to plant roots, in solution. The "organic" materials used for feeding plants are products of the animal kingdom and need to be broken down in the soil before becoming available and consequently some time must elapse before the roots can absorb the chemicals as plant food. For this reason the organics are normally regarded as slow acting while the inorganics may be looked upon as giving a more tonic effect.

Some have said that roses are "gross feeders" but I think this is an exaggeration; while they respond to suitable feeding, overdosing can easily upset the plants, resulting in growth which can be too lush and which may succumb more easily to disease. Tender growth, made too late to ripen can be seriously affected by winter frosts.

For the favoured few, then, who are able to obtain stable or farmyard manure in sufficient quantity, the feeding problem for garden display is, to my mind, a very simple one. At some time during the winter, a dressing of bone meal, as coarse as possible, should be scattered evenly over the beds, at the rate of 4–6 ozs per sq. yd. If obtainable bone grist, which consists of very small pieces of splintered bone, gives a very slow but steady supply of phosphate. Gloves should be worn when handling bone products as it is just possible for the anthrax baccillus to gain entry through skin abrasions.

This should be followed by the application of the manure, which should be rotted, to a depth of about 3 in. (2 in. will do if supplies are limited) and this mulch may extend right up to the stems of the trees. I have never had any trouble in this full cover of the ground provided the dung is not hot. In late August follow this with a dressing of Sulphate of Potash (not Muriate of Potash) at 2 ozs to the sq. yd. If your soil is decidedly alkaline (chalky) it may be desirable to spray with a sequestrene, once a year in the spring, and to give a watering with Magnesium Sulphate (Epsom Salts) at 1 oz. to the gallon of water, applied to 2 sq. yds of soil in early summer. Give this treatment annually and you need do no more—remember we are thinking of roses for garden display.

Now for the great many, for whom stable or farmyard manure is something to hear about only; what can be done to keep the garden roses healthy and free flowering? To reiterate, the first necessity is to be sure that the soil is well supplied with humus. On a chalky soil particularly, humus seems to disappear very quickly and must be regularly replaced both to keep the soil in what we call "good heart" and to form a reservoir of absorbed fertilisers, later applied, on which the roots will feed. Again in well drained soils—sands and gravels—unless humus is present, nutrients will be washed quickly beyond the reach of the roots. On heavy soil humus is necessary to keep the soil open, otherwise it becomes compacted and drainage suffers and so do the roses. You may well ask, why this insistence on the provision of humus, when the article is said to be on the feeding of roses? The plain answer is that, except for very temporary benefit, the application of fertilisers, particularly the inorganics, to soil lacking humus is wasteful and almost useless.

The first application of fertiliser is the bone meal or bone grist, put down in November/December at 4–6 ozs (according to your purse) per sq. yd, left on the surface for the weather to wash in.

About the middle of May, or a week or two earlier in a very forward season, a dressing of fertiliser at 2 ozs to the sq. yd should be applied, followed shortly afterwards by the peat mulch, to a depth of at least 2–3 in. if you can afford it.

A further dressing of fertiliser is put down in late June, followed in late August by Sulphate of Potash, 2 ozs to the sq. yd.

Now as to the fertiliser mixture to use. There are, as I have said, very many, all somewhat similarly based. One of these mixtures, recommended by our Society, and used successfully for many years is:

Nitrate of Potash	6 parts by weight
Sulphate of Ammonia	3 parts by weight
Superphosphate	16 parts by weight
Sulphate of Potash	8 parts by weight
Sulphate of Magnesium	2 parts by weight
Sulphate of Iron	$\frac{1}{2}$ part by weight

On chalky soils the magnesium and iron should be doubled and on heavy clay soils 6 parts of Sulphate of Calcium (Gypsum) will help to condition the soil.

A very well known and well proved formula was propounded by a Mr Edward Tonks and is made up as follows:

Superphosphate	12 parts by weight
Nitrate of Potash	10 parts by weight

> Sulphate of Magnesium   2 parts by weight
> Sulphate of Iron   1 part by weight
> Sulphate of Calcium   8 parts by weight

Tonks recommended an application of the above in early spring at 4 ozs to the sq. yd. If time and energy permit I prefer the application made at two separate times, one in late April or early May and one in late June, 2 ozs to the sq. yd on each occasion.

These mixtures can be made up by the amateur, at home, but complete mixing is very difficult. If the constituents are not equally spread throughout the mixture some parts of the garden will get an excess of one chemical and others will be short of it. Though slightly more expensive the machine mixed fertilisers supplied by the specialist firms are better. Fairly recently some of these firms, whose names are well known to all gardeners, have produced some brand named complete rose fertilisers which include many of the well tried chemicals and some new ones, including the trace elements in the minute quantities required. These fairly new products are excellent and their analysis shows them to be well balanced. It is, I hope, scarcely necessary to underline that they should be used strictly in accordance with the manufacturers' instructions—remember "a little more for luck" can sometimes do much more harm than good.

I have, at times, for a change, used fish manure in place of the dressings already mentioned. This is normally based on fish but has other balancing chemicals added. Peat and fertiliser may be mixed together thoroughly and applied in May as mulch and feed. A successful mixture of this kind is peat and John Innes Base Fertiliser. Two essential points are that the peat should be damp when the mixture is put down and the application should result in a dressing of the fertiliser at the rate of $\frac{1}{2}$ lb to the sq. yd.

A final touch in the feeding programme, if you want to feel that you are really doing the best for your trees is to give one or two foliar feeds, again with proprietary brands, of which there are now many available. These may normally be used in conjunction with sprays against aphids and disease and therefore entail little extra work.

To sum up I would say that if you are able to get stable or farmyard manure, apply it, well rotted, in spring to a depth of 3 in. Dress the ground with 2 ozs Sulphate of Potash to the square yard in late August and with coarse bone meal or bone grist at 4 ozs to the sq. yd in November or December and your ground will be well supplied with all the food that your roses need. If you can do this annually, and your aim is first-class roses for the garden and home, you need do no more.

If you cannot obtain the animal manure, apply the fertiliser in early May and mulch with peat in late May 2–3 in. deep. In late June add the second dose of fertiliser, in late August the dressing of Sulphate of Potash and in November/December the bone meal or bone grist. Alternatively, the fertiliser may be mixed with the peat before application in which case the total fertiliser applied must be the equivalent of 4 ozs to the sq. yd or the amount stated by the makers if a proprietary brand is used.

As stated already, it is important that the peat should be well moistened before it is put down, otherwise it may well blow away in high wind and it is difficult to wet when on the soil. If really long lasting dry weather follows the application of fertilisers they should be well watered in.

I have written of roses for garden decoration and for cutting in this article. With regard to the hybrid teas of course, the greatest display of colour will no doubt come from plants which are not disbudded, while for cutting for the house at least some disbudding must be done to provide blooms with good stems. According to your requirements you will no doubt compromise on this point. For myself, while I do not restrict the number of shoots carrying a bloom, I do, with the hybrid teas, disbud to give each bloom a reasonable length of stem for cutting.

With many of the floribundas, particularly those with rather crowded heads of bloom, I like to take out the central terminal bud of the truss quite early in its growth. This enables the surrounding buds to open more nearly together and to my mind gives a more pleasing result.

TO A ROSE

A tender rosebud here is born,
Just kissed by glistening May,
In sweet simplicity at morn,
To greet the dawn of day.

This lovely flower so truly Queen,
So delicately cast,
Symbol of love and peace has been
All through long ages past.

Soft petals to the sun unfold
And beauty yields to all,
The perfect features I behold
Her loveliness extol.

Oh that this flower could ever stay
In her perfected prime,
But youth too soon is flaked away
By ever fleeting time.

                                        IRIS WHITTAKER

Re-designing the Garden at Bone Hill

HARRY G. CLACY, M.Inst.R.A.

An article in the *Rose Annual* for 1962 described the early stages in the development of the property to form the headquarters of the Society and to provide its own Trial Ground and Display Garden.

A plan was then drawn up which provided for the erection of a pergola in the form of two quadrants with the existing pond and its surrounding trees as their centre; curved beds followed the inner line and large beds radiated from the outer line. The erection of the pergola was postponed, but sufficient room was left for its eventual erection.

With the advent of Plant Variety Rights it became obvious that more land would be required to accommodate all the new seedlings which might be produced and submitted for trial. A growing and urgent need for a large car parking space had also to be met.

After considerable negotiation with the owner, the Leaseholder and the tenant farmer an area of land of approximately 4½ acres, was purchased adjoining the eastern boundary of the property.

When fencing in the new land the opportunity was taken to set back the line along the Chiswell Green Lane frontage sufficiently to allow the grass verge to be incorporated in the roadway and the formation of a grassed bank outside the fence to match that on the original frontage. With the generous cooperation of the County Highways Authority the surface of the additional width of roadway was made up, surfaced and drained. This has added much to the appearance of the front and to the convenience of those visiting the gardens and the public using the lane. The post and wire fence will soon be covered by the rugosa bushes which have been planted outside the fence.

A space 380 ft long and averaging 60 ft in width was divided off and prepared for car parking and should accommodate over 100 cars. The car park has properly constructed entrance and exit crossings with gates.

The new Trial Ground was prepared by ploughing, sub-soiling and sowing with grass seed; a service road was constructed along the east and south boundaries, giving easy access to a working area where manure and mulching materials can be stored, and where it is proposed to build a large shed to house the various machines required for the work of the garden. Beds were prepared for the reception of the 1967–8 incoming seedlings and these are now well established.

With the removal of the plants on trial which are now in their third and second year, the whole of the previous trial ground will be incorporated in the Display Garden. With this in view, and in consultation with Mr Gault and Mr Graham Thomas, I was asked to draw up a comprehensive scheme of development, dealing with the whole of the space available and which could be carried out in three or more progressive stages. The scheme was drawn up and, after some opposition, it was agreed by the Council. The plan is reproduced to illustrate this article, but of necessity reduced to a very small scale.

In planning the lay-out some important points had to be taken into consideration, such as the provision of a new entrance to the garden (the previous approach being across the forecourt of the offices); to provide ready access to the Trial Ground from the offices and other parts of the garden; to provide paths of sufficient width to take the machinery to all areas; to show various ways of training roses, especially to gain height in an otherwise level site; also to provide space for a representative collection of species and older varieties.

The new entrance will be *via* the turnstile along the main drive through a semi-circular pergola and along a path between beds of newer floribundas to a catenary erected with cedarwood columns connected by rope. This marks the crossing of the path with that which will provide direct communication between the offices and the Trial Ground.

From the catenary the path continues southwards, sweeping around circular beds in the centre of which a sundial will be placed. Referring to the plan at this point and looking to the left, or eastwards, it will be seen that it is proposed to open up a wide area as far as the boundary of the Trial Ground by the removal of the middle section of the existing shrub rose border.

This space is planned to provide a wide grass walk leading up to a pavilion, proposed to be erected to the memory of the late secretary, Henry Edland. The pavilion and the terrace in front of it will be raised above the level of the land to give a view over the whole of the garden. The grass walk will be flanked by very large beds set at an angle and each planted with one variety to give massed colour effect.

The pavilion will provide shelter for visitors and also for members of the Seedling Panel carrying out their work in the trials. Borders on both sides of the pavilion will be planted with pillar roses on tripods, filled in with shrub roses. Beds of hybrid tea roses are planned alongside the paths surrounding this pavilion garden.

Continuing the walk from the entrance through the catenary and past the sundial beds, the lower cross path is reached near the Courtney Page memorial gates. This path will be extended to the boundary of the Trial Ground, the gates being taken down and re-erected to form a new entrance.

Crossing the lower cross path one enters the recently erected pergola formed by a double row of brick built piers, surmounted by oak beams over a gravelled path and sweeping round in a quadrant to the new constructed pond. Before this work could be carried out it was necessary to remove the old pond and all the trees and shrubs surrounding it. At the same time it was decided to remove the whole of the trees on the southern boundary, many of which were old and diseased. This has opened up a fine vista over the surrounding countryside. Young trees have now been planted 40 ft apart along the whole of this boundary.

The new pond, constructed in concrete, is 35 ft in diameter and 2 ft deep; a fountain jet is fixed in the centre and it will later accommodate aquatic life.

A stone-paved path surrounds the pond inset with four rose beds already planted. The path joins up with the paving of the Princess Mary walk with its floribunda borders, a successful feature of the original lay-out.

The pergola is carried half way round the pond in a single line of piers and when the climbers are established and the roses in the beds in flower, a good reflection of colour should be seen in the surface of the pond.

Beyond the pond the pergola and path are continued in another quadrant to join up with the path leading to the Visitors' Lounge and the walled garden.

The beds radiating from the pergola towards the southern boundary, hitherto filled with award-winning varieties, will be increased and each filled with one variety. The award winners will be found in future in a border formed around the perimeter of the Trial Ground.

In addition to planting trees on the southern boundary a border has been prepared varying in depth from 16 ft to 25 ft, and this will be planted with pillar and shrub roses, mostly repeat-flowering, replacing those removed from the existing border mentioned above.

In order to make the garden as comprehensive as possible, and to add historical and botanical interest, a representative collection of rose species and the older garden types is to be selected and arranged by Mr Graham Thomas, in the spaces to the north and south of the pavilion garden. Space for some of the largest-growing bushes will be found along the east side of the Trial Ground.

It is anticipated that it will be another two, possibly three years before the whole of the development can be completed in accordance with the plan, but sufficient has been carried out for visiting members to visualise the completion.

It was very gratifying to all concerned to hear the many appreciative remarks made by the overseas delegates when they visited Bone Hill during the Fourth International Conference.

Every stage in the working out of the scheme has received the very careful consideration of the Garden Management Committee, and the cooperation of Mr Turner and the Garden Superintendent has been much appreciated.

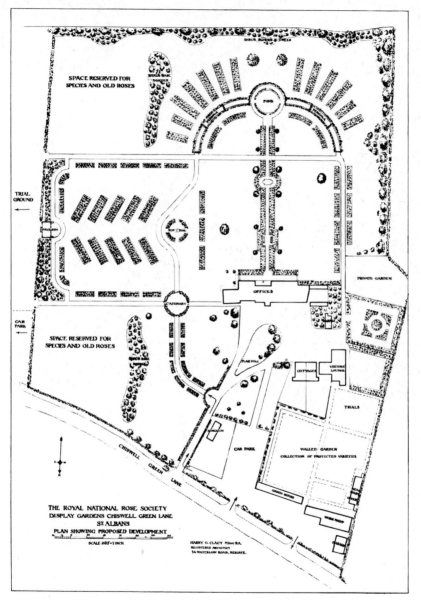

Proposed Development at Bone Hill

'CRIMSON GLORY' (see page 33)

'PEACE' (see page 30)

An Immortal Quartet

HARRY MURRAY
Past President, National Rose Society of N.S.W. Australia

How often have you asked yourself, or been asked "What is the greatest rose ever raised?" It is a question that cannot be answered authoritatively on everyone's behalf, as so many factors of personal taste and inclination are involved and even when one confines oneself solely to the roses that have been released since the end of World War II, it is still a perplexing problem.

There is such a wide choice of literally hundreds of compellingly beautiful roses, bedecked in hues that almost span the full range of colour of the rainbow, with varying habits of growth and diverse foliage and stems. The task is further complicated because of the suitability of different varieties for contrasting climatic and soil conditions. As if this wasn't enough, we also have to contend with the fact that some cultivars are far more disease-resistant and vigorous than their equally desirable sisters.

But one should not, and in fact cannot, confine the choice to varieties that have been introduced only during the past twenty to twenty-five years, as there are many claimants whose life spans far exceed this period. Roses of the calibre of 'Mme Caroline Testout', 'Ophelia', 'Lady Mary Fitzwilliam', 'La France', 'Antoine Ducher', the very recent 'Super Star' and many others can all lay claim to this title for each of them, in its own way, has been a great step forward.

Then again, some roses which in themselves have not been truly outstanding, have earned the accolade because of their staggering propensity for producing progeny of breath-taking beauty. Still others have been the patriarchs of families that have constituted magnificent and radical departures from the accepted standards at the time of their introduction.

I would not presume to be dogmatic as to the identity of the candidate for this high honour, for who can honestly say that he or she is qualified to speak on behalf of the whole world of rose lovers? So, somewhat tentatively, I nominate four contenders for inclusion in the ranks of the immortals. I know that there are numerous others equally well qualified, but space is at a premium. However, I hope that the history of my nominees will prove sufficiently interesting.

Mme A. Meilland—A Living Memorial

With the coming of the First World War a young rose hybridist, Private Antoine Meilland, went from his native city of Lyon to fight for the glory of France leaving his young wife, their five-year-old son and his beloved roses. Throughout the long years of conflict Madame Antoine Meilland rose

29

very early each morning to commence a day of back-breaking labour digging, hoeing and growing the vegetables (required for the war torn country's
larder) which occupied most of the nursery where formerly grew the Queen
of flowers. Many were the tasks heaped upon her slim shoulders each day,
not the least of which was the necessity to push a heavy hand cart loaded with
vegetables to the market over several miles of rough country roads. Despite
the magnitude of her labours, Madame Meilland still found time to tend a
few rose bushes which she knew would be of such importance to her
Antoine when he returned from the battlefields, and her son Francis did all
he could to help his mother with her tasks.

Upon his discharge, Papa Meilland found these few bushes in excellent
condition, thanks to the efforts of his wonderful wife and son, but ahead of
him stretched a long hard fight to restore his depleted nursery and many lean
and difficult years. Throughout this time his wife was by his side to encourage him and share the burdens. Young Francis spent most of his leisure
time in the nursery and at the age of seventeen, after a visit to the garden of
a distinguished hybridist, he became imbued with a burning desire to raise
new roses and this all-absorbing passion was to remain with him for the rest
of his tragically short life.

Then followed year after year of careful crossings, intent observation and
plain hard work by the devoted father and son who suffered a terrible blow
with the unexpected death of Madame Meilland.

In the spring of 1936 there rested in a bed of some thousand new rose
seedlings, an insignificant plant of no outstanding character which bore the
label 3-35-40. In June 1939 the Meillands invited to their nursery some of their
best foreign clients and there, amongst all its contemporaries, stood a magnificent bush with dark green glossy foliage, topped by regal blooms of soft
yellow, fringed with delicate shadings of pink. Around the stem of this bush
was a label which carried the legend 3-35-40. Could these magnificent blooms
which possessed an ethereal quality, possibly be the product of that seedling
which just three short years before was so insignificant?

The visitors were extravagant in their praise and anxious to distribute this
gem. However, the dark clouds of war were once again gathering over
Europe and these were to burst just three months later, but fortunately not
before consignments of budwood, including the still unnamed 3-35-40,
had been despatched to Germany, Italy and America.

Very soon thereafter the Meillands decided that this outstanding rose
could bear no name other than that of Madame A. Meilland, that brave and
courageous lady who through the long hard years had done so much to
encourage and inspire both father and son. But with France occupied and
devastated by war, the rest of the world did not know of this decision, so in
Germany 3-35-40 was named 'Gloria Dei' (Glory to God), in Italy 'Gioia'
(Joy) and in America 'Peace'.

The progeny of 'Peace' are almost innumerable and include such well-known varieties as 'Anne Letts', 'Garden Party', 'Grand'mère Jenny', 'Isabel de Ortiz', 'June Park', 'Karl Herbst', 'Memoriam', 'Michèle Meilland', 'Mischief', 'Rose Gaujard', 'Royal Highness', 'Sterling Silver', 'Super Star', 'Tzigane' and many other beautiful varieties and sports.

In 1958 the world was left very much the poorer by the death, at the age of forty-six, of Francis Meilland, one of the greatest rosarians, visionaries and hybridists ever to tread its good earth. But both Francis and his father Antoine are blessed, in so far as they will be remembered by rose lovers of many future generations and 'Peace' is and will continue to be, a living memorial to the imagination, skill and labour which they both gave so freely and generously to the world of roses.

Général Jacqueminot—A Worthy Warrior

In southern France during the early part of the nineteenth century there lived in the sleepy little village of Montpelier, Monsieur Roussel, a very kind and highly respected gentleman. He was a man of not inconsiderable means who as a boy had developed an affinity for "la bonne terre" and had spent almost the whole of his life growing roses, which were his first and most abiding love. Monsieur Roussel left the care of his extensive garden to the tender ministrations of his gardener (whose name by a curious coincidence happened to be Rousselet) whilst he occupied himself with his hobby of breeding rose seedlings.

At this time there were several hybrid perpetual roses in commerce, but unfortunately there was no outstanding crimson rose amongst their number. Although Monsieur Roussel raised many fine seedlings, in his opinion none of them was fine enough to grace the catalogues of the world's rose nurserymen. So, without realising the worth of his labours, this gentle and humble man sought continued pleasure in his hobby until his death in 1850.

Monsieur Roussel bequeathed to his devoted gardener Rousselet his beloved seedlings, amongst which was a rich glowing crimson with a heavy almost overpowering fragrance, whose buds had most attractive shadings of scarlet and black. As Monsieur Roussel had not bothered to keep records of his crossings, the parentage of this wonderful rose will for ever remain a mystery, although the most widely held opinion is that one of its parents was the crimson china rose 'Gloire des Rosomanes'.

The good gardener, being a man of foresight, immediately perceived that this rose was of great significance, as it represented a major departure from the type of bloom grown at that time. All the earlier, and indeed many of the later, hybrid perpetuals, because of their multiplicity of short petals, either had rather flat shapeless blooms or flowers with confused formless centres. But this new rose had only 25 to 30 long petals which resulted in a large globular flower with a tight centre. Its brilliant crimson colouring was subsequently to become a yardstick by which to measure the perfection of other roses of similar hue.

Rousselet moved north to Paris and in 1853 he introduced his former employer's seedling as 'Général Jacqueminot', being so named in honour of one of France's generals who was the hero of the hour.

To its other many virtues 'Général Jacqueminot' was to add what to the rose breeder is the cardinal virtue—the ability to transmit its good characteristics both as a prolific pollinator and seed parent. So successful was it in this role, that there are more than 520 recorded roses directly descended from it and, in addition, there are probably dozens or even hundreds of other unrecorded crosses in which it figured. In fact, almost all of the great crimson hybrid perpetuals of the Victorian era were offspring of this truly great rose. As late as fifty-four years after its introduction, it retained an honoured position in the first half of the National Rose Society's list of the twenty top crimson roses.

The part played by Général Jacqueminot in his country's history was of minor importance and of short duration and although the general won a degree of renown on the battlefield, he achieved real fame in the rose gardens of the world. Both he and the rose which bears his name proved to be, in the full sense of the words, "worthy warriors".

Crimson Glory—The Head of a Royal Line

Although there were over 40 crimson roses in commerce in the early 1930s, all of them were lacking in one or more of the essential qualities that are desired in a really good rose. The search for a rose with a rich crimson colour, velvety texture, classic form and haunting fragrance had been unsuccessfully conducted for many years. But this search was soon to end with the introduction in 1935 of a truly great crimson rose.

The tragic economic depression of the 'thirties showed no signs of lifting and the people of the world in those black days had little about which to be happy. The sale and introduction of roses had been reduced from a stream to a trickle and the ranks of the seekers after the perfect crimson rose were thin indeed, but numbered amongst them was a dedicated German hybridist, Wilhelm Kordes, a native of the small village of Sparrieshoop in the state of Schleswig-Holstein.

Herr Kordes had for some years been using the renowned 'Mme Caroline Testout' as a parent in various crosses as he wished, if possible, to pass on its characteristics which he found most desirable in a rose. In the late 'twenties he crossed the "Testout" seedling 'Superb' with the American-raised scarlet rose 'Sensation' and one of the issue of this union was the crimson 'Cathrine Kordes' which was released in 1930.

But Kordes was still not satisfied and he continued to press on with his crosses and experiments, which by now were reaching staggering numbers and

'BIRMINGHAM POST' (H.T.)
'Queen Elizabeth' × *'Wendy Cussons'*
Raised by Watkins Roses Ltd
TRIAL GROUND CERTIFICATE 1968
See page 184

'SUPER SUN' (H.T.)
Sport from 'Piccadilly'
Submitted by W. Bentley & Sons Ltd
TRIAL GROUND CERTIFICATE 1968
See page 185

involved hour after hour of tedious and painstaking study, research and labour, rewarded only by frustrating failures. But undaunted, with unshakable determination he continued to strive to attain what must at times have seemed to him to be a hopeless goal, the creation of a crimson masterpiece. In 1930 a rose called 'W. E. Chaplin' won a Gold Medal and Kordes, much impressed by its splendid form and colour, used it as a pollen parent in a cross with a seedling from his own 'Cathrine Kordes'. The result was three seedlings, one a light pink, another a blood red and the third a heavily perfumed, generous blooming rich deep crimson rose which in recognition of the attainment of his goal he called 'Crimson Glory'.

This rose received a Gold Medal in 1936 and immediately jumped into the list of the twenty most popular European roses. It later topped the list for an incredible period of eight years and subsequently remained in this list for a further eleven years until it was deposed by its own offspring in the early 'sixties.* Even today, thirty-two years after its introduction, in some parts of Australia it is, when well grown, one of the very best reds.

Notwithstanding its phenomenal popularity, it will be as a parent of magnificent roses that Kordes' creation will always be remembered, as it possesses the rare ability to produce better roses than itself.

'Charlotte Armstrong', 'Ena Harkness', 'F. W. Alesworth', 'Josephine Bruce', 'June Park', 'Red Ensign', 'William Harvey', 'Show Girl', 'Burning Love', 'Fashion', 'Frensham' and 'Vogue' are just some of the progeny of this rose amongst roses.

Red roses, possibly more than any other colour, possess a very strong appeal and mystique of their own which entitles them to be described as "the royal family of the genus"; if this be so, 'Crimson Glory' is truly the head of a Royal line.

Soleil D'Or—A Golden Harvest

In the latter part of the nineteenth century there were several yellow perpetual-flowering roses amongst the teas and noisettes, but all of them had delicate constitutions and rapidly faded to an unattractive cream. A number of species roses possessed the coveted yellow colour stability and although hardy, they had but a solitary, much too short, period of flowering. Notable amongst these was the 'Persian Yellow' (*R. foetida persiana*), a fully double deep yellow rose that had been brought from Persia in 1838 by Sir Henry Willock, the then British Envoy at Teheran.

For years the purity of colour of the 'Persian Yellow' had intrigued a dedicated French hybridist, Joseph Pernet-Ducher, who lovingly tended his roses near the city of Lyon. What if, by some miracle, he could combine

---

* It had disappeared altogether from the tables of The Rose Analysis based on the 1961 season and had occupied only a lowly position for several years previously. But in Australia it remained popular for a longer period. *Ed.*

the magnificent colour of this species with the repeat flowering character-istics of the garden hybrids? What indeed—as the 'Persian Yellow' was an almost sterile rose, extremely difficult of propagation which for years had defied many efforts to breed from it. Undeterred, in 1883 he determinedly set about his chosen task which although disarmingly simple to propound, was to prove almost impossible to achieve.

Pernet-Ducher favoured the red hybrid perpetual 'Antoine Ducher' and, using this variety as a seed parent, he made literally hundreds of crosses with pollen from the 'Persian Yellow'. The result was hundreds and hundreds of failures, until finally after five heart-breaking years he obtained a few seeds "begotten by despair upon impossibility".

Some three years later he noticed that one of these seedlings, a semi-double pink with a deep yellow reverse, carried the characteristic scent of the 'Persian Yellow' and, although it was not the much sought after deep yellow, it was certainly a step in the right direction. This seedling was duly planted and Pernet-Ducher thought no more of it for a further two years when, to prove its existence to a dubious friend, he went to gather a few of its flowers. As he bent over the bed he could hardly believe his eyes, as there, growing by the side of the original plant, was a tiny seedling with fully double flowers of a rich orange-yellow. Nature had, by this chance second generation seedling, completed the miracle for which Pernet-Ducher had for so long laboured.

This rose was shown for the first time at the Lyon Horticultural Exhibi-tion in 1898 as 'Soleil D'Or'. It took the show, and subsequently the whole of the continent, by storm and just prior to its release in 1900 the French Horticultural Society, in recognition of its importance and the accomplish-ment achieved by Pernet-Ducher, classified it as the first of a new Pernetiana class so named in honour of its originator.

Without 'Soleil D'Or' the world would not have seen any of the deep yellow, orange or flame-coloured roses that have done so much in recent years to delight the eye and uplift the heart. Over twenty years ago there were no less than 513 varieties which were traced as direct descendants of this magnificent rose and today it is estimated that at least seventy-five per cent of all modern roses carry 'Soleil D'Or' in their ancestry.

The importance of its existence is immeasurable and its creation is a tribute to the patience and persistence of one man who, for almost a quarter of a century, strove so heroically to achieve the richly deserved fruits of his labour, a golden harvest indeed.

Well, that is my quartet and I feel that each of them is justly deserving of its place. Whether or not you agree, I am positive that on one point we shall be in full accord—the rose is indeed the Queen of flowers and her beauty, charm and appeal will never be surpassed.

No Roses, by request

LEWIS WILSHIRE

"What about roses?" my wife asked. "They seem to do very well here-about." "No doubt," I replied, "but the rose is one flower I can do without. They have thorns, their foliage is sparse, they don't flower until midsummer and they want too much attention. No roses for me."

We had just moved into a new house. The garden was fairly small, and I had planned it as a labour-saving entity: shrub and herbaceous borders, lawns, a rough-stone wall for alpines and rockery-plants, an arch for honey-suckles and clematis, and a small vegetable garden. And that was it. No roses. I was much more interested in flowering shrubs than in roses.

In due course, the garden was laid out, builders' rubble and surplus stone removed, clay broken up, paths laid . . . the garden began to take shape.

"Looks very nice," was the wife's comment, "but something's missing." She pondered. "I know what it is," she went on, "we've surrounded the house with trellis-topped fencing, but we haven't any roses on it."

I argued that ramblers could never be induced to ramble the right way, that they couldn't be planted among shrubs, and that they only bloomed for a short period. Also they had thorns. "Well," she said, "it's your garden and I don't want to interfere, but a garden doesn't seem a garden without at any rate a few roses."

Reluctantly, I said we would have one or two ramblers.

That, of course, was the end.

In order to buy a few ramblers one had to find out which. That meant writing for catalogues; and rose catalogues, as every gardener knows, can be fiendishly persuasive. I quickly discovered that there were now perpetual-flowering climbers, and in a very short time had acquired 'New Dawn', 'Elegance', 'Maigold', 'Danse du Feu', as well as 'Albertine', 'Dorothy Perkins', 'Cl. Shot Silk', 'Paul's Scarlet', 'Albéric Barbier' and 'Excelsa'.

"Very nice," was the comment, "but couldn't we have a few bush roses?"

"No room," I pointed out. It was quite true. There wasn't any room anywhere.

At this point, a personal tragedy occurred which was to have a profound effect. My mother died, leaving me a fine old grandfather clock and eight unnamed rose trees, of which she had been very fond. Naturally, I couldn't allow a stranger to have her rose trees. So, although the season was well advanced, I dug them up and transferred them to my vegetable garden. For long it looked as though they would not survive, but I kept them soaked in water (the weather was dry—it was May) and they began to recover. Inside a month, their survival mattered so much that not a day went by without a

35

close inspection. I had second thoughts about the vegetable garden. Supposing I laid a lawn, made a pergola, created a rose-garden. . . . How could mere vegetables compete against that sort of vision?

It was after the lawn was laid, and the pergola erected, that Nature struck— first Mildew, then Black Spot showed me that roses don't grow without intelligent preparation and occasional treatment. By this time, however, I was not deterred, I was stimulated. My mother's eight roses (one of which turned out to be a shrub rose and another a well-known hybrid perpetual) were receiving more attention than all the rest of the garden put together.

"I wish I'd never suggested you grew roses," was my wife's comment.

"It's your fault," I said, "I knew this would happen. My grandfather was a rose-grower. They aren't as other men. I'm afraid you will now have to spend the rest of your life with a rose-bore."

She smiled, thinking that when autumn came, my enthusiasm would decline.

Well, she knows better now.

I have a very fine collection of rose catalogues. I have spent more than we can afford on those beautifully modelled, delicately coloured hybrid teas, those glorious floribundas. Their evocative names and promised perfumes have—in anticipation, for I am still awaiting delivery—gone to my head. I am a member of the R.N.R.S., know a very little about a great many roses, have learnt something of form, habit—the face and the foliage. I cannot write easily, at the moment, because I have a particularly nasty thorn in my index finger. (I have ordered 'Zéphirine Drouhin'.)

There is a moral in this, somewhere; it has to do with the femininity of the rose, I think. She is beautiful but she is barbed. She can be wholly captivating, but she cannot be taken for granted. She may come into your life as an afterthought, but she will not consent to remain a back-number.

Keep not your roses for my dead, cold brow:
The way is lonely, let me feel them now.

ARABELLA EUGENIA SMITH

Roses and Genetics

RONA HURST

Now that genetics, in partnership with biophysics and biochemistry, and under the new name of molecular biology, has become so publicised, it is interesting to remember that during the 'twenties and 'thirties cytogenetical work with roses played a considerable part in the earlier researches in this subject and especially in opening up new aspects of the study of evolution. In no other genus could such a comprehensive and comparative study be made, falling as it does into many different categories which could only be investigated otherwise by using a number of different genera.

The enormous number of wild-growing ROSA species, many of which are so well depicted for us in Miss Willmott's splendid monograph, extend widely all round the north temperate zone while several, by accident or design, have followed man into the south temperate zone. Certain species, very sweet-scented and with a propensity for doubling their petals, attracted the attention of man in the early stages of his civilisation and through the centuries were domesticated by him. These gradually, like his animals and foodcrops, produced new forms for his careful selection. The Greeks and Romans were particularly fond of these roses and by mediaeval times a firm basis was laid for what we now call the old-fashioned bush roses. During the last century the famous French rose-growers in particular evolved from these the hybrid perpetuals through hybridisations with *Rosa chinensis* and the tea roses, which eventually were to blossom forth into our magnificent hybrid teas of today.

Added to these is another completely distinct group of ROSA species, the briars or *Canina* roses, growing wild in Europe and Western Asia and important horticulturally as stocks. These have a most peculiar cytogenetic behaviour and geographical distribution, more or less coinciding with the greatest extension of the ice sheets of Pleistocene times, pointing to the fact that they are probably ancient hybrids of that period. Consequently there are many interesting evolutionary problems connected with them.

So, within one genus, we have every stage from the purely wild species, through the early cultivated forms to the most highly evolved garden forms of today, artificially created by the concentrated efforts of many great rosarians. Genetics was certainly not in the minds of the early breeders since its principles were unknown until 1900; nevertheless mutants were carefully preserved and many of their hybridisations were of great future genetic importance, especially the introduction of the previously elusive yellow shades by Pernet-Ducher at the turn of the century by using the yellow *Rosa lutea* from S.W. Asia and its magnificent mutant 'Austrian Copper', with

37

petals coloured rich nasturtium-red on the inner surface, providing the basis for the long line of bicolours which are so popular today.

The Abbé Mendel had carried out his famous experiments on heredity in peas in the 1860s, but these were disregarded and forgotten until they were rediscovered in 1900. Put very briefly, he had proved that normally every individual carries two complete sets of hereditary characters, one received from the father and one from the mother at fertilisation. At the formation of its own germ cells these will again contain only one set of characters, but these, although unchanged, will have been reshuffled so that any differences between the original parents will segregate out in subsequent offspring, giving different combinations.

Through crossing different varieties of peas Mendel found that in the case of equivalent characters such as yellow or green seeds, tall or dwarf stature, one would be dominant over the other (the recessive), hiding it when they are both present together. Only when two recessives come together can this character show itself under ordinary conditions. By the laws of chance this can theoretically happen once out of every four times, which is also true for the meeting of the two dominants, both the pure dominants and the pure recessives resulting obviously breeding true. In the remaining two, however, the dominant will meet the recessive, but outwardly only the dominant will show so that out of every four there will be three apparent dominants to one recessive. This famous 3:1 ratio for the inheritance of any one pair of characters and the purity of each unit character involved, were the key principles for Mendelian breeding.

In England William Bateson and Miss E. R. Saunders at Cambridge, and C. C. Hurst in Leicestershire had been working on similar lines at the end of the century without discovering the whole truth, though they were very near to it. The R.H.S. was extremely interested in this work and as it was realised from their results that the secrets of heredity could only be discovered by minute observations on hybrid behaviour, the Rev. W. Wilks, then Secretary of the Society, arranged an international conference on hybridisation in 1899 at which the three English workers and others at home and from abroad read papers on the subject. Much interest was aroused and when Mendel's lost paper was discovered the next year it was seen that it held the missing clues in dealing with each character as a separate unit, retaining its individuality from generation to generation.

Experiments were put in hand in many countries during the next decade to test the truth of Mendel's Principles in various animals and plants and they were found to hold true in all those examined. Mendelism was rechristened *genetics* and the unit characters *genes*: the next step was to discover what these mysterious entities were which appeared as pairs in any individual and singly in its germ cells, fertilisation restoring the paired condition in the new individuals arising. Microscopists who had been examining the cells in animals and plants had discovered that each cell contained minute worm-like bodies which took up dyes so readily that they were named "chromosomes" or coloured bodies. As work proceeded it was found that each bodycell contained the same number of chromosomes in any individual, and usually in every individual of a species though it might be different in other species, but when they examined the germ cells they found the number was reduced to half. Putting two and two together it was suggested that here was the perfect mechanism for Mendel's segregation of characters, but this had to be proved. During the second decade T. H. Morgan and his colleagues in America set out to do this, using the minute fruitfly, Drosophila, which could be bred in enormous numbers and most conveniently possessed only four pairs of chromosomes which made the work less complicated. If the genes were carried by the chromosomes they should therefore work in four groups in the germ cells of this fly and by an immense number of experiments this was not only proved but many of the genes were actually "mapped" for their positions within these four chromosomes.

Genetics had arrived thus far at the end of World War I; there was considerable disbelief in the new ideas, as was the case in the early days of Mendelism. Hurst, who had always believed in the chromosome theory, returning from the war in late 1919, saw that this new work had also to be extended to other animals and to plants in the same way that the Mendelian work had been. Before the war he had had an extensive experimental station for this at Burbage in Leicestershire, where his researches covered horses, rabbits, poultry and many different kinds of plants, including roses. Already some workers in America were starting on various species of plants to correlate the chromosomes with the genetic characters, but Hurst felt that it was necessary to go beyond this. He was extremely interested in the problems of evolution and he realised that if the genes were located in the chromosomes an examination and comparison of the chromosomes of the various species in a large genus should give considerable enlightenment on this too, pointing out ways by which they had evolved.

This was where the roses came in. He had a large and representative collection of species and cultivated roses from all over the world and genetical work was already in progress with some of them. He determined to extend this by investigating the chromosomes too and in 1922 we went up to Cambridge for the necessary laboratory accommodation and facilities. Fortunately just about this time a Swedish botanist, G. Täckholm, published an account of work he had done on ROSA chromosomes which was extremely useful since, in addition to those he had worked with in Scandinavia, he had done a number of those in the very excellent collection of species then at Kew, largely the result of the great pre-war collections made in that hotbed of speciation of S.E. Asia, though there were many from other areas. His work showed that ROSA chromosomes were amazingly interesting, far beyond anything Hurst had hoped for and likely to prove most profitable for his research. For ROSA proved to be one of the genera containing many species known as polyploids in which there are more than two complexes of chromosomes in an individual. The basic chromosome number is seven (haploid), and in the ordinary diploid condition 14 chromosomes are present in the body cells of the individuals of the many species belonging to this category; but there are also tetraploids with four sets of chromosomes (28), hexaploids with six (42), and octoploids with eight (56).

The *Caninae* roses, some forms of which were also examined by Blackburn and Harrison in Newcastle about this time, showed a very queer state of affairs since they were pentaploids with five sets of chromosomes (35), of which only two sets—14 chromosomes—paired together, the remaining three—21 chromosomes—continuing unpaired. In the pollen cells the seven pairs divided normally giving a varying percentage of healthy pollen grains with seven chromosomes; the unpaired chromosomes were most erratic, a few getting included in some of the main grains, others forming small grains themselves, in either case causing sterility. The formation of the eggcells was curious in the extreme, for in this case all the single chromosomes tended to be included with one of the sets of the reducing pairs so that female germcells had 28 chromosomes which, when fertilised by pollen carrying 7, restored the original number of 35 in the progeny.

Actually these roses are very largely apomictical (i.e. setting seed vegetatively without reduction or fertilisation) which accounts for their rich harvest of heps in spite of much gametic sterility. Nevertheless the hybrids which occur from time to time show that this irregular fertilisation can take place. The great point is that here too the chromosomes are working in sets of seven, which made them very useful for experiment.

The chromosomes of the garden roses at that time were not so complex as might be expected, most so far as examined being diploid or tetraploid, with some triploids occurring as hybrids between these and a few higher polyploids arising through crosses with *R. canina* (*R. alba*, etc.), in the Penzance Briars (hybrids between *R. rubiginosa* and various garden roses), and a few others. The work done with these was described by Hurst in the R.H.S. Journal in 1941 under the title of *Notes on the Origin and Evolution of our Garden Roses*, and reprinted in *The Old Shrub Roses* by Graham Thomas (1955).

There must be far greater complexities now after another forty years of intensive hybridisation by many rose growers and through the introduction of other species. Hurst himself set out to incorporate into the garden roses the desirable qualities of the strong-growing and beautiful American species *R. nutkana* (a hexaploid), crossing it with a popular garden rose of the 'twenties, 'Red Letter Day', with a very high proportion of *R. chinensis* blood which made it extremely free and perpetual flowering.

The result was the shrub rose, 'Cantab', which gained the Cory Cup at the

R.H.S. in 1940. This is illustrated in Edland's *Pocket Encyclopaedia of Roses* (1963, p. 111, No. 345). The bush, which runs up to a considerable height, covers itself with large single flowers up to 4 inches across, of a rich carmine pink. It is also fertile and inherits the late, hard-fruiting habit of *R. nutkana* so that it puts up another display in late autumn. Although it is only summer flowering itself it carries the recessive character for perpetual flowering from 'Red Letter Day' and it was intended to breed from 'Cantab' to raise perpetual-flowering bush roses, but due to the war this was not possible. One hopes that use will be made of this first generation hybrid which contains other desirable but hidden recessive qualities including the double flowering of 'Red Letter Day' and the robust caney habit of *R. nutkana.*

To return to the wild species: polyploidy, now so much a part of plant genetics, had scarcely been recognised at the beginning of the 'twenties. A very few plants which showed gigantism in all their parts had been found to have double the number of chromosomes and Japanese botanists had found a polyploid series in *Chrysanthemum* species, but the implications of this were not realised even by those involved, much less by other biologists. Chromosome number had always been regarded by most as merely another systematic character in the days before Morgan had shown that the chromosomes carried the genes and this was not by any means universally accepted as yet, so little having been done from this standpoint except in Drosophila.

During 1922–23 the material Hurst had taken from his own collection, and in the wild, was examined and we found that it completely agreed with Täckholm's work. By this time quite a considerable number of species and garden forms had been covered and Hurst was able to correlate these results with the systematic position in ROSA. He began to realise that the wild-growing polyploids were not just plain duplicated diploids as was found for some garden roses, but appeared to contain the characters of two, three or four diploid species according to whether they were tetraploid, hexaploid or octoploid. This was an entirely new idea, though one or two cases were known in cultivated plants in which a sterile hybrid had produced a fertile form by the duplication of its chromosomes. These first ROSA results were reported at the British Association at Liverpool in 1923.

One of the greatest conundrums of the early geneticists arose from the fact that in their experiments it seemed as if much variation proceeded from an "unpacking" of a considerable number of genes contained within a wild species, especially under domestication. If this were so, how did they get packed up originally? It has to be remembered here that for many people special creation was still by no means forgotten. Linnaeus had believed that species were specially created but varieties arose afterwards. Darwin's great work on the origin of species by the natural selection of variations had been against this idea, but so little was as yet known as to the causes of variation that there was still no definite proof of this and Darwin's theories were being questioned by a number of people in consequence.

Hurst saw that in these polyploids there certainly was a very considerable opportunity for this packing up by the bringing together of less complex species to form more complex ones which, through the greater number of chromosomes and genes contained, had far greater powers of mutation and also of response to differing environments. The work of other people, too, was beginning to show that not only were whole chromosome complexes involved in this build-up, but duplications of single chromosomes could occur, of parts of chromosomes even, all adding to the complexity of species and creating the condition which had so puzzled the early workers.

The rose work went forward rapidly. We visited and took material from all the famous gardens, including the fabulous Roseraie de l'Haÿ near Paris. Much interest was aroused, especially in America, and a vast amount of criticism everywhere. Only the most advanced biologists had as yet reached the point of accepting that genes might be carried by chromosomes; that they could occur in such complex groupings was another big pill to swallow. Although the rose work received much attention and many people came to see the experimental collections at Burbage and Cambridge, few people were conversant enough with the systematics of this very large and difficult genus to be able to follow it easily.

In July 1928 Hurst gave an outline of the experiments to date at the great International Rose Conference in London, an extended and fully illustrated paper being published in *The Rose Annual* for 1929, showing that the classification of ROSA species could be correlated with the chromosome numbers, explaining the many difficulties experienced by earlier rosarians in dealing with this very complicated genus, rendered so by reason of its polyploid condition which creates much otherwise inexplicable overlapping.

By this time the chromosomes of 674 species, varieties and hybrids had been examined and it is probably still true to say no other genus has been so widely covered. During the next few years this was increased to over 1,000 by ourselves and others. Unfortunately most of the great collections of the very beautiful rose species have been lost during this very disturbed century, Miss Willmott's being destroyed during the first war and the greater part of the one at Kew during the second, with smaller ones falling victims to the lack of labour. Unfortunately there is no present hope of replacement of the great Asiatic species owing to political conditions. The fatal habit of Botanic Gardens of distributing seeds from open flowers has resulted in various hybrids being perpetuated as the real species, of which very few now remain except as illustrations in the great pre-war rose monographs.

The work on the chromosomes of various other plants and animals was steadily advancing everywhere, giving fresh proofs of the possible courses of evolution. Wheats in particular showed diploids, tetraploids (macaroni wheats) and hexaploids (bread wheats) which were eventually traced out as ancient species hybrids in which the chromosomes had become duplicated. Today this production of new species by hybridisation and the duplication of the chromosomes of the sterile hybrid to make a fertile new species is a commonplace, both by artificial experimental means and as occurring naturally in the wild; but it was in ROSA that this was first realised as an evolutionary factor opening up new possibilities in the creation of new and more adaptable species, as has been occurring in nature through long aeons of time.

Hurst was assiduously collecting information on all the various types of chromosome and gene changes which were being discovered, many of which were also found in ROSA, showing how these could bring about the many changes necessary to build up all the complexities of the higher animals and plants—"from amoeba to man". Bringing all this together with the rose results he published it as a book, *The Mechanism of Creative Evolution*, in 1932 which certainly hit the world headlines for all the new ideas it contained.

No other genus could have shown so conclusively the proofs of the progress of evolution, not only naturally but, in later centuries, in the great florescence of garden roses, through human controls, thus illustrating how man has increasingly taken over and speeded up these processes by his domestication and breeding of animals and plants and the making of better environments for their success. The future of creative evolution now lay in the hands of man, for better or for worse, according to how he used his new powers. The final and most important control man has yet to exercise is upon himself and unless he can do this very quickly, both in the control of human populations and of his greed for power, extending to the danger of annihilation by starvation or by atomic or biological warfare, his new knowledge, which could be so beneficial for all, will be of no avail.

With the cooperation of biophysicists and biochemists, together with the new refinements of electronic techniques in the laboratories, the mystery of the actual genes themselves has been revealed during the past fifteen years, showing them to be real molecular entities acting as chemical codes, or messages, handed down by the chromosomes from generation to generation, and from cell to cell, giving the information for the various processes through which the development of a complete organism can be achieved.

With the new genetical knowledge gained in recent years man becomes increasingly in control of biological development and the alleviation of disease, in addition to the earlier genetic methods of breeding better food animals and plants. This has frightened some people into the belief that science might tamper too much. This belief stems largely from ignorance and the misrepresentations of facts by reporters, who make terrifying assertions without scientific knowledge.

It is pleasant to think that the rose, so beautiful and well-beloved, should have played such an important part in the unravelling of the genetic problems so necessary for the future betterment of man and his environment.

Gloire des Mousseux

DEREK A. WILSHER

A title which any French-speaking rosarian will easily interpret! Many will aspire to greater erudition: perchance there are those who in the stead of interpretation will offer definition: Centifolia Moss Shrub rose. Such a rose, by such a name was first brought into existence in or about the year of the Great Exhibition; the expert tells us that Laffay was the accoucheur. It is, indeed, a Moss-rose. What wealth of conjecture does that title *not* enkindle? The serenity of a summer's day, pink flowers nestling amongst green foliage, the hum of the bees as they buzz busily from one silken chalice to the next . . . the moss-like growth surrounding the calyx serves to enhance its appearance, as well as give it its name. An old fable tells us how the moss-rose gained such a collar . . . perchance this fable dates from those days—2,500 years ago—when "burning Sappho" named her Queen of Flowers, a title the intervening years have done naught to diminish. . . .

. . . In those far-off days when the world was young, and Gods mingled freely with Mortals, the young God of Love one day descended from Olympus to wander through this terrestrial sphere. It was a warm, spring day; the air was heavy with the scent of flowers. Violets and forget-me-nots sprang beneath his feet; the rose smiled a welcome from her leafy bower, the sun shone and the birds sang in chorus. By and by the young God of Love became weary; a pleasant grassy, moss-strewn, flower-bedecked bank offered an inviting couch . . . Cupid sank down thereon easily. . . . Not even Olympians are immune from all human frailties . . . lulled by the chorus, caressed by the breeze, Cupid closed his eyes, and soon slumbered peacefully.

The slumbery silence was soon disturbed by a soft murmuring which arose from the flowers on that grassy bank. "The little God Cupid is sleeping here" whispered a violet to a primrose: "how gentle and sweet he is," whispered the primrose. "Such a handsome boy," commented the dog-daisy. Their comments spread. Soon all the flowers of the countryside knew that the little God of Love was sleeping on a grassy bank . . . and one by one they crept stealthily to see him and gaze on his fair young beauty.

With the others came the rose. Tall and upright, modestly blushing, she came. "How sweet he is," said she, "But how warm with the sun shining over him—I'll provide him with some shade." She gently raised her branches, and arched them over his head. The foliage sheltered him from the sun's hot rays, the shade was soothing; Cupid smiled in his sleep. "How fortunate you are, Rose, to be able to shield the dear little God," murmured the other flowers.

At length Cupid stirred; he opened his eyes, and awoke. "How pleasantly shaded I am here," said he. He turned to the rose. "Thank you, Rose, for your shade. You are the loveliest of flowers; you are also as kind as you are beautiful." The rose blushed a deeper shade of pink, and modestly bowed. "Tell me, Rose," continued Cupid, "What I can do to thank you for your kindness." The rose pondered a moment, then with a mischievous smile murmured "Make me yet more beautiful!"

Cupid started back and anger blazed from his eyes. "What, coquette," cried he, "Possessed of all charms, do you yet demand more? You have the loveliest colour, the sweetest scent, the most delicate form . . . do you demand more? *This* shall you have for such insolence." He grasped a handful of moss from the bank and threw it over the rose's lovely head. The rose started back, faltered, and fled—to hide her shame. "Oh why," she sobbed, "Did I make such a request? I was the loveliest of flowers, but now my beauty is all gone. Who now will look at me again, my head, my crown, my pride, all covered with that low, horrible, common green moss?" In her despair she fled to the deepest forest, but her way was blocked by a river. She halted, and looked about her. Her gaze fell on the water at her feet . . . she looked, started, and looked again. There, mirrored in the limpid water, was her own *new* self. Her sobs ceased, the tears stopped trickling down her cheeks . . . in full amazement she gazed, and gazed again.

"How lovely you are, Rose," said the stream. "I've never mirrored a more lovely sight. But what new charm is this, the halo of delicate green lace around your head?" The rose smiled happily. "I asked the little God of Love to make me more beautiful," murmured she, "and he gave me this. . . ." The other flowers drew near and they, too, said "You look lovelier than ever now, Rose. . . ." Only one cheeky little daisy murmured "*Moss*-Rose."

> The morning rose that untouched stands
> Arm'd with her briers, how sweet she smells!
> But pluck'd and strain'd through ruder hands,
> Her sweets no longer with her dwells.
>
> SIR ROBERT AYTOUN, 1570–1638.

The Care of Cut Roses

MARGARET L. VICKERY

There is nothing more beautiful than a vase of freshly arranged roses, heads held high, each petal crisp and glowing with colour. But so often by the next day heads are drooping, petals limp and dull. This is a double tragedy if the roses have also been grown by the arranger (or her husband!). Yet there is no need for this to happen, if some simple precautions are taken to ensure that the blooms never lack the water so necessary to their health and well-being.

I think it not too fanciful to compare the removal of a rose bloom from the bush with a major operation. For once the stem has been severed the bloom is deprived of its source of nourishment and supply of water. The cut shoot should therefore be regarded as an invalid and treated as such. It is cruel to arrange the bloom immediately on cutting and it should be allowed to rest for several hours in a cool, dark, airy place in deep warm water, the stem being immersed to the neck of the bloom, if possible. The reason for this will become apparent if we consider why it is that water is so important to plants.

Just as we perspire, so a plant transpires water from all its surfaces. The rate of transpiration depends on atmospheric conditions and is greatest when the weather is hot and dry, most of the water being lost from the undersides of the leaves. This is often evident in hot weather when leaves wilt whilst flowers remain erect. The wilting, in itself, serves a purpose as it ensures that the undersides of the leaves are in the shade and away from direct sunlight. This mechanism will operate whether the source of heat is the sun or a current of hot air from a fire or radiator. Thus, one way of guarding against wilting is to make sure that the arrangement is standing away from direct sunlight or other sources of heat. The removal of all the leaves would, of course, reduce transpiration considerably, but here I feel we must compromise, as a completely defoliated rose looks unnatural and loses much of its beauty. However, should the stem carry an abundance of leaves then the judicious removal of a few will help to prolong the life of the rest. All leaves that come under water in the arrangement should be removed, as these will rot, causing an offensive odour and encouraging bacterial attack of the stem, thus shortening the life of the bloom.

Transpiration will also be reduced if the leaves are given a light spray of water after arranging, as this will establish a damp atmosphere within their vicinity. This trick is particularly useful for show work where conditions can be most trying.

From the foregoing it is obvious that once a bloom has been cut it should never be out of water for more than a few minutes. But this is only half the story, as the mere placing of the stem in water does not ensure that absorption will be sufficient to prevent wilting. A rose stem is classed as "woody", meaning that the surface cannot absorb water. The outer skin or bark should therefore be removed for about half an inch up from the cut by gentle scraping with the serrated edge of florists' or kitchen scissors. Alternatively, it can be gently peeled away. To increase the surface area of the stem in contact with water, two cuts at right angles to each other should be made for about half an inch up from the base. If this is done there is no need to hammer the stems; although this breaks the surface bark it also bruises the stem and may kill some of the tissue, which will then decay in water, shortening the life of the bloom. Should a bloom have been out of water for more than a few minutes about half an inch of stem should be removed and the above process repeated, before placing in water. This should always be done when roses are purchased and have to be carried home without water.

Florists' roses are often forced and these are much more susceptible to wilting than the hardy outdoor varieties. As an extra precaution the stems should stand in 1 inch of boiling water for two or three minutes, with the blooms protected from steam by wrapping them in tissue paper. The container is then filled to the brim with cold water and the blooms left in a cool place for several hours. It is not necessary to repeat the treatment with boiling water when arranging, but if the stems are shortened they should be scraped and cut, as described above.

When roses are arranged it is usually necessary to have both buds and open blooms. Should buds only be available, as is often the case when roses are purchased, then a few can be encouraged to open quickly by placing in hand-hot water and leaving them in the light for several hours. Those required as buds should be placed in cool water in a dark place.

These steps in the care of cut roses can be summarised as follows:

1. (a) After the removal of the stem from the bush scrape off a little bark and make two cuts at right angles to each other up the stem from the end.

    (b) If purchased, on reaching home remove half an inch of stem and continue as in (a).

2. Place in deep, warm water. If the roses are forced or the stems limp treat with boiling water.

3. Leave in a cool, dark, airy place for at least twelve hours.

4. Arrange, remembering to repeat the removal of some bark and the right-angled cuts if the stems are shortened.

The foregoing may seem complicated at first reading but with a little practice it soon becomes second nature to "condition" your roses before arrangement. The results are well worth the effort.

A Shower of Roses

SUSAN BONE

Although I had always liked roses it wasn't until four years ago when we moved to a bungalow with a fairly large garden that I felt a compulsive urge to grow them, and I bought a modest three dozen bushes. Two years later we moved to a flat in an old rectory owned by my husband's parents, situated in the Breckland area of East Anglia, and I moved the bushes with me—in July—and all but one survived, though more by luck than judgment. The soil here is very sandy with a moderate content of flint overlying chalk. By this time I realised that I was not interested in the sundry other plants, shrubs, etc. which adorn gardens, and by chance came across a glossy illustrated catalogue of a leading rose nursery. I spent hours poring over this, and slowly but inexorably came to the conclusion that I had to grow roses. Lots of them.

Another fortuitous discovery sealed my fate: I borrowed from our local library the book *Growing Roses* by Jack Harkness.

"Then felt I like some watcher of the skies
When a new planet swims into his ken."

Apart from the astonishing variety of rose bushes commercially available, I learnt that roses could and should be nurtured; and that the process did not involve long hours of toil, but enjoyable pottering.

The first move was to survey my garden. A 50 ft square facing east, hemmed in by overgrown box trees on the north side, the west perimeter 3 ft deep in an assortment of nettles, ground elder, kerria and two dubious looking rambler-type roses which did not flower. On the south side was a promising looking small bed which once had served a greenhouse, and further along a banked bed with a very untidy sycamore tree. A quarry tile path (also ex the greenhouse) separated this from a bed 21 ft × 6 ft supporting a monstrous privet hedge. Also against a south-facing wall is a very large bed, over which sprawled the branches of one of the box trees, searching for light and air.

The privet hedge went first, and the roots had to be excavated with a pick-axe. The sycamore tree went next. Initially I was merely going to plant a few bushes in front of it, but Mr Harkness in his book deprecates the practice of growing roses near or under trees. Removal was complicated by the fact that the bed comprised a dense carpet of ground elder bedded in a sprinkling of earth over an astonishing quantity of bricks and rubble. This, then, was where the greenhouse material settled, apparently. However, I was quite a dab hand with a pickaxe by now, so I set to work.

'ADAIR ROCHE' (floribunda—H.T. type)
'Paddy McGredy' × 'Femina' seedling
Raised by S. McGredy IV, N. Ireland
TRIAL GROUND CERTIFICATE 1968
See page 184

'FRED GIBSON' (H.T.)
'Gavotte' × *'Buccaneer'*
Raised by John Sanday (Roses) Ltd
TRIAL GROUND CERTIFICATE 1968
See page 185

Peter, my husband, thought I had completely taken leave of my senses, and this opinion he voiced frequently and with alarm. I stolidly excavated on, and by August, to quote his family, our garden looked as if it had been blitzed. In the meantime I had been collecting catalogues of roses from nurseries, and while resting from my labours would study these avidly. I made copious lists of varieties I wanted—there was no time to visit the nurseries to see the roses for myself—I depended entirely on the exotic descriptions accorded the varieties. All that remained was to finance the operation. Peter's limit of expenditure on gardens amounted to a few ninepenny packets of seeds, and anything over that he considered grossly extravagant and frivolous. Not surprisingly, he turned ashen when I presented my request. Looking back, I think that he paid up so quietly because he had been in a state of acute shock, and anxiety.

Against the advice of the pundits I finally purchased 150 assorted varieties of hybrid teas, floribundas, climbers and shrubs. I had measured out the beds, and from the lists I made selected the most promising looking varieties by colour and height and split them into blocks. The beds were double-dug in the course of excavation, and I obtained a load of topsoil from a nearby building site which gave them the benefit of an additional 4 in. depth.

Planting commenced at the end of October: I had placed orders with several nurseries, which spaced out arrivals nicely and permitted planting to be carried out with a minimum of fluster.

During the long winter evenings I browsed through any book I could get hold of on the subject of rose growing, and the more I read the more I realised what an art rose-growing is, and how very little I knew about it. I also discovered that the experts did not always agree—two warned against hard-pruning newly-planted bushes in sandy soil. At this time I was half-way through pruning—hard—and frantically consulted the Secretary of the Royal National Rose Society, who reassured me that bushes should indeed be pruned at least down to the first three eyes. I also read that varieties should be planted individually in beds, or well and truly mixed, but that different varieties of the same colour should not be placed cheek by jowl. This gave me a severe jolt, as I had painstakingly arranged all 150 bushes in blocks of colour. I moved about a dozen around at a very late stage in a despairing attempt to break up these colour blocks.

Experts agreed, however, that horse manure was advantageous, and that a minimum mulch of 2 in. over rose beds was desirable. This was delightful to learn as I have a source of supply in my daughter's pony. After pruning (mid-March) I spread a 2-in. layer of stable manure over the banked bed (15 ft × 15 ft) and resorted to a well-known proprietary rose fertiliser, 4 oz. per square yard, for the rest.

The 21 ft × 6 ft bed runs in front of my kitchen window and lightened many hours of labour at the sink: it was a joy to see the leaflets appear, sprout, and then put forth their buds. I tottered down one morning at the beginning of July, and drew back the curtains to survey the state of development only to see gaunt stalks where only the night before had poised clusters of tantalising buds. Words cannot express how I felt. My source of horse manure had got out of its stable during the night and consumed the first buds of some 60 rose bushes altogether. The pony did not die of colic, much to my rage, and just to think about the bushes set me cursing my fate afresh. I had nursed them along, keeping all manner of pests at bay, feeding them, weeding them, only to provide a vile pony with a midnight feast. The stable exit has been reinforced now, and our garden fenced in, which rather spoils some of the effect I was hoping to achieve, but if the pony can get in and eat roses again, she deserves to. Anyway, the bushes seemed to redouble their speed of growth as a result of this cavalier treatment and they bloomed before July was out.

The two rambler-type roses flowered, bearing miniature buds the colour of an egg-yolk along their arching stems.

The first-year bushes threw a shower of roses. Judging from their performance in my garden I found the catalogue descriptions had been reasonably faithful, and I am indebted to those nurseries which included a note of warning concerning disposition towards disease among their descriptions. The few I had moved in with had been dumped haphazardly rather than planted, and though manured as freely as the novices they have been niggardly and shy with their foliage and flowers. A combination of proximity to the box trees and not preparing the bed before planting, no doubt. The difference is startling. The three-years old 'Perfecta' grew barely 18 in. high and threw only three blooms: the first year bush of the same variety flowered sooner, abundantly, and grew to an exuberant 3 ft.

Bushes and climbers I had moved and planted late in March are pigmies even now in comparison with the others, and flowered meanly at the end of July.

The bushes with the 2 in. blanket of stable manure flowered briskly and continuously, and have been a source of constant delight from early June onwards. They are altogether taller, bushier and healthier looking than the bushes treated only with the proprietary fertiliser.

Plants of the genus Rosa are very beautiful in all stages of their cycle of growth to my besotted eyes. I wish I had sufficient space to grow them in groups, instead of singly, in more variety, and with a more congenial aspect than east; but within the restrictions imposed on the bushes I have acquired, both from position, soil and climate, they have been lavish in their beauty.

I have indeed been showered with roses in this my first year of growing them. I regularly and earnestly beseech the Supreme Creator who made their existence possible (with the adept co-operation of those magnificent stalwarts, the hybridisers) to deluge me with roses in future, in spite of my often misdirected ministrations.

In quest of her infinite variety

C. W. ELLICK

Nearly four decades ago when I was first initiated into the knowledge and love of the genus Rosa, my tutor and mentor likened rose breeders to a band of indefatigable adventurous pioneers who, to be successful in reaching their goal, must be endowed with the heart of a lion, the wisdom of Solomon and the patience of Job.

The names of Norman, Meilland, Kordes and Tantau are immortal, to mention but a few, and their names are also synonymous with the beauty of our heritage. We take so much for granted and accept it as our natural right. How many of us realise when we pay a mere pittance for a new rose, that it may have taken a master craftsman seven to ten years to produce it?

One does not have to be a scientist or a botanist to become a hybridist, but a knowledge of the genetics and the characteristics of the roses to be used as parents is essential. The cells which form the tissues of the living rose contain bodies called chromosomes which contain a selection of units of heredity, as in every living thing, known as genes. These genes are capable of transferring inherent characteristics such as colour, fragrance, vigour, resistance to disease and over a thousand complex features to succeeding generations.

The odds against a breeder producing a new rose are utterly fantastic. Mrs G. Fisher, the well known American hybridist, over the period of the last twenty years has made some five hundred crosses each year, and each successful cross would have produced anything up to approximately forty seeds. In all that time, despite her tenacity and perseverance, Mrs Fisher has produced only about twenty seedlings of any commercial value. Her most famous, perhaps, is 'Sterling Silver'. However, you too can become a hybridist; the operation in itself is simple in the extreme. A greenhouse is not absolutely essential, as I have proved, though in this climate of ours it is a decided advantage.

If the roses to be used as parents are potted up into nine-inch pots and taken inside during November, they will grow more vigorously than in the open garden. You will be able to make your crosses at least one month earlier; moreover, the resulting seedlings will be thicker and stronger, therefore easier to bud on to your stocks. Few if any amateurs can bud the eyes from their seedlings if they are as thin as a needle.

The male sex organs of the rose consist of the anthers and filaments by which they are attached on the outside of the embryo seed pod or receptacle. The female organs consist of the stigmas which are attached to the styles, which in turn are joined to the ovaries at the base of the receptacle. When fertilisation takes place a pollen tube is formed which makes its way down the style to the ovary. Natural fertilisation takes place in two ways; first, by the transfer of the plant's own pollen from the anthers to the stigmas; secondly, by the transfer of ripe pollen from other nearby roses by pollen-carrying insects. A chance seedling *could* become a rose of the calibre of 'Super Star' or 'Peace'—such is the fickleness of Nature.

When you embark on the great adventure choose a warm sunny day when the pollen is active and several flowers are opening on the rose to be used as the seed parent. The bloom to be used should be three-quarters open, no more. Very carefully unroll and remove the petals. Ensure that no small pieces of broken petals remain as this would invite the fungus disease known as Botrytis, the scourge of all breeders. Next, with a sharp penknife or a small pair of scissors remove all the anthers by cutting through the filaments at or near their base. They are unmistakeable as they are taller than the stigmas and they must all be removed if the operation is to be a success. Then cut off the sepals. These can be left, but their removal assists the ripening of the pod. The prepared receptacle is then covered with a muslin or polythene bag to avoid pollination by insects.

It is usual to leave the seed parent about twenty-four hours, although on a warm sunny day this may not be necessary. The stigmas will go shiny and sticky when they are ready to receive the pollen. The pollen may be transferred from the anthers of the male parent by the forefinger, a piece of muslin or a sable, squirrel or camel hair brush. However, I prefer to take Mohammed to the Mountain and, holding the petals back, use the anthers themselves to transfer the pollen. The cross is then labelled, with the date on the reverse of the label, which is then attached to the pedicel or footstalk. The bag is then replaced for a short period to enable the pollen to set, but should not be left too long as transpiration inside a polythene bag could encourage Botrytis.

Should the marriage be consummated, in October or November you will be rewarded with a nice ripe seed pod. It is then removed with the label still attached and kept in a box of moist peat, or peat and sand, outside, to be stratified by the weather. In late January or early February the seed pods are removed from the boxes and the seed extracted. I have a glass of water by me and the seed is dropped into it. The infertile seeds, the "floaters", are then eliminated.

The fertile seeds, the "sinkers", are then sown in boxes 2 in. deep and the same distance apart. If the temperature is kept at about 40° F. germination should take place in a very short space of time, although some varieties will take six to eight weeks or even longer. There is nothing to be gained by having a higher temperature and the boxes can be quite safely taken outside when the mean temperature is above this optimum level. It is not advisable to leave the boxes outside during the night, even in high summer, because of marauding cats and other predators.

The seedlings should be pricked out into 3-in. pots as soon as they are large enough to handle or, alternatively, they may be put into Vencel troughs or other similar receptacles about 6 in. apart. There are many good seed and potting composts on the market and the medium to be used is largely a matter of choice, but if you use a John Innes compost do ensure that it comes from a reputable source.

In about twelve weeks from sowing, with a little luck, the great day will dawn when your seedlings burst into flower. Should you be ambitious and see yourself as an embryo McGredy, Dickson or Harkness you will have many disappointments. Boxes of singles are the rule rather than the exception. Console yourself and be proud that each and every one is your own creation. You can use your best seedlings to re-cross with other roses of your choice and will find the subject most fascinating and rewarding. Who knows? the rose of the century may be just around the corner.

Should you think you have a winner and are not skilled in the art of budding, call in an expert. Three years from the cross some fifty trees of your rose may be in existence. The growth, habit, flower formation and disease resistance will be appraised. In the event of it proving to be a possible commercial proposition, the rose will be named and registered with the International Rose Registration Authority through the auspices of our own Society. Six trees may be sent to the Trial Ground at St Albans to take their place for three years with those from the nurseries of the famous hybridists of the world, whose names are household words and to whom we owe so much.

With experience you will get to know the best seed parents. Some roses are reluctant brides and some are completely sterile. It is necessary to keep written records, particularly if you have some definite breeding programme in view.

The toast, Ladies and Gentlemen, is to the rose breeders of the world, dedicated to her infinite variety.

Not so very long ago?

GEOFFREY J. BURFOOT

Ever since I came across the following verse "On New-blown Roses" some years ago (Mediaeval Latin Lyrics, Helen Waddell, Penguin Classics) I have felt an affinity with its author, Ausonius, a rose lover of *circa* 380 A.D. Of antiquity, perhaps I would have said, until I read Ruth Borchard's article "Of Very Ancient Roses" in the 1966 *Rose Annual,* wherein she takes us back most interestingly and intriguingly into the remote and unimaginable past in tracing the origins of rose species millions of years ago and later, much much later, their culture. For me, she puts matters Rosa into a different perspective.

Perhaps 380 A.D. is not so long ago as all that for rose growers. There must have been great rosarians long before the Romans as, by their time, it seems to have been quite the usual thing to plant Villa gardens with roses. As they, the Romans, conquered and colonised, they took plants with them for their new dwellings. Ruth Borchard instances this in her explanation of the finding of rose species in France not indigenous to the country. However, her article renewed my interest in the poem and its writer, Ausonius, a Roman who possibly had done this very thing, thereby introducing some new strain to the West. Re-reading the verse, he seemed again so very human and understanding about roses. I imagine him taking his early morning walk in his garden, refreshing himself both physically and spiritually before the heat of the day, browsing among his roses, much in the same way as our contemporary enthusiast takes a quick but lingering look around his rose beds, fortifying himself before dashing off to catch the 7.55 to the City and its intolerable heat on a hot June day.

Now what variety were Paestum roses? I looked it up and found "Paestum —City of Lucania. Founded by Greeks *c.* 600 B.C. Came under Roman rule *c.* 273 B.C. when name altered to Paestum. Famous for its roses." Evidently they were specialising in those times and not content with just anything in the way of roses.

The translator tells us that Ausonius, man of letters and poet, one time tutor to the son of the Roman Emperor Valentinian, released from his high offices of state (Governor of Gaulle and later Consul) had returned to his old home in Bordeaux with its "walled gardens and quiet paths". Then in his seventies, he was able to enjoy his remaining years at the villa, "the nest of his old age" as he called it, when he may have written the poem facing this page.

I, for one, cannot help liking Ausonius. I think he was one of us.

On New-blown Roses

Spring, and the sharpness of the golden dawn.
Before the sun was up a cooler breeze
Had blown, in promise of a day of heat,
And I was walking in my formal garden,
To freshen me, before the day grew old.

I saw the hoar frost stiff on the bent grasses,
Sitting in fat globes on the cabbage leaves,
And all my Paestum roses laughing at me,
Dew-drenched, and in the East the morning star,
And here and there a dewdrop glistening white,
That soon must perish in the early sun.

Think you, did Dawn steal colour from the roses,
Or was it new-born day that stained the rose?
To each one dew, one crimson, and one morning,
To star and rose, their lady Venus one.
Mayhap one fragrance, but the sweet of Dawn
Drifts through the sky, and closer breathes the rose.

A moment dies: this bud that was new-born
Has burgeoned even fold on even fold;
This still is green, with her close cap of leaves,
This shows a red stain on her tender sheath,
This the first crimson of the loosened bud.

And now she thinks to unwind her coverings,
And lo! the glory of the radiant chalice,
Scatt'ring the close seeds of her golden heart.
One moment, all on fire and crimson glowing,
All pallid now and bare and desolate.
I marvelled at the flying rape of time;
But now a rose was born: that rose is old.
Even as I speak the crimson petals float
Down drifting, and the crimsoned earth is bright.

So many lovely things, so rare, so young,
A day begat them, and a day will end.
O Earth, to give a flower so brief a grace!
As long as a day is long, so long the life of a rose.
The golden sun at morning sees her born,
And late at eve returning finds her old.
Yet wise is she, that hath so soon to die,
And lives her life in some succeeding rose.
O maid, while youth is with the rose and thee,
Pluck thou the rose: life is as swift for thee.

Roses in Regent's Park

A. G. L. HELLYER

No doubt many people have forgotten, if indeed they ever knew, that within the Inner Circle of Regent's Park there was once a privately owned botanical garden. It was leased from the Crown by the Royal Botanic Society and it contained, amongst other things, a huge conservatory known as the Winter Garden. Because the whole area was railed off and visitors had to pay a small fee to enter, it was a very convenient place in which to hold exhibitions and for years the National Rose Society, as it then was, used it for its Summer Show, displayed in great marquees set out on the lawn. I used to attend these shows in the 1920s as an exhibitor, but since the firm for which I worked grew scabious and not roses, we were relegated with the sundries to a glazed corridor at the back of the Winter Garden.

When the Royal Botanic Society's lease of this ground expired in 1932 it was not renewed. Instead the Winter Garden and corridor were demolished and the whole area within the Inner Circle was redesigned as part of Regent's Park, freely open to the public. What more fitting than that one part of this garden should be devoted entirely to roses?

I have heard several different versions of the way in which this venture began but they all have this in common. There was a widespread feeling in government as well as in horticultural circles that the British rose growing industry needed and deserved help and that a fine display garden in the heart of London would be of considerable assistance to it. So in 1932 a gift of rose bushes was made to Regent's Park by the British Rose Grower's Association probably, I think, at the suggestion of the Empire Marketing Board, and further gifts followed in later years.

These rose bushes were used to form the circular rose garden now familiarly known to the Regent's Park gardeners as "the cartwheel". Though I do not think that any of the varieties grown there to-day would have been found there in the 1930s, the design of this part of the garden remains virtually unchanged. It was so successful that very soon King George V consented to a suggestion that it should be known as Queen Mary's Garden and under that name it has become familiar to rose lovers in all parts of the world.

No great changes were made during the war years nor in the years immediately after the war, though with the aid of purchases and gifts the varieties grown were kept reasonably up to date. Sometimes varieties were grown which had been strangely neglected by the public and I particularly remember one magnificent bed of 'Pilar Landecho', a vigorous buff yellow rose raised just as the war was starting and perhaps for that reason overlooked by many rose growers. Well, there it was at Regent's Park, full of growth and flower every summer, a living reminder to all visitors of how easy it is to overlook what is good in pursuing what is merely new.

But the really big developments in Queen Mary's Garden came after Mr Simpson. Millar Gault was appointed Superintendent of Regent's Park in August 1955. Since by the time this article appears Mr Gault will have retired, and since I have known him well for a great many years, it is fitting that I should give a brief account of him before describing the many changes and additions he has made to the garden.

Mr Gault's term of office at Regent's Park has brought him so much fame that it has tended to obscure what he achieved before. In fact there are few gardeners who have had such a wide and varied experience, which has included periods in private service as well as in commercial and public gardening. It all began, so he assures me, when he was five years old in Caithness in the extreme north-east of Scotland, about as unfavourable a locality, one might imagine, as could be found in the British Isles to engender a love of gardening. But Millar must have been born with gardening in his blood for at that early age he was already growing flowers and digging up daisies from the fields if he could find nothing better to grow.

He began his professional career as an apprentice at Crathes Castle in Aberdeenshire in 1919 just about the time when the garden was beginning to undergo those changes which have made it one of the most famous among plant lovers in the whole of Scotland. He stayed there for a couple of years, went on as an improver to Taymouth Castle, where he learned to love and value magnificent trees, left when it became a hydro hotel and thereafter held a number of posts, first as journeyman, then as foreman, until in 1933 he became head gardener at Stoke Place, Slough to Sir Richard Howard-Vyse, Gold Stick in Waiting to the Queen. In the meantime he had worked under glass and in the open, had become familiar with the cultivation of flowers, fruits and vegetables, above all had learned to appreciate the value of soil cultivation and feeding as the only recipes for success in gardening.

There followed a period as head gardener at Cliveden when Lady Astor was at the height of her fame and the great house was the meeting place of politicians from all parts of the world. Neville Chamberlain was a frequent visitor keenly interested in the indoor plants, especially the orchids.

Mr Gault left Cliveden to become head gardener at St Andrews Hospital, Northampton. Six months later war broke out and for the next few years he had to devote all his very considerable energy and knowledge to the task of producing more home grown food. Typically he soon decided to do far more than was absolutely necessary and to exhibit vegetables as well as grow them. He brought 50 varieties of potatoes to a Royal Horticultural Society show and won a Silver Knightian Medal at his first attempt. Next time he had more varieties and a Gold Medal and the culmination of this period of his career came in 1948 when he put up four exhibits of vegetables in London, all of which were awarded Gold Medals and the last of which received, in addition, the Lawrence Medal as the best exhibit of the year at a R.H.S. show. It was these successes which determined me later on to commission him to write "Vegetables for Exhibition", out of print now but still in my view the best book on quality vegetable growing since Edwin Beckett's.

Mr Gault left St Andrews Hospital to become deputy manager at Suttons of Reading and two years later moved on to Bees Sealand Nurseries near Chester to take charge of the seed trials there. Had Mrs Gault liked Flintshire, he might have been there today, a very distinguished gardener but relatively unknown to rose growers. In fact she disliked it and persuaded her husband to apply for the post of Superintendent of Greenwich Park. He was duly appointed and launched on another, and in some respects the most important, phase of his remarkable career.

Greenwich provided a breathing space and a stepping stone to Regent's Park where he succeeded Mr Austin as Superintendent in August 1955.

First he improved the planting around the original circle, putting in more vigorous climbers such as *Rosa filipes* and *R. longicuspis* to clothe the ropes that link the encircling pillars and throw their scent over the whole garden. He also replaced the small beds near the Jubilee Gates with much larger rectangular beds set lengthwise to flank the entrance path. For some years now the carmine red floribunda 'Ohlala' has made a magnificent display in two of these beds.

From these improvements it was a natural step to link the beds near the Jubilee Gates with the circle by means of a series of fine rose beds all along the path and these have now been extended in the opposite direction right to the new restaurant beside the path leading out of the Inner Circle and down past Bedford College and the large lake to the Clarence Gates.

More beds were made flanking the smaller lake in the Inner Circle itself and this gave the garden a new, more informal, look linking it firmly with the general landscaping of this part of the park. Shrub roses were used in places here and also in a long border which follows the boundary of the Inner Circle all the way from Chester Road to the new restaurant. This development is still continuing and now, as one drives around the Inner Circle, roses peep out at one in many places through the railings.

Another innovation was that, in this new informal planting, roses were underplanted with many small shrubs and herbaceous plants. For this purpose Mr Gault has used several ornamental varieties of sage and rue, the lower growing geraniums such as *G. endressii* and "Johnson's Blue", hostas, *Hebe pageana* and many more. This has been so successful that some underplanting is now done around the edges of beds even in more formal parts of the garden.

A wide path cuts through the Inner Circle from the Jubilee Gates to a large statuary group in bronze at the far end. This surrounds a fountain, is set in a large formal pool and was erected in memory of Christian Hubert

Gortz, a benefactor of the park. As it nears this impressive memorial the path is flanked by eight large beds angled like the feathers of an arrow.

Even the density of the rose planting has been increased from an average of 2 ft apart for varieties of normal vigour to 1½ ft. The effect of this, combined with the great increase in the area of the rose garden, has been to raise the number of roses from about 10,000 in 1955 to 40,000 at the present time.

But it is not simply in size and number of roses grown that Queen Mary's Garden has developed in the last thirteen years. The proportion of new roses has also increased to so remarkable an extent that many rose lovers now look upon it almost as another trial garden. In this Mr Gault has been helped by the fact that, as a member of the R.N.R.S. Judging Committee, he is able to see new varieties well before they are placed on the market. He can then ask for early supplies of those that appear to have the vigour and freedom he requires, and since he enjoys the confidence of the trade and many rose growers realise the publicity value of a good display in Regent's Park, he is usually able to get what he wants.

During 1968 it was possible to see, amongst other new or newish roses in Queen Mary's Garden, 'Duke of Windsor', 'Peer Gynt', 'Summer Holiday', 'Blessings', 'Jubilant', 'Timothy Eaton', 'Beatrice', 'Orange Silk', 'City of Belfast', 'Shepherdess', 'Brasilia', 'Altissimo', 'Fred Loads', 'Swan Lake', 'Escapade', 'Bonsoir' and 'Bantry Bay'. Visitors were thus able to form a very good idea of the garden quality of these roses as seen growing side by side with older and better known varieties.

None of this has been permitted to interfere with quality, indeed if anything standards of cultivation now are higher than they have ever been. Where once only perhaps two rose beds were completely remade each autumn now the number is about twenty-five. All preliminary cultivation is to a depth of 2 ft and great quantities of new soil are brought in annually to replace that which has become tired through growing roses. Farmyard manure is used freely and so are fertilisers, though Mr Gault insists on his own mixture, which is John Innes base fertiliser plus Keiserite to provide extra magnesium. He also applies sulphate of potash in July to ripen growth and sometimes fish manure as well.

Pruning is spread over a period of three months from January to March and Mr Gault says the only difference he sees is that the early pruned bushes start to flower first.

For his many services to horticulture Mr Gault was awarded the Victoria Medal of Honour by the Royal Horticultural Society in 1963 and was made a Member of the Order of the British Empire in the New Year's Honours list of 1964. By a happy coincidence he actually received both awards on the same day in February 1964, going to Buckingham Palace in the morning to receive his M.B.E. from Prince Philip and to the Annual General Meeting of the R.H.S. in the afternoon to receive his V.M.H. from Lord Aberconway.

Amateur Detective

OLGA WEST

Mrs West is best known in this country as the raiser of the rose 'Africa Star'

Today it is difficult to pick up a rose book, magazine or annual which does not contain some article on hybridising. Many of these articles are now written *for* the amateur hybridiser, but not so many *by* amateurs, so I shall make this my excuse for writing—I am an amateur.

In referring to my first efforts at hybridising as those of an amateur, I mean this in every sense of the word; not only was I, by the dictionary definition of an amateur, "one who cultivates any study or art for the love of it, and not for money," but my efforts were amateurish—by the same dictionary defined as "clumsy and unskilled".

In fact, so great was the depth of my ignorance that, setting out to do my first crosses, I quite fearlessly declared my objective to all who would listen. Fortunately for my self esteem at that time, none of these had much more knowledge on the subject than I had, so I was not laughed out of court before I could begin! There I was, stating outright that my intention was to work towards producing the "blue rose"! Time and experience have brought enlightenment, however. One soon learns what a gulf usually exists between the rose of one's dreams and the result of any particular cross one makes, and also how elusive the true blue rose remains.

I now realise the great element of luck that favoured me, and enabled me to produce, among my earliest efforts, a rose of as good a colour as 'Africa Star'. At that stage, however, my ignorance was blissful. Having boldly declared my objective, I now had to do something about it, and as no one in this part of the world had any experience that would assist me I had to set about acquiring a little more knowledge from books, so after reading up the technical side of rose breeding, the techniques of cross pollination, after-ripening the seeds, planting and post-germination care, I turned for theory to what I can only call the hybridists' Bible—*Modern Roses*. For those who do not know it, this book is an amazing compilation of essential facts about practically all known and available roses—including their names, breeders, dates of introduction, and most important of all to the would-be hybridist, their parentage.

Here was the key to the past and, I hoped, to the future. Before trying to produce a "blue" rose, I must find out what had gone to the making of the roses already available in that colour range, so I began delving into the ancestry of roses.

I decided to concentrate on hybrid teas and floribundas in the lilac, lavender-blue group, and leave out of consideration all old roses, species, shrubs and climbers, and omit even modern roses such as 'Baby Faurax', a dwarf polyantha (and later 'Blue Boy' and 'Lavender Lassie', listed respectively as a Centifolia and a Hybrid Musk). I felt that once I crossed the line I would never be able to stop, and would be completely engulfed in old purples (beautiful as they are), non-remontants, miniatures and slow-to-flower or small-flowered climbers.

All my investigations and findings, therefore, refer exclusively to hybrid teas and floribundas.

The year was 1957, and I had available *Modern Roses IV*, published in 1952, and of course N.R.S. *Rose Annuals* and Select Lists. It is quite interesting to refer to these ten-years-old lists, and compare them with those of today, and note developments in this particular field of rose-breeding. In *Modern Roses IV* there were only six "blue" roses listed! (Today we have 42!)

The six listed were:

O I. 'Grey Pearl' 1945 (no parentage given at that time but I later found it given as ('Mrs Charles Lamplough' × seedling) × ('Sir David Davis' × 'Southport').

O II. 'Lavender Pinocchio' 1948 ('Pinocchio' × 'Grey Pearl').

III. 'Lavender Queen' 1951 (unnamed seedling × unnamed seedling).

X ★ IV. 'Lilette Mallerin' 1937 ('Charles P. Kilham' × unnamed *R. foetida bicolor* seedling).

X V. 'Tristesse' 1951 (again no parentage given at that time, but since then listed as 'Charles P. Kilham' × 'Betty Uprichard').

X ★ VI. 'Pigalle' 1951 ('Fantastique' × 'Boudoir').

When I looked back into the ancestry of these six, I found a few interesting facts beginning to emerge.

'Grey Pearl's' parentage I traced back for a century and a quarter, through over two dozen "ancestors", and I could find only reds, whites and pinks, except for one possibly significant variation, a rose called 'Ophirie', produced in 1841 and described as "reddish copper" and "rose and fawn".

Lilette Mallerin first brought to my attention the red-orange 'Charles P. Kilham' 1926 (parentage unknown), which was crossed with a *R. foetida bicolor* seedling—orange scarlet and yellow—to produce the mauve pink "Lilette".

In **Tristesse** 'Charles P. Kilham' again appeared and **Pigalle** gave 'Charles P. Kilham' and a mixed ancestry again, including *R. foetida bicolor*.

In fact, out of the five whose ancestry was given or partly given, 'Charles P. Kilham' appeared in three, and *R. foetida bicolor* appeared in two. Independently, 'Lavender Pinocchio' shared 'Grey Pearl's' ancestry.

To simplify future detection I now labelled 'Grey Pearl' O, 'Charles P. Kilham' X, and *R. foetida bicolor* ★.

By the end of 1957 another dozen "blues" had been produced. These were: 'Amy Vanderbilt', O; 'Esculor Clara', X ★; 'Gletscher', O; 'Lavender

Lady', O; 'Lilac Time', —; 'Magenta', O; 'Prelude', X ★; 'Royal Tan', X; 'Simone', O X ★; 'Sterling Silver', X ★; 'Twilight', O; 'Violetta', X ★.

Hot on the trail, I examined the family trees of the new dozen, and decided to mark them O, X, or ★ according to whether 'Grey Pearl', 'Charles P. Kilham' or *R. foetida bicolor* appeared in their backgrounds, at the same time keeping an eye open for any other significant facts which might come to light.

Now a real pattern emerged, as can be seen in the details shown above. Either 'Grey Pearl', 'Charles P. Kilham' or *R. foetida bicolor* appeared in eleven out of the twelve. 'Lilac Time' was the only outsider—all the others included in their make-up either one, two or all of my special three.

At that time I had 'Lilac Time', 'Lavender Pinocchio', 'Prelude' and 'Pigalle' in my garden, and I used these as the basis for my original crosses. Very unfortunately, the labels of one lot of crosses were lost, and out of this batch came 'Africa Star', so I cannot be absolutely sure of its parentage. I can fairly safely say, however, that its parentage included either 'Lavender Pinocchio' or 'Prelude'. So that 'Africa Star' is marked on my lists either O, or X ★ or both.

In the last ten years another 23 "blue" roses have been introduced. Again I have classified them O for 'Grey Pearl', X 'Charles P. Kilham' and ★ *R. foetida bicolor*.

The new list reads:

'Blue Diamond', X; 'Heure Mauve', X O ★; 'Intermezzo', O X ★; 'Kölner Karneval' ('Cologne Carnival); 'Lavender Bird', —; 'Lavender Charm', X O ★; 'Lavender Garnette', O; 'Lavender Girl', X ★; 'Lavender Love', ★; 'Lavender Pompon', O; 'Lavender Princess', O; 'Lilac Charm', † —; 'Lila Tan', O X ★; 'Lila Vidri', X ★; 'Mainzer Fastnacht' ('Blue Moon', 'Sissi'), X ★; 'Mauve Melodee', X ★; 'Orchid Masterpiece', O; 'Pigmy Lavender', O; 'Purpurine', X ★; 'Royal Lavender', O; 'Tutu Mauve', —; 'Violette Dot', X ★; 'Overture', O X ★.

Of these I have been unable to find the parentage of four.† Every single one of the other 19 contains either 'Grey Pearl', 'Charles P. Kilham' or *R. foetida bicolor* in its ancestry.

Summing up the results of these investigations, we have 42 modern "blue group" roses. Of these, I know nothing of the ancestry of five, 'Lavender Queen', 'Kölner Karneval', 'Lavender Bird', 'Lilac Charm' and 'Tutu Mauve'.

This leaves us 37 whose parentage we can trace, at least partially. Of these, 19 (or a possible 20, including 'Africa Star'), share *'Grey Pearl's'* ancestry; 21 (or possibly 22, again including 'Africa Star'), have *'Charles P. Kilham'* in their pedigree; and 19 (or 20 with 'Africa Star' as another possible) have *R. foetida bicolor.*

† One parent was 'Lavender Pinocchio', so this should be coded O. *Ed.*

Only two are derived from neither 'Grey Pearl' nor 'Charles P. Kilham', these two being 'Lavender Love', which does include R. *foetida bicolor*, and (still the odd one out) 'Lilac Time', which includes none of the three; but possibly also of significance, it does have R. *foetida persiana* in its ancestry, and this rose also appears in the background of a number of others listed above.

According to *Modern Roses*, 'Charles P. Kilham' was a red-orange colour, and R. *foetida bicolor*, orange-scarlet with a yellow reverse. 'Grey Pearl' had all the usual reds, whites and pinks in her past, but also included 'Ophirie', reddish-copper, rose and fawn.

These are the facts—perhaps some hybridists with greater knowledge and experience than mine will draw some interesting conclusions for us from these facts,† and perhaps some other amateur seekers for the blue rose will find this summary useful for future breeding programmes.

I am left with plans and dreams and a kaleidoscopic mental picture of red-orange, orange-scarlet, reddish-copper and rose and fawn—but where, oh where, did the blue come from?

Author's Note: Since writing this article I have received the 1968 *Rose Annual*, in which mention is made of Mr Harkness's new Certificate of Merit floribunda 'Escapade'. Here the lilac colour comes from 'Baby Faurax', a violet dwarf polyantha of unknown parentage, omitted from the above lists as it was neither a hybrid tea nor a floribunda.

This Annual also includes Mr Harkness's very interesting article on his breeding programmes. His new "blue group" roses all appear to come from 'Lilac Charm', 'Africa Star' and 'Sterling Silver'—all referred to above. It is interesting to note that 'Lilac Time' (the only "outsider" in my lists) has given him no worthwhile results. This has been my experience too, so far.

O. A. W.

† See Mr. Le Grice's paper on "Breeding Blue and Brown Roses", read to The Fourth International Rose Conference. *Ed.*

R.N.R.S. Award-winning Roses in Australia

L. V. LAWRENCE

Imagine if you can roses growing in a land where the summers are moderately hot and dry whilst the winters are comparatively mild and wet. Such are the almost ideal climatic conditions under which rose lovers in the southern parts of Australia can grow and enjoy this fascinating hobby of rose growing. A well-grown rose plant generally reaches an average height of 5 ft and a width of 4 ft with an abundance of flowers in keeping with the size of the plant.

Here in Melbourne our average annual rainfall is 26 in. and about three-quarters of this rain falls between May and October, the beginning of winter to mid-spring. During the winter months our rose bushes are almost dormant. The main flush of roses comes during late October and early November, but this spring blooming period varies slightly depending on the locality. Adelaide and Sydney are a little earlier, whilst Hobart is two weeks later. Most of the rose shows are held during this time. The main spring flush is followed by a second blooming about Christmas. By judicious summer-trimming in February and a general feeding of the plants our rose bushes produce yet another flush in autumn which equals, and with some varieties is superior to the spring blooming. It is true that some roses can be picked throughout the year but these are the three main blooming periods.

Our pests and diseases include aphids, thrips, Mildew, Black Spot and Rust which is increasing.

Having explained the different climatic conditions under which we grow our roses here in Melbourne, you will appreciate that the behaviour patterns of the cultivars which have won some of your major awards in the United Kingdom may be affected to some degree. Australian rosarians would appear to get the best of two worlds, as most of the best new roses from both Europe and America reach our gardens within a season or two. Thus, most keen rose lovers here are avid readers of your English publications, particularly when the awards in your wonderful trials are announced. We cannot plant these new beauties in our gardens quickly enough, especially if they promise to be suitable for exhibition. Some of your top roses have been superb in our conditions, whilst others have left a lot to be desired.

The following comments on some of the roses which have been successful in your trial grounds and which are now growing in my garden may be of interest.

As it is premature to comment on your latest winners, I shall begin with 1966. The President's International Trophy was withheld in that year and no Gold Medals were awarded, but 'Charm of Paris', the first winner of the

'AFRICA STAR' (see page 60)

'LILAC CHARM' (see page 62)

S. M. Gault

Roses and the lake; Queen Mary's
Garden, Regent's Park. (*see page 58*)

Henry Edland Memorial Medal, has shown good promise. The unusual shade of pink is attractive and the hot drought conditions of our 1967–68 growing season suited this cultivar, although it does seem to "spot" badly in rain or dew. I think that 'Redgold', a very striking red and yellow floribunda from Dickson's, will be very popular. Massed displays at some of our recent shows have drawn very favourable comments.

The 1965 President's Trophy winner, 'Grandpa Dickson', became available in this country in 1967 and already some good blooms have been seen in our gardens and at our shows. The colour is paler than reports indicated, probably due to our warmer conditions. Some growers (mostly in New South Wales) report that it is prone to Black Spot, but this has not been evident in my own garden.

'Ernest H. Morse' has settled into our gardens and I think it is the only red variety I have ever grown which is completely free of mildew. This bright red rose with its healthy upright growth has the one weakness that the petals have a tendency to curve in instead of reflexing when picked. This fault has disappeared on more mature plants.

'Apricot Nectar' is a most attractive new colour in floribundas although, from overseas descriptions, I had expected a deeper colouring—it is a pale buff with me. Moreover, although I do not see much Black Spot in my garden this cultivar was infected last season, but it has grown well.

Turning to 1964 we have that outstanding variety 'Duftwolke' ('Fragrant Cloud') which has fulfilled every promise we read about it. The growth is healthy and very quick to repeat whilst the flowers are stable in colour and very sweetly scented. I can understand some people not being able to classify it, as typical growth of both hybrid tea and floribunda appeared on my plants during the season but, with disbudding, it will reach show bench standard and has already been in many winning exhibits. It does get a little Black Spot.

'Blue Moon', which won a Certificate of Merit, has not grown well with many Melbourne rose lovers. I find difficulty in separating this variety from 'Kölner Karneval' and, whilst neither of these varieties is first class, they are still probably the best of this colour grouping at the present time.

One rose which was only named in 1964, although it received a Trial Ground Certificate prior to 1963, was 'Norman Hartnell' and it has proved itself to be an exhibitor's real delight. It is a consistently good exhibition rose in our climate and, at our large convention show in 1967, it was frequently included in the stands of winning exhibits.

In 1963 the floribunda, 'Elizabeth of Glamis', won the highest honours in the trial grounds. My own plants have not grown as vigorously as most other bushes but as regards colour and disease resistance it is good. The colour is wonderful with no fading in our sunshine. Of the other three varieties which won Gold Medals in 1963 I rate 'Evelyn Fison' as the finest red floribunda in my garden, with 'Europeana', a Certificate of Merit winner, next. 'Casino' is a good yellow climber, but I much prefer 'Royal Gold' which is the best yellow rose I grow. We are lamentably short of good yellow roses, so perhaps 'Grandpa Dickson' and 'Winefred Clarke' which I have planted recently, will fill this need.

Another Certificate of Merit winner, 'Pascali', has proved to be, in my opinion, the finest white rose over recent years. Unlike most whites it does not succumb to mildew and the neat flowers are favourites with most floral arrangers. 'Violet Carson', another award winner, is a delightful floribunda with a very soft unusual colouring which does not fade in our warm conditions.

'Uncle Walter' and 'Evensong' are not popular because the former does not bloom well after the initial spring flush, whilst the latter has not enough petals in our conditions.

Because the President's International Trophy was withheld the British top awards for 1962 were three Gold Medals. The three winners were 'Isabel de Ortiz', 'Chinatown' and 'Pink Parfait'. 'Isabel de Ortiz' is not widely grown now because the blooms are too large and coarse. There were very few plants of 'Chinatown' released because most of the budded plants developed a virus, but 'Pink Parfait' is one of my best floribundas. It blooms continuously right through the season until mid-winter.

I shall conclude by naming a few of your roses in addition to those already mentioned which I have found most satisfactory to grow. These include 'Silver Lining', 'June Park', 'Ena Harkness', 'Josephine Bruce', 'Ophelia', 'Mischief' and 'Piccadilly'.

Slaves of the Rose Garden

DR A. DICK

How good is the modern rose and how long will it survive? Some time must elapse before the answer to these questions is known. Quite apart from the qualities of the rose its survival is often dependent on publicity at the time of introduction and on its subsequent popularity. It may even happen for some reason or another that a new variety may fail to attract the public eye and disappear from catalogues in a short time, although in all other respects the rose is regarded as first rate.

My first recollection of my father's rose garden of some 350 bushes dates back almost 50 years and I now recall the names of several varieties (arranged alphabetically) which I then regarded as excellent garden roses.

'Daily Mail Rose', 1913	'Mme Abel Chatenay', 1895
'Dorothy Page Roberts', 1907	'Mme Butterfly', 1920
'Duchess of Wellington', 1909	'Mme Caroline Testout', 1890
'General MacArthur', 1905	'Mrs A. R. Waddell', 1908
'George Dickson', 1912	'Mrs John Laing', 1887
'Harry Kirk', 1907	'Mrs Wemyss Quin', 1914
'Hugh Dickson', 1904	'Ophelia', 1912
'Kaiserin Auguste Viktoria', 1891	'Pharisäer', 1903
'Los Angeles', 1916	'Richmond', 1905

This list is representative of the varieties grown some 50 years ago; they offered a limited range of colourings, but all were regarded as good roses which could be used for indoor decoration or some for specimen blooms. It would be of interest to note just how many of these old roses have survived and are still growing today. Some, as we shall see, are still available from several nurserymen.

I have sufficient knowledge of many of the old varieties to be able to identify most; accordingly, during the summer months I have scrutinised roses grown in gardens or parks in an attempt to find out which varieties introduced before 1950 are most frequently encountered today. These I shall sub-divide to include the hybrid tea type, the floribunda and the climber in its various forms. Space permits only the briefest description of some of the varieties which I list chronologically according to the year of introduction, but I shall try to bring out the chief virtues which have permitted the variety to survive for so long. Finally, I shall venture to predict which varieties introduced subsequent to 1950 will live to a "ripe old age".

Hybrid Tea Type

The lovely pink 'Mme Caroline Testout' (1890) is still widely grown both in bush and—perhaps more profitably—in climbing form. The blooms are full and slightly globular but are freely produced and remarkably resistant to rain. This is one of the older roses which I consider well worth growing.

Next, I include 'Frau Karl Druschki' (1900) regarded by many exhibitors as the best white variety. It does well if lightly pruned and makes a good specimen bush or covers a short pillar or low wall. Apart from pink on the outer petals it is certainly our purest white, of perfect form, and is remarkably hardy; unfortunately it is marked by rain and subject to mildew.

Two red roses, 'Hugh Dickson' (1904) and 'George Dickson' (1912) are still prominent in older rose gardens. The former was introduced by the Belfast firm bearing its name while the latter came from Alex. Dickson of Newtownards. "Hugh" is the more vigorous and is very effective when the long shoots, which it produces freely, are pegged down. It is a healthy scented red rose, but not too free flowering by modern standards. The deeper 'George Dickson' can produce massive blooms of a delightful fragrance but how it hangs its neck!

'Ophelia' (1912) is a very fine decorative rose which is a delight to grow and, apart from its proneness to thrips early in the season, it is worthy of a place in any rose garden. Two sports 'Mme Butterfly' (1920), which also sported as 'Lady Sylvia' (1927) are of a deeper pink but I prefer the pale flesh pink 'Ophelia'.

'Mme E. Herriot' (1913), better known as the 'Daily Mail Rose' is unique, as it was the first flame-coloured hybrid tea rose. Not a vigorous grower, it makes an excellent buttonhole rose and is one of the earliest varieties in bloom. While the bush form is rarely propagated nowadays the climbing sport is readily available and does well on south facing walls.

An outstanding variety after World War I was undoubtedly 'Etoile de Hollande' (1919). This was an excellent crimson garden rose, fragrant, healthy and wet resistant, but not too vigorous. Like several of the above varieties its climbing sport has proved more satisfactory and blooms profusely.

The inter-war years saw the introduction of very many excellent varieties from the famous Irish hybridisers. From Alex. Dickson came 'Betty Uprichard' (1922), 'Shot Silk' (1924) and 'Dame Edith Helen' (1926), while from Sam McGredy III came 'Mrs Sam McGredy' (1929), 'Picture' (1932), 'McGredy's Yellow' (1933) and 'Hector Deane' (1938), to mention a few of the most popular varieties.

Space does not permit detailed description, but the fact that several are still in demand speaks for itself. Of the Dickson seedlings 'Shot Silk' is doubtless a very fine rose, healthy and wet resistant; it is still widely cultivated today and I consider this to be one of Grandpa Dickson's very best.

Of the McGredy varieties which have survived longest it is interesting to note that the majority are essentially decorative roses, by which I mean those not normally large enough for exhibiting in the specimen bloom classes. The exception is, of course, 'McGredy's Yellow', probably the purest yellow rose yet available and an excellent variety if it is well cultivated. Of the others, I would single out two, 'Mrs Sam McGredy' for its lovely bronze foliage and copper-salmon blooms. It is not too hardy in the north, but as a climber against a sheltered wall it is well worth growing. 'Hector Deane', because of its wonderful fragrance and vigour, deserves special mention. Perhaps I should be interested in this variety; it was named after the Irish surgeon who removed the tonsils of Sam McGredy IV! Unfortunately, it is susceptible to rust and should not be grown in affected areas.

The Irish roses certainly dominated the British market in the 20's and 30's, but several American varieties proved popular, especially the tall and vigorous orange-yellow and pink 'President H. Hoover' (1930) and clear pink 'The Doctor' (1936), both of which are still widely grown. The latter, however, is susceptible to Black Spot and is at its best in town gardens.

In the next decade three really outstanding varieties were introduced, 'Peace' (1942), 'Ena Harkness' (1946) and 'Eden Rose' (1950). These three need no further introduction, and for at least 15 years they were to remain the most popular and widely grown garden roses; in fact, 'Peace' probably still holds its supreme position. Many red roses have appeared since 'Ena Harkness', but I doubt if any has shown much improvement; if the stems had only been firmer one could hardly have faulted this rose. 'Eden Rose' recently has lost some popularity largely due to apparent lack of freedom of flowering in some areas, but I have not found this to be so in Scotland.

Floribundas

The story of the floribunda rose, as we know it today, differs vastly from that of the hybrid tea. Prior to 1924 we had a group of dwarf bedding roses known as polyantha pompons which had limited appeal.

We must thank Svend Poulsen for his pioneer work on the modern floribunda. He introduced 'Else Poulsen' (1924), 'Kirsten Poulsen' (1924), 'Karen Poulsen' (1933) and 'Poulsen's Pink' (1939), all of which are vigorous free flowering varieties still found in many gardens and parks. Unfortunately, they are liable to mildew and have declined in popularity.

A British hybridiser to whom praise is also due is E. B. Le Grice. His famous "Maid series" started in 1938 with 'Dainty Maid'. At the recent Autumn Show I admired several bowls of this wonderful bi-colour pink variety and thought what a real beauty it is. 'Dainty Maid' is widely grown in Scotland and stands up well to wet weather.

Soon after World War II the floribunda rose was to find its feet again and before long was to take a foremost place in rose catalogues and prove more popular, for bedding, than the hybrid tea. Some of the American introductions from Eugene Boerner proved to be outstanding and in a short space of time he introduced 'Fashion' (1946), 'Vogue' (1949), 'Masquerade' (1950), 'Ma Perkins' (1952) and 'Spartan' (1954).

In 1946 Albert Norman introduced 'Frensham' while in 1956 E. B. Le Grice contributed 'Allgold'; these were to prove the most popular red and yellow floribundas for over a decade. The popularity of 'Frensham' is now declining owing to its susceptibility to mildew, again reflecting our insistence on having disease-resistant varieties.

One cannot yet be critical of the very numerous more recent floribunda introductions which flow continuously from such famous growers as McGredy, Dickson, Harkness, Tantau, Kordes and Meilland to mention only a few. I must, however, include amongst the really outstanding floribundas two varieties introduced after 1950 which have already made their mark and set a very high standard on which to assess future tall-growing and vigorous floribundas; I refer of course to 'Queen Elizabeth' (1955) and 'Iceberg' (1958).

Climbers

Of the older climbing roses still extensively grown I include 'Gloire de Dijon' (1853), 'Zéphirine Drouhin' (1868) and 'Mme Alfred Carrière' (1879). The first is a vigorous and very fragrant creamy-buff tea rose which blooms early in summer and again late in the autumn. 'Zéphirine Drouhin' is the thornless scented pink Bourbon climber well known to all rose lovers and not too rampant; it makes an excellent pillar rose. 'Mme Alfred Carrière', a personal favourite, is a vigorous, pale pinkish-white noisette climber which is markedly fragrant and is rarely out of bloom all season. It is healthy and hardy and can be used to cover pillars, pergolas or walls.

Turning to the wichuraiana ramblers which bloom only once a year and are frequently used to cover fences or walls, 'Dorothy Perkins' (1901), 'American Pillar' (1902) and 'Excelsa' (1909) have proved the most popular. I think they are now going out of favour because of their restricted flowering season and strong susceptibility to mildew. They have survived for sixty years and I think they have had their day.

Other early introductions which are still popular include 'Dr W. Van Fleet' (1910) and its very excellent repeat-flowering sport 'New Dawn' (1930), 'Paul's Scarlet Climber' (1915) and 'Albertine' (1921). Of these I would particularly recommend 'New Dawn' and 'Albertine', both hardy climbers of pale flesh pink, and coppery pink colouring respectively.

In the 20's and 30's I have already mentioned in the section on hybrid teas that many such varieties were more profitably grown in climbing form. As examples of this group of climbers still giving great satisfaction I include the 'Daily Mail Rose', 'Mme Butterfly' and 'Mrs Sam McGredy' as three of the best and certainly the most popular.

After the Second World War climbing roses were to enter a new era of popularity and improvement, much as the floribundas did. One of the earliest successes was 'Danse du Feu' (1954) and this was to be followed by excellent varieties from several hybridisers in Britain and, in particular, from Kordes in Germany. These new varieties proved hardy and very free flowering. Some of them may lack the fragrance and charm of the early climbers and I think there is much to be gained by striking a balance to include the old as well as the new.

Conclusions

In a non-statistical survey it is impossible to be dogmatic, but I feel reasonably confident that I have included the best of the earlier introductions which have grown well in Scotland and survived for so many years.

It would appear that the modern hybrid tea rose is more vigorous, free flowering and disease resistant than a lot of the older varieties and many are strongly scented.

Modern varieties are certainly produced in a wider range of colourings and at present demand appears to favour bright shades or bi-colours.

The modern floribunda is vastly superior to the older polyantha rose for mass bedding, and is fairly disease resistant and hardier than the hybrid tea.

Some of the modern climbers are free- if not perpetual-flowering but they lack the charm and perhaps fragrance of old climbing varieties.

Rambler roses are gradually disappearing and have limited use in the modern rose garden.

It is frequently stated that too many new varieties are introduced each year. With an ever increasing number of hybridisers the annual output is likely to increase, not diminish. This is as it should be, because no rose is yet perfect, and there are not too many top quality roses. The work of the hybridiser must therefore continue, not cease. I suggest there is at present a real need for further short-growing floribunda roses in a variety of colourings.

If the modern rose is so good, we might reasonably expect many to survive for a very long time. This however, is unlikely to be so because, in a world which enjoys and demands changing fashions, only the best of our present varieties are likely to survive upwards of 25 years; the others will be replaced by future introductions possessing superior qualities. Varieties which have proved successful and seem destined to survive for some time yet seem to me to include 'Super Star', 'Fragrant Cloud', 'Pink Favourite', 'Rose Gaujard', 'Piccadilly', 'Mischief', 'Sutter's Gold' and 'Wendy Cussons'.

I have already commented on two outstanding floribundas, namely 'Iceberg' and 'Queen Elizabeth'. Other varieties in this class which have proved highly satisfactory in Scotland include 'Evelyn Fison', 'Lilli Marlene', 'Pink Parfait', 'Paddy McGredy' and 'City of Leeds'. New climbers of considerable merit are 'Maigold', 'Golden Showers', 'Casino', 'Pink Perpetue', 'Bantry Bay' and 'Copenhagen', but time is necessary to assess how these varieties will compare with their counterparts of 50 years ago.

A Note on Systemic Fungicides

E. F. ALLEN, M.A., Dip. Agric. (Cantab.), A.I.C.T.A.

Systemic pesticides have such obvious advantages over more traditional types that the advent of systemic insecticides some years ago was welcomed by farmers, growers and gardeners everywhere. Not only were such materials more long-lasting because they could not be washed off foliage by rain, but also they clearly presented a reduced hazard to beneficial insects such as ladybirds. Two examples of such insecticides will be familiar to rosarians— namely formothion (Toprose Systemic Spray) and dimethoate (Boots Systemic Greenfly Killer).

For many years plant pathologists have looked forward to using systemic fungicides so that plant diseases could be controlled more effectively and with fewer spray applications. Such chemicals would be of especial benefit in a very wet year and many rosarians must have wished for a systemic fungicide during 1968. However, the production of these chemicals has presented many technical problems. Griseofulvin was perhaps the first in the field and was under study more than a decade ago. This interesting antibiotic certainly possessed systemic capabilities but its effective life within the living plant proved to be too short to be really satisfactory. Nevertheless it has been used in recent years by growers of both lettuce and chrysanthemums.

Probably the first really efficient systemic fungicide became available for test purposes in this country only in the summer of 1968 under the code name of Du Pont 1991, later to be called Benlate. This is a 50 per cent wettable powder formulation of the methyl ester of 1-(butylcarbamoyl)-2-benzimidazole carbamic acid. I am indebted to a friend in New Zealand (Dr K. R. W. Hammett in litt.) for first drawing my attention to this material as he had been able to demonstrate activity against Rose Powdery Mildew from soil incorporation at rates as low as 2 ppm by weight of soil, with a useful range between 50–100 ppm in pot trials.

In an outdoor trial in my own garden I was able to make four spray applications between 25 July and the end of August. The concentrations used were 5 and 10 oz. of the formulation per 100 gallons water plus 8 fl. oz. of a special wetting agent called Surfactant F. The higher rate, certainly, proved to be eradicant on newly established Powdery Mildew on both 'Frensham' and 'Iceberg'.

In a replicated trial on 'Anne Letts' results were less conclusive because all twelve bushes, including the unsprayed controls, remained free from Mildew even on the flower stem necks although a little had been present in early July.

I have not yet been able to demonstrate systemic action on rose bushes growing outside. However, tests on small pot-grown seedlings showed that the systemic acaricidal effect was quite rapid under glasshouse conditions, the action being ovicidal on *Tetranychus telarius,* the Glasshouse Red Spider Mite. The systemic movement within the plant is apparently only upward and it is sufficient to provide protection against Powdery Mildew on rose seedlings, but I noted eradicant action only with direct spray application to foliage.

Benlate is expected to be on the garden retail market in 1970 and it should be under test at the Society's Trial Grounds during 1969. It seems to be a very remarkable material and is active against a wide range of fungus parasites, including Black Spot and Verticillium Wilt. It is, however, inactive against bacteria and the Phycomycetes, which include Rose Downy Mildew and Potato Blight. Preliminary tests indicate that activity against Rose Rust is insufficient to give control. As regards the use of Benlate for Black Spot control I have not yet made a satisfactory evaluation.

At least four other systemic fungicides have been available for trial during 1968 and two of these, Plantvax and Vitavax, have been included in my trials against Rose Rust. Plantvax, the less developed of the two formulations, gave very good Rust control but Vitavax was ineffective although it provided systemic protection against Black Spot. In my view both of these materials show considerable promise, but they probably require further development. I look forward to testing improved formulations in the future.

The Fourth International Rose Conference 2-4 July 1968

Lectures delivered at the Hilton Hotel, London W.1
from 2-4 July 1968

CONFERENCE SUB-COMMITTEE

B. W. W. Sampson (CHAIRMAN)

E. F. Allen	E. V. Elwes	Maj.-Gen. R. F. B. Naylor
R. C. Balfour	F. Fairbrother	Bertram Park
F. M. Bowen	J. L. Harkness	Brig. C. E. Lucas Phillips
J. Clarke	J. W. Mattock	H. Wheatcroft

INTRODUCTION

The following extracts are taken from the article of welcome, written by the President, which was included in the Souvenir Programme issued at Alexandra Palace on the occasion of "The Great Summer Rose Show" immediately prior to the opening of the Conference.

"First let me welcome on behalf of the Council of The Royal National Rose Society all those, and in particular those from overseas, who are attending this, our 89th Summer Rose Show and the Fourth International Rose Conference.

In 1858 the Reverend S. Reynolds Hole, with the help of a small band of enthusiasts, organised in London the first National Rose Show. After three years, the organisation of this Show was handed over to the Royal Horticultural Society and it was not until 1876 that another distinguished cleric—The Reverend Honywood D'ombrain decided that the time had come when a National Rose Society should be founded to concentrate solely on the Rose. Accordingly, with the help of some of the leading nurserymen and amateurs he launched the National Rose Society in 1876 with the Reverend Reynolds Hole as its first President.

The first Summer Show was held at St James's Hall, Piccadilly, in 1877, at which 100 exhibitors exhibited some 10,000 blooms. Much water has flowed under the bridge since then and at our Summer Shows now some 300 exhibitors stage 47,000 blooms.

Many leading amateurs of those days grew roses by the thousand—the record going to H. V. Machin of Worksop who in the '80s and '90s of the last century grew upwards of 40,000. Roses in those days were not nearly as floriferous as they are now and some varieties had to be grown by the hundred to secure the blooms required on the day of the show.

It is interesting to note that our Amateur Champion of 1967, Colonel W. B. Wright of Instow in Devon, grows only about 400 rose bushes and cuts 150 blooms for the show.

Since its inauguration in 1876 the Society's membership has grown as follows: in 1878 there were 320 members; in 1900—500; in 1914—6,500; in 1927 (50 years old)—14,000; in 1947—16,000 and in 1967—116,000 (including 16,000 new members.) In the 10 years since the last International Rose Conference was held the membership has almost doubled.

And now a few words about the Conference. International Rose Conferences have been held by the Society in London in 1928, 1938 and 1958 and it is our intention to hold the next one in 1976 to coincide with the centenary of the foundation of the Society.

The object of the Society when it was founded was laid down as:

"The extending and encouraging by every means and power, the cultivation and exhibiting of the Rose, and of uniting all who are interested in it in one bond of Union."

and it remains basically the same today.

The aim in holding these Conferences is to bring together leading rosarians, amateur and professional, from all over the world to discuss together how the culture and cultivation of the rose may be improved. At the same time they will have an opportunity of seeing our roses and of making new friends in the rose world, a world that knows no barriers."

Delegates from overseas included representatives or parties from Australia, Belgium, Canada, Denmark, Eire, France, Germany, Holland, Italy, Israel, New Zealand, Poland, Rumania, South Africa, Switzerland, and from 25 states of the United States of America. The largest party of 90 came from New Zealand and 85 from the U.S.A.

With the gracious permission of Her Majesty the Queen an afternoon Reception was held in St James's Palace on Monday, 1 July for delegates from overseas, which our Royal Patron Her Majesty Queen Elizabeth The Queen Mother honoured with her presence. This proved a memorable occasion which ensured a successful start for the Conference.

Rose Propagation
Chairman: E. J. Baldwin

DAVID E. GILAD
Department of Floriculture, Ministry of Agriculture, State of Israel
Rose Propagation in Sub-tropical Areas

The subject of propagation of roses in sub-tropical areas has quite a limited application to people in your climatic conditions.

We have what we call summer sub-tropical conditions, which means that we have those typical sunny and warm summers with very mild winters, and I would say that this applies all over the Mediterranean area more or less.

Our rainy season starts only in late autumn, sometimes the middle of November. We do not have more than thirty days of rain during our winter season, which ends some time in February or March. So you see our conditions are quite different. Because of that we have to take a different rootstock. We are working with the *Rosa odorata* var. Indica Major rootstock which belongs to the Indicae Group.

This rootstock is propagated as hard wood cuttings in our conditions. When our nurserymen first came into the country some time in 1928, they started propagating in their nurseries using the same methods and systems and more or less the same timetable as was used in Europe. So they used to plant their cuttings some time around November, budding only in late spring or the beginning of summer— sometimes it was about the end of April or May if good weather was available. Generally in the old days they did not know the cold storage system for bud work, and things were much more difficult. Naturally budding in mid-summer did not help matters, and the "take" was not so good.

The plants were dug the same year, around December/January, at the latest in February. Naturally those plants did not become dormant enough. They were quite green and tender. So, looking around and watching how other places managed, we tried to combine a method of propagation used in the west coast of the United States with some techniques we thought would suit our conditions.

So now our system of work is quite different. We in effect shifted our seasons and fitted our propagating techniques to our difficult climatic conditions.

Under our old way of working we planted the cuttings about the middle of November, budding them only in April or May, and then we cut back the rootstock immediately. We had to lap over the stock, letting the bud grow gradually. The main difference was that it used to have the stub, and we could not cut the stub in our conditions without getting die-back of the plant.

Now the new system, compared with the old one, is shifting the seasons, as I have said. First of all we plant the cuttings in mid-summer, in our greatest heat, from mid-August to the beginning of September. Of course, we cannot do it without irrigation, and we use sprinklers to irrigate overhead and give us light sprinklings two or three times a day according to the weather. We get a very fast rooting system, therefore, and in eight weeks the cuttings are ready for budding.

They are budded some time at the end of October, during November and, according to the weather, it could even extend into December. Now those stocks are left as dormant buds, though not all stay dormant, until the end of February, the first signs of spring in our conditions, and then they are just topped or cut back to the bud itself without leaving any of the stock, and the buds are just allowed to grow out. These plants grow through the summer naturally, and then in autumn, towards winter, they are ready for digging out and selling.

That is the difference between the two systems. Naturally you will realise that shifting to the new system, which we call autumn budding, compared with the old system of spring budding, gave us two or three extra months of growth, and this might seem to be a disadvantage. But under our conditions we do not get the stub woody enough or hardy enough, so we felt that those two or three extra months would do a lot of good to the plants. We found out, also, a few more advantages, but I will mention them later.

We keep our mother plants of Indica Major separate. We think that segregation is good also for other reasons, especially as I mentioned the mosaic virus that, in certain techniques in using or re-using cuttings from plants that have been budded, you could spread quite widely. So we keep our mother plants in separate blocks. We use only one-year-old growth for our cuttings. When we feel they are ripe enough—it would be some time around July—we cut down our irrigation, and let them defoliate themselves the natural way, to stop their growth, in order to get really woody cuttings for our season.

And here you can see the cut back plants brought to the shed where, if any foliage is left, it is removed, and the cuttings are prepared by tying and bunching them together. In the smaller nurseries they will cut them with the clippers, with a pair of scissors to 20 cm., and in the larger scale nurseries they will do it with a band-saw in the regular way. These cuttings are turned over to the next station, where they de-eye them and leave only two buds at the top. All the rest of the buds are de-eyed to avoid suckers in the future.

Here we have the root cuttings which were de-eyed except for the two top buds. They are then planted in the field. In the matter of distances, it depends on the type of nursery and what they are doing. I have not mentioned yet the system of rooted cuttings with dormant eyes, which is part of that method of propagation, and I refer to it later.

As already mentioned, eight weeks after planting the cuttings are ready for budding. It is the budding with the T shaped slit, taking off the buds with a piece of wood and using the same blade for cutting the bark and opening at the same time. Here you see the T shape cut. This shows taking off the bud with some wood in it—we are not separating the wood as that makes it easier for us, and we can manage to do a better job. This shows inserting the bud straight from the blade direct into the slit. We tie our buds with plastic polyethylene strips as we find these best under our conditions. They retain the moisture and set the bud well. We have tried different types of rubber, but did not find them suitable for our climate, because either the rubber dried out and broke too fast or sometimes it would not give a good tie and the buds would split out from the rootstock.

Although I said we are budding using the dormant bud system, even so lots of the buds might grow out quite fast. So we have to take care during winter and, if certain buds grow out too fast, we have to pinch out the tops to harden them a bit and to ensure that they will not be broken by winds or rain.

Then early in spring, some time around February—it might be the end of February—as soon as the climate permits, we cut all the rootstocks down, back to the bud itself, shortening the bud where it has grown out to the second or third leaf, and that is the job completed. Thereafter, we just try to keep our nurseries clean, using Simazine, which we find satisfactory, and the following December the plants are ready for sale.

That was the system I described earlier of producing maiden plants with the Rosa Indica Major cutting rootstock under our conditions. Now a new system was developed three years ago, as we were interested to meet the demand for the cut flower trade for greenhouses, and using the same cuttings, prepared and budded in the same way, we tried digging them much earlier, before the buds grow out, as rooted cuttings with dormant buds. Another way, when our growers were interested to receive plants later and still obtain a crop of flowers in the winter, was

to dig them with a started bud and cut them back to two buds. Actually this is the halfway stage between the two methods already mentioned. Again, the seasons are the same more or less; in this case, of course, we operate only from mid-August until at the latest the middle of February when dealing with dormant buds, and the season might extend into March with started buds.

Naturally we plant much closer under this system, about 27,000 cuttings to a thousand square metres, so it would be four times as many, or approximately 100,000 to an acre. The plants are dug with the new blade system, the same system as the big plants. They are pulled out with gloves and brought into the shed. In the shed, of course, we try to keep them in water, to be sure they won't dry out. You see, on a typical February day the sun is almost like here in July.

They are graded, cut back and cleaned; every bud is inspected to see it is sound, and the plastic is removed. In this case we try to keep the bud dormant by tying it with polyethylene strips round the bud itself, and that is the finished product. You can see we have a pretty good root system considering the only time we had to develop it was from mid-August to the middle of February at the latest, and the bud is well-taken, well-heeled, dormant and ready for planting. Actually at this stage we leave this stub to afford protection against dying back.

Our latest experiments are with mist propagation methods.

RALPH S. MOORE
Sequoia Nursery, California
Propagation of Miniature Roses

My climate is somewhat similar to Mr Gilad's in that we don't have any really harsh winters in the area in which I am growing, as you can judge by the fact that we can grow such things as oranges nearby and we have a variety of other crops.

Our own propagation methods and procedures may be divided into three parts, namely seeds, cuttings, and budding or

grafting. I will speak of seeds first, as this is where all varieties start.

Some kinds, or strains of roses, including miniature or baby roses, can be and are grown from seeds. Some of these, such as species, or selected strains, as, for example, *Rosa polyantha nana*, are quite often propagated by the seed method. Of course there is always some variation. That is expected and for certain purposes, seed propagation uniformity is not required. However, for the most part, growing from seed has very little application in the propagation of miniature roses except in the breeding process to secure new improved kinds desirable for garden cultivation.

In this case, the breeding of new varieties, variation is desirable and in fact is initiated by careful hand-crossing of desirable parent varieties and species. For this reason, I would like to dwell a bit on the breeding of new miniature rose cultivars. It is here that the ease or difficulty of propagation can be guided or determined. It is senseless to develop a new variety which cannot be easily and economically propagated and grown. In fact we have discarded numerous seedlings solely because they could not easily be propagated.

Whilst this may appear to be a loss or a waste, it is usually only a matter of time until a similar variety, and maybe even better, appears in a succeeding lot of seedlings. Quite often we may have two or more which are very similar. We have just recently discarded a variety that we were developing—a selection that we had built up for several years. Then another new seedling appeared from very similar parentage, and so we had to choose one or the other. We chose the one which showed the least defects and the most of desirable characteristics. Other things being equal, only the best should be selected for introduction, and this might be determined in the final analysis by the ease or difficulty of propagation.

How does one go about breeding for this desired quality of ease of propagation? First, we should start with the parents, and this may involve such things as knowing that the parents are easily propagated. In the case of miniature roses, we feel it should imply ease of striking roots in the proper medium such as sand, soil or possibly a mixture of peat, sand or other media. This is not enough to ensure that a variety can be economically propagated. Some varieties will root quite readily from cuttings, but they won't produce enough high quality cutting wood to propagate any considerable quantities. In others, the best rooting may occur within quite a narrow range, that is, a short period of time during a growing season. Some plants only give a high percentage of rooting when weather, condition of wood or other factors are at the optimum state, and this is sometimes difficult to determine because what holds one season may be entirely different another season. Anyone who propagates from cuttings realizes this, so we try to eliminate the temperamental kinds.

Another difficulty is that some varieties may produce the quantity of growth, that is shoots that will bloom, but there are not sufficient eyes from which to propagate. Sometimes we overcome this by keeping all the blossoms off, inducing new tender growth, because we do grow from cuttings. Sometimes, as I said, the variety may produce quantities of flowers but the ends of shoots, as you get to the flower cluster, just don't have the growth buds or eyes. The variety 'New Penny', which some of you know, is one of this type, although here in England I have seen quite a bit of it grown and of course you graft it. But in our experience it is not one that you can grow in a great quantity from cuttings. We have found, though, that it is a good pollen parent, and will produce seedlings of beautiful colour shades. Several of the new ones will have this variety 'New Penny' in them.

On the other hand, from identical parentage came the variety 'Eleanor', a coral pink which many of you know. It propagates easily as it will produce the little growth buds or eyes almost underneath the flower, so you can get a quantity of cutting material from any plant.

Yet another problem, and one which the breeder tries to eliminate or at least minimise, is susceptibility to disease, and by this I mean to include all the ills to which roses may be heir, such as mildew, black spot, crown gall and sundry other ailments. Of course, no variety is perfect; if it were, we would just quit trying to grow new varieties of roses.

And what do we mean by a perfect rose? We may have one of which we say "Well, that rose is just perfect". It may be white, and somebody says, "I hate white roses", so you don't have the perfect rose! We say we want roses which are hardy —roses that might be hardy in your climate, or in New England or Canada but we should qualify this. Hardiness to cold is one thing which we tend to think of first of all, but there is also hardiness to heat—what will that rose do in the 115 or 120 degree temperature of Arizona? How will it do in Israel? What will it do in other places where you have an entirely different set of conditions?

Another thing that we have to consider is soil. If this plant is going to grow on its own root (because we don't normally put it on another stock) it means that it has to tolerate great variations in soil conditions. Sometimes, particularly in the southwestern part of the United States, we have considerable alkalinity in the soil and this is further complicated by the use of fertilisers and often times water which is not of the best quality. All these variations must be taken into account whenever we speak of successful propagation.

In breeding, to fit at least some of these facts, we must go back to parents which can pass on at least some of the most desired qualities in more than average quantity to the offspring. In my own work I have endeavoured to breed into miniature roses such hardy and easily propagated roses as *Rosa wichuraiana* and other species roses. Also included are many varieties and hybrids. Sometimes these come ready-made in such varieties as 'Little Darling', which is a floribunda, 'Floradora' (floribunda), 'Golden Glow' (large flowered climber) and many others. More often the best parent varieties are made by crossing species or seedlings of commercial varieties, and selecting one or more plants from seedlings which have proven that they will pass on to the offspring a number of these better qualities.

The main purpose of it all is to obtain new kinds of miniature roses (and other types) which are not only desirable for their beauty, but which are easy to propagate and grow.

Now then, as to seed propagation. As I stated, propagation from seeds covers three separate areas at the present time.

(*a*) We sow from 25,000 to 40,000 hand-hybridised seeds each year. These are from many different crosses. Sometimes they are exploratory, that is we may make only 50 pollinations, and sometimes we make 1,000 pollinations. We have to see into which direction these crosses will lead us. From this lot of seedlings each year, we will select what look to us seedlings of promise, and then we begin to propagate from the best a few plants from cuttings. Later on I will show some colour slides which will illustrate some of the propagation methods we are using.

(*b*) Then in our breeding programme, there is a great deal of work being done with moss rose hybrids; this year half of the crosses cover moss rose hybrids, and this means growing seedlings and propagating these for testing. Now normally we bud these in order to get a stronger plant and hurry the testing.

(*c*) I am also doing work to improve seed-grown strains of *Rosa polyantha nana*. The hope is that we can produce relatively true breeding strains in pink and white, possibly later other shades or colours, which will give a higher percentage of doubles than can be obtained from the mixed seeds generally available today. Sometimes you see advertisements in papers and magazines, "Grow your own miniatures from seed". If you've tried it, you are usually very disappointed. We have already made significant steps in this direction, and while the *Rosa polyantha nana* strain is only of relatively minor importance, I feel it could be of value to gardeners who like to experiment and do a little growing of their own. Now these don't run exactly true to type, but you can have fun growing them from seed anyway. The seeds sprout quite readily, and if you get a plant that is the colour or the shape you like it can be easily propagated from cuttings. In my breeding work with this type, we have selections now which will produce at least 50 per cent with double flowers; some are very double. We are trying to select improved forms that we can grow in quantity from seeds. If you wanted to get pink or white, we hope to give you these by colour, and they would probably run 80–90 per cent true to colour and at least 50 per cent doubles. Now, among these present selections we found the year before last a seedling which was lavender, out of the pink ones. It is quite double. We may even propagate this one as a commercial variety from cuttings, because it is a very nice little rose and fragrant. I must say that *Rosa polyantha nana* does produce a fair amount of seed, in sharp contrast to most of the miniatures of the 'Eleanor' type, and it seems that, other than the *Rosa polyantha nana* types, all the other miniatures are more or less sterile. Usually they are very sterile, and production of seed to sell would be prohibitively costly.

Now then, propagating from cuttings: Because of the smallness of the plants and limited quantity of suitable propagating material, it would appear to me that cutting propagation is the most logical to use in growing nursery and garden plants of miniature roses. That is quite in contrast to what you are doing here in England. And so, as I said earlier, it seems logical to select and breed new varieties of miniatures which will lend themselves to cutting propagation. In recent years, new and improved methods and techniques, including the use of root-inducing hormones, mist propagation and so forth have greatly aided the plant propagator, and these are not confined just to the commercial grower, but can be used by home gardeners as well.

In propagation of miniature roses from cuttings a number of things should be taken into consideration. Among these are the difference of rooting responses; the timing—that is, using the proper time of the year to make the cutting root the best; the condition of wood that is best for cuttings, whether it is hard or soft or in between; the types of cuttings, whether short, long, branched or tips. We have found that some varieties, generally those that have very short internodes, do much better from very short cuttings.

Sometimes the removal of flower buds helps a great deal. Mist propagation as I have mentioned is used. New plants can be propagated in beds, flats, flowerpots, or

what have you. We treat cuttings with hormones (powder) and we also dip all the cuttings in a chlorox solution—to you household bleach. This is done for sanitation reasons, and then, in addition we use certain other fungicidal treatments.

The choice of rooting material—sand, soil, peat, Pearlite or a mixture of these and other materials—is important. Use the one that is best in your area or locality. Then again, hardening off: after cuttings have rooted under the mist, you have to harden them off so that they can be easily transplanted. And in potting, use the type of soil mixture that you find best. We have found in our growing that a mixture of one-third soil, one-third peat moss and one-third Pearlite is best, but you can substitute sand for the Pearlite.

Pots of various kinds may be used. Some have had difficulty in using plastic pots because they didn't drain well. In other areas, such as ours, we like them because they don't dry out so quickly.

Other things to take into consideration are light, heat, shade, water, fertilising and so on. We find that cuttings root best in a high light intensity under misting and I was interested to know that Mr Gilad was using sprinklers in rooting other cuttings. We do a good deal the same thing, using fine misting nozzles and more recently we are using some which are just small revolving type sprinklers.

In budding and grafting—and I understand that this is the practice in most of Europe—you have to use an understock that is suitable. We don't use budding or grafting except in propagation of the little standard tree roses. Our method of growing these miniature tree (standard) roses is to bud canes, the young shoots coming out from the understock we are using. We bud them at the proper length allowing at least two eyes or leaves above the budded eye. Then after the bud has taken we cut this from the plant—I will show you pictures of that—and then we root this cutting under mist. We cut out all eyes (buds) below the eye we insert of the miniature rose. After rooting these cuttings are transplanted. This year we are coming up with some other innovations—

'PAUL'S SCARLET CLIMBER' (*see page 70*)

'MME BUTTERFLY' (*see page 68*)

Climbing Rose 'MME ALFRED CARRIÈRE' (*see page* 70)

HM Queen Elizabeth the Queen Mother, receiving D. S. Butcher, President of the Rose Society of New Zealand, and Mrs Butcher at St James' Palace on 1 July 1968. L. A. Satterlee, President of the American Rose Society, and Mrs Satterlee are also in the group

I don't think I have pictures of all of them.

These long canes, the understock, are budded while they are attached to the stock plant and then, about three weeks after they are budded, we sever from the plant and de-eye and place under the misting. Then we have another innovation— a tool which is called a Multi-Rooter, which was developed in our nursery. All it does is cut four slits about one inch long (vertically) at the base of the cutting. This helps to produce more roots, and it spaces the roots better, we find.

Some nurseries here in England, on the continent and down in Australia have welcomed these tools to use in the propagation of cuttings, particularly hardwood cuttings, because it does help to produce a lot more roots.

Then after these cuttings are rooted we generally put them into peat moss pots and get them well established. We don't try to force the budded eye out immediately. We let the wild understock eye grow until roots are thoroughly established in the peat moss pot, and then we move it into a larger pot, a square plastic pot about five inches across. We then start cutting back the understock. So that it won't die back into the bud we leave a bit of the wild shoot and if it sprouts out again we rub that off. After the budded eye starts growth we pinch the tender tip to get a good branched head.

Yet another reason for budding certain miniatures may be to propagate desirable but difficult to propagate kinds, and that is where the method you are using here in England does come in, because you can propagate varieties which would not be propagated readily from cuttings.

Now, briefly, successful propagation should begin with the breeding process. One should use parents, not only kinds which give desirable plants and flowers but care should be taken to ensure production of new kinds that will grow easily and economically from cuttings. To obtain such results, we have for years selected parents that will produce such offspring. This has involved studying the pedigrees and details of many varieties of roses of all types. It has meant the rooting, or attempts

to root, cuttings of many varieties, hybrids and seedlings. It has meant the hybridising and growing of numerous seedlings useful only for future crosses. It has meant the planting of seeds and growing many seedlings just to evaluate the parents for possible large-scale work with miniatures, in the breeding process. This has been true with the miniatures, and also it is true in the breeding work on the moss roses with which we are working. We hope before long to have ever-blooming bush-type moss roses which will essentially be floribundas and hybrid teas in habit, but will have the moss buds in a wide range of colours that you can grow in the garden with other roses. In fact, this next season we have scheduled to introduce the first ever-blooming miniature moss rose. This is the culmination of about twenty years of work with the Mosses.

Second part—the growing of miniatures from seeds is limited for practical purposes to *Rosa polyantha nana* and to the experimenter or plant breeder. All named cultivars are first produced or grown as seedlings from crossing selected kinds chosen as parents. In late December we plant the seeds in shallow nursery flats in an unheated greenhouse. We don't care to force seedlings, but prefer to let them develop naturally, and these will be in bloom at about the same time as the normal roses will be in bloom in the spring. We plant in a mixture of one-third peat, one-third Pearlite, and one-third sand, and then we put a covering of peat moss over these seeds about three-eighths of an inch or about ten millimetres deep. Over this we put on a layer of similar thickness of horticultural grade Pearlite. When this is watered down, the total thickness is somewhat less than is indicated. We find this is the best covering we can give because it doesn't inhibit the sprouting of the seeds and they come right on through.

From cuttings. Cutting propagation appears to me to be the most logical method of propagating miniature roses in our country. We use hardened wood during winter, the dormant season, but as soon as it is available we use soft or semi-soft wood for making cuttings. We have been using a mixture of half peat moss and half Pearlite as a rooting medium. Half sand and half peat moss appears to work just as well, and recently we have been rooting quite successfully in our standard potting mixture—equal parts of soil, Pearlite and peat moss.

Cuttings vary, but for the most part we prefer material about two to three inches long. Cuttings may be straight, single stem or branched. Some varieties, such as 'Yellow Bantam', do much better if cuttings are very short. In fact, we find that cuttings about one inch long root better than cuttings three inches long in that variety. All foliage is retained for the fastest rooting, that is under misting. Soft wood cuttings are rooted under the mist. The time to root varies with the variety, hardness of wood and time of year. We root cuttings outdoors all year. In winter, with hardwood cuttings, the rooting time is as long as three months. In the warmer time of the year, it may be less than three weeks. All our cuttings are dipped in a chlorox solution, then into Captan solution before planting, and each cutting is treated with a hormone powder. In our nursery, budding miniatures is confined to the production of miniature tree or standard roses.

B. E. HUMPHREY
Hillier & Sons, Winchester
Hardwood Cuttings

I should like to say at the outset of my talk that I do not consider that the propagation of the vast majority of cultivars of roses by cuttings is likely to supersede the traditionally accepted method of propagation by budding, despite what we have heard so far this morning. There is not really time here to go into all the reasons why I hold this view, but the most important, I think, are as follows:

Firstly, in most cases we do not know how the varieties commonly under cultivation will thrive over a period of time on their own roots and over a wide variety of soil conditions. There are indications that certain varieties do not thrive after a three or four year period on a thin calcareous soil, but the long-term trials undertaken by the Ministry of Agriculture should yield interesting information. They have roses on their own roots at a number of centres throughout the country now.

Secondly, the cost of production from propagation to sale is unlikely to be reduced by the softwood cutting technique. Neither is this technique likely to aid management by changing the period of peak work load, which could be an advantage were this possible.

Thirdly, hardwood cuttings could show advantages over budding in production costs—I think everyone would agree on that—but they have disadvantages in the substantial quantity of plant material required for this method, and the increased difficulty in getting satisfactory percentages of rooting.

And fourthly, propagation by cuttings does not have the same "expansion potential" as by budding. What I mean by that is that fewer plants can be produced in a given period of time from a given quantity of propagating material if propagation is by cuttings instead of by budding.

However, we must put the other side of the case as well. There are advantages in producing roses from cuttings and the more important might be considered here. There is no suckering problem, so that you produce a more desirable article from the customer's standpoint. Everyone has seen roses which have been overtaken by the root stock at some later stage. The special skills of budding are not required when producing by cuttings. Plants produced by cuttings are especially well adapted for the subsequent operations involved in containerising, in that they do not have a disproportionately large root system in the early stages of development. This could, of course, be overcome in the case of budded stocks, by hard pruning back the existing root system, but the point still stands I feel.

To come back to economic considerations, if softwood cuttings are the chosen method, then I personally do not believe that rooting on benches under mist, followed by subsequent potting, is justifiable in a production chain for field production, though this method could be considered for raising container plants. Striking cuttings directly into beds under mist propagation as at our own nurseries of Hillier & Sons is certainly more acceptable.

In 1962 and 1963, I carried out a detailed experiment on the behaviour of hardwood cuttings of just one rose variety, the floribunda 'Frensham', under different environmental conditions. I will now describe this experiment in some detail, in the hope that it will give some guidelines for future work in this direction.

The methods used were based on the storage techniques described by Hatcher and Garner, East Malling Research Station for fruit plants and I am going to assume that the audience is familiar with some of this work.

The experiment which I carried out was properly replicated and it was statistically analysed and the significances were worked out at the 0·1, 1 per cent and 5 per cent level. Four Garner Bins were built and maintained at different temperature levels, 65, 55, 45° F. and an unheated control in which a minimum temperature of 29·5° F. was recorded on 25 January 1963. The Bins were considered as blocks, each of which was divided into half, giving two plots per block, one plot being filled with cuttings treated with 50 mg/litre solution of I.B.A. in water and this was applied to the cuttings as a 24 hour soak. The other plot was filled with cuttings which were not treated with growth substance rooting hormone. Each plot had six replicates of ten cuttings, making a total of 480 cuttings for the whole experiment, a fair number to base some results on I would say.

Cuttings were inserted on 21 and 22 November 1962, and half the surviving cuttings from each plot were taken out and planted under field conditions into a medium-textured silty loam soil on 26 February and 20 March 1963 respectively. At 14-day intervals, sample cuttings were removed from these stores, and they were drawn so that I could study the growth and development during the storage period.

Now for the results. Counts of rooting and survival were made when cuttings were field-planted on the 26 February, the remainder being similarly recorded at the second planting date on 20 March. For rooting and survival during storage, the following results were noted:

The combination of prolonged high storage temperature and growth substance treatment significantly depressed rooting and survival; for instance, storage at 55° F. of treated cuttings resulted in 96·6 per cent survival, whereas storage at 65° F. with the same treatment reduced the survival rate to 56·6 per cent, which was considered highly significant.

As far as rooting goes, storage at 55° F. of treated cuttings resulted in 86·6 per cent rooting, but storage at 65° F. of treated cuttings—the planting date was prolonged, in other words until 20 March —resulted in a reduction in rooting down to 56·6 per cent, which again was considered significant. If storage was prolonged at high temperature, rooting was depressed but not significantly if this was not combined with treatment. In other words, untreated cuttings stored for a long period at the highest temperature were not significantly depressed in their rooting ability—80 per cent at 55° F., 76·6 per cent at 65° F., so the combination of hormone treatment plus high temperature plus long storage was deleterious on the rooting and survival of the cuttings.

Regarding development, as one would expect the highest temperature gave the most development of root and shoot growth. The basal buds of all the cuttings showed retarded development due possibly to the gaseous content of the rooting medium; in other words the CO_2 content was higher at the bottom of the medium and this inhibited bud growth.

The apical buds of all the cuttings were retarded, presumably due to a temperature effect—the cuttings obviously encountered lower temperatures in the upper layers of the rooting medium. Now the really important part is the field establishment after planting, and the results are as follows:

Prolonged storage resulted in a higher percentage of field establishment, although this effect was not significant in treated cuttings where short storage was compensated by growth substance treatment. In other words, instead of storing cuttings for a long time one could treat the cuttings with I.B.A. and obtain the same effect.

There was no significant difference in the levels of establishment of untreated cuttings for prolonged storage at 45° or 65° F. The prolonged storage under warm conditions ironed out the difference in temperature. There was no significant difference between prolonged storage at 45, 55 or 65° F. Results were similar.

In all but one case, field establishment was depressed significantly by a storage temperature at 65° F. The overall figures for field establishment from cuttings in the unheated control bin were significantly lower than for those warm-stored, indicating the value of controlled temperature storage conditions for the rose, and this to my mind was one of the most important points of the experiment.

Now, as an interesting development here, I compared the results of rooting in storage—in other words, what was rooted when I came to plant out—with the final figures of field establishment. In all cases, high levels of rooting in storage were significantly reduced by losses in field establishment, emphasising the critical importance of field conditions in the early stages after planting out. For instance, in one case we had 93·3 per cent rooted in storage, but the final figure for field establishment was only 36·6

per cent—heavy losses after planting.

Where low levels of rooting in storage were evident, growth substance treatment significantly increased field establishment. Cuttings poorly rooted when they were lifted from the storage bins which were treated with growth substance rooted after planting into the field. If they were not treated with growth substance this effect was not so significant.

The general conclusions which can be drawn are that there appears to be a correlation between rooting in storage and establishment in the field, unless extreme divergencies in conditions are encountered —and to come back again to this 93·3 per cent rooting in storage and this 36·6 per cent final field establishment, we had here an extreme divergence in that these cuttings were taken from 65° F. and planted straight into an extremely cold, heavy wet field, on 26 February, and the cuttings responded badly to this treatment. Not too surprising really, being rather a shock for anyone.

The higher the percentage of rooting in store, the higher is the percentage of establishment in the field, and this is extremely interesting because it ties in quite closely with recent work which Dr Howard has shown with apple stocks at East Malling. Although you lose cuttings after planting out from the store, the higher the percentage of rooting you can achieve in store the higher is the general percentage of final field establishment, and if one can ensure that conditions in the field are optimum, then one would expect the difference between percentage rooting in store and final field establishment to be at a minimum.

Disease Control

Chairman: E. F. Allen

J. T. FLETCHER
N.A.A.S., Cheshunt
Diseases of Glasshouse Roses

My contribution to this session is concerned entirely with diseases of the cut flower crop grown under glass. First I will outline the industry in the United

Kingdom to set the background to the talk, and then discuss one or two of the disease problems which occur fairly frequently.

The acreage of this crop in 1966 was approximately 160 acres. In 1967 this had fallen to just over 100 acres, and this decrease was largely due to the demolition of a lot of old glass in the Lea Valley, particularly in the Cheshunt area. This change has, I think, caused a number of other major changes in the rose industry—for instance, many of the producers now planting the crop for the first time will be growing a smaller acreage than those large producers in the Cheshunt area, and this in itself will bring about a certain number of fairly fundamental changes.

Looking at the picture from the European point of view, the position is somewhat different in that the acreage under glass has increased considerably in most countries. The only accurate figures we have are for Holland, where in 1966 just over 600 acres were grown for cut flowers and at present it is estimated that there are over 800 acres. A similar trend is taking place in West Germany, France and in the Scandinavian countries.

I would like to consider the disease problems of this crop in relation to a cropping cycle:

diseases, downy or black mildew and grey mould are diseases that can be extremely important and very serious, but they are more sporadic in their occurrence. I have mentioned the other two because I think they are diseases that could become more important, particularly the nematode transmitted virus diseases.

Diseases of roses under glass have not been as important economically as diseases of other glasshouse-grown crops, but this is not because there are no diseases on this crop. Numerous diseases have been recorded on roses, and it is interesting to speculate why disease problems have generally not been important. A consideration of the traditional cropping cycle may throw some light on this matter.

Propagation

Traditionally, roses under glass have been propagated on the seed-raised rootstock *Rosa canina*, but there is now a trend towards the use of vegetatively propagated rootstocks. This change is just beginning, and it is difficult to see at present how far it will go, but obviously these rootstocks have in many respects

Traditional Cropping Cycle for glasshouse grown roses

PROPAGATION
R. canina rootstocks
raised from seed

Glasshouse environmental control

PLANTING
Steam sterilized border soil

PRUNING and WINTER REST

CROPPING
Fumigation with sulphur
and high volume spraying

and point to the changes that are occurring in the culture of this crop or are likely to occur during the next few years which may possibly affect disease incidence and control.

The diseases which occur most frequently are: Powdery Mildew (*Sphaerotheca pannosa*); Downy Mildew (*Peronospora sparsa*); Grey Mould (*Botrytis cinerea*); Verticillium Wilt (*V. dahliae*) and virus diseases. I have not attempted to put them in any order of importance, although I think it is fair to say that powdery mildew is found on all crops grown under glass. Of the other

considerable advantages. One immediately obvious is the increased vigour and therefore increased yield. However, seed-raised rootstocks have certain advantages as far as disease control is concerned. For instance, most virus diseases are not transmitted through the seed. Also vascular wilt pathogens are not seed-borne, but this is not the situation with vegetatively propagated rootstocks. Although these rootstocks can be equally disease-free, it is obviously a point which needs careful attention, and efforts must be made in order to avoid build-up of virus diseases and vascular pathogens in these rootstocks.

The increased vigour that we get with such rootstocks as *Rosa chinensis var. indica* and *Rosa chinensis var. manettii* could also give rise to increased canker problems. *Botrytis cinerea* cankers have been more common during the last two years, but it is a problem I do not wish to over-emphasise because so far it has not been severe.

Planting

Traditionally, the soil is well steam-sterilised before planting—I am sure a very good insurance for a very long-term crop. Very recently, the Lea Valley soils have been examined for free-living nematodes by Mr A. Winfield our Nematologist, and he has found that many of the sites have high populations of a number of different free-living nematodes. We have only recently realised that these nematodes cause damage, but even more important, I think, is the fact that a number of them transmit viruses. One instance has been found in which the nematode vector and the viruses it transmits (Strawberry Latent Ring Spot) caused considerable damage in one particular crop. On most of the other nurseries the vectors are present, but the viruses are not. If the situation ever arises where the two are put together, as could occur with virus infected vegetatively propagated rootstock, considerable crop loss could occur.

A move in the right direction, I am sure, is the use of soil sterilants such as D.D. and the metham-sodium types, together with steaming, in order to control the nematodes. With the increase in labour costs, sheet steaming is becoming more popular and this need not be less efficient than the traditional methods. In fact, I think it could be even more efficient, particularly when combined with the use of chemicals.

Cropping

Fumigation and high volume spraying have been the traditional methods of controlling foliar diseases during the cropping period, and most rose growers use sulphur vaporising lamps. These are mainly used for the control of powdery mildew. This disease has considerable effects both on the quality and the quantity of flowers produced. Sulphur vaporising lamps are cheap to run, and on the whole give a fairly efficient control. The sulphur is placed in the top of the lamp and with gentle heat the sulphur is vaporised and a fine deposit left on the foliage. These lamps are used for anything from four to twelve hours per night, and spaced at about 30-ft intervals in a 30-ft wide house which is usually sufficient to give a good control of powdery mildew. High volume sprays can be used to supplement high volume spraying, and the dinocap type of materials are the most widely used for this purpose.

There have been some very interesting recent developments in the production of systemic fungicides, and I understand that there are a number of materials now being tried on roses for the control of rose powdery mildew. Any development in this direction would be welcomed, I am sure, but I think we ought also to bear in mind that, if we get a good control of powdery mildew with systemic fungicides, it would be unwise to abandon the use of sulphur vaporising lamps. Over the years the use of sulphur has almost certainly contributed in no small measure to the low level of disease incidence in the glasshouse-grown crop. Perhaps it is not surprising that black spot, for instance, is not a problem of the crop grown under glass. But if sulphur vaporising lamps are abandoned in favour of good systemic fungicides, it may well be that these very specific fungicides will not be so effective for the control of such diseases as black spot, other leaf spots and rust.

Glasshouse crops are of course grown with a certain degree of environmental control and, if manipulated correctly, this can help disease control very considerably; this is particularly so with black mildew or downy mildew. This disease first appears as necrotic spots on the leaf and when leaves showing this symptom are gently tapped many of the leaflets drop off. If the undersides of these leaflets are examined carefully with a hand lens, it is possible to see the fungus producing its sporing structures. They are not always visible, but can usually be found on some of the affected leaves. This disease, if severe, causes almost complete defoliation of the crop, and therefore can be very serious, but it can be very readily controlled if the humidity within the house never exceeds approximately 85. Humidity control is best achieved with heat and ventilation.

At the time of the introduction of carbon-dioxide as a new technique, there were one or two instances where downy mildew did become a problem. In an effort to keep carbon-dioxide trapped in the house, the ventilators were not opened as regularly as they should have been which resulted in an increase in relative humidity in the house producing very favourable conditions for disease development. Dithiocarbamate sprays like Zineb and Maneb also help to control downy mildew, but they are usually not necessary, providing the humidity is maintained at a reasonably low level.

Pruning

Finally, in the cropping cycle we come to pruning, where there has again been a change in technique. The winter rest period has been eliminated by some growers, which means the leaves are on the plant all the year round and there is no break in the cycle. This change in technique could present new problems in the control of foliar diseases.

I would just like to mention one physiological disorder, and that is the problem we know as Baccara Leaf Drop. This problem very often looks like downy mildew, the same sort of scorched appearance is evident on the upper surface of the leaves, together with defoliation. It very frequently occurs soon after forcing begins early in the year and also again in the autumn, often connected with a drop in temperature. From observations we have made on a number of nurseries, the trouble seems to be associated with a sudden increase or decrease in temperature. For instance, when forcing begins, if air temperatures are very rapidly raised it

may be that the root activity is unable to keep up with the sudden burst of top growth, which is perhaps at the expense of stored food within the plant. There may come a time when the nutrients and water uptake are not sufficient to supply the foliage produced, resulting in water and nutrient withdrawal from the older leaves to supply the growing shoot. These older leaves produce necrosis and eventually drop.

It is perhaps more difficult to apply this theory to the autumn-grown crop, but again the trouble occurs when lower night temperatures occur. Nutrients and water uptake may be reduced as a result of the temperature drop and may not be sufficient to support the amount of foliage which the plant has produced throughout the summer.

In the spring, the way to get over this problem is to raise the temperature steadily, if this is possible, and again in the autumn attempts should be made to try and lower the temperature steadily, rather than to have sudden fluctuations one way or the other. It would be interesting to see whether undersoil heating, perhaps in raised beds, could be used to minimise this problem.

If I may just summarise the points that I have attempted to make; firstly, that there are considerable changes taking place in the rose cut flower industry in this country and these changes could affect a situation which over the past, I think, has been fairly stable and fairly satisfactory, as far as disease control is concerned; that the introduction of vegetatively propagated rootstocks needs careful watching, as far as virus diseases and vascular wilts are concerned; I think the use of the systemic fungicides should not mean the abandonment of the sulphur vaporising lamps, for fear of building up foliar diseases, and the same really applies to summer pruning, which is again a point which could give rise to increased foliar diseases. Soil sterilisation and the trend now towards the use of chemicals in addition to steam is a step in the right direction, particularly for the control of nematodes and especially those that are virus vectors.

PROFESSOR L. BROADBENT
Bath University of Technology
Aspects of Plant Pathogenesis in Roses

I, together with one of my colleagues, Mr Firman, wrote an article in the 1968 *Rose Annual* which outlined what we hoped to do at Bath and, in particular, the philosophy behind that work. I do not want to reiterate all I wrote there but I would like to state again that our aim is to understand the biochemical, the physical and the physiological changes that occur when a rose becomes diseased.

For too long most of the plant pathologists of the world have been paying attention to the diseases, to the pathogens or the pests that cause those diseases, and have tended to neglect the host plant. If we are going to make any great progress in understanding and controlling disease, we have got to know much more about the host. Why does a plant sometimes react to the presence of another organism with disease? What is the basis of tolerance, or resistance to a pathogen?

I hope that this work will not only be of academic interest, but that it will be of great benefit to rose breeders, and indeed to breeders of other plants, because if they know exactly what they are attacking and why they are attacking it, they should be in a much better position to achieve resistance or tolerance.

We began our studies only recently, so there is not a great deal to report yet, but I am going to outline the work that is being done by our two post-graduate students, one of whom is being supported by the great generosity of our chairman and his late father, and the other by the Royal National Rose Society.

We decided to begin at the beginning. This is not always done in scientific investigations. We started by looking at the micro-organisms on the leaf surface because any pathogen, or any pest for that matter, that attacks the rose from the air has to penetrate through the cuticle, and first of all it has to battle with the organisms that are present on the leaf surface (phylloplane).

Mr Stevens has been working on this problem for nearly two years. The work is not easy, and in fact most people have fought shy of tackling a comprehensive study of plant pathogenesis, which means the whole ecological set-up behind disease in the plant. It might be several years, of course, before we have any results that are going to be of use to the rose grower, but on the other hand there may be some valuable information just around the corner. It is one of the fascinations of research that one never knows what is going to turn up next. At Bath we are primarily interested in research that will benefit the grower, but inevitably we have to work on fundamental problems because most of the easy work has been done in the past.

Mr Stevens is attempting the difficult task of characterising and studying the ecology of the different bacteria, yeasts and fungi that occur on the surface of the foliage. These have to be removed before they can be studied. This is a field of biological endeavour which is expanding, but that nevertheless is not well established and he had to spend considerable time testing the different methods that were described in the literature for removing the micro-organisms. Unfortunately, most of these methods proved unsatisfactory, usually because they tended to select one group of organisms in preference to others. But I think everybody who is not familiar with this field is always amazed at the number of micro-organisms on the leaf surface.

I said that one method was less effective than another. To give you an example, washing leaves in distilled water gave 600 organisms per square centimetre—I think we are all getting used to the metric system, so you can now envisage a square centimetre, about the size of a drawing pin. But the same leaves were then macerated by being ground up with water, and a further 21,600 organisms were found which had not been washed off. The highest count obtained so far by macerating is 400,000 organisms per square centimetre.

The leaves of the rose, like the leaves of every other plant, are absolutely crawling with micro-organisms, and it is through this barrier that the pathogen has to penetrate.

The work that was done showed that most of these organisms are on the leaf surface, not inside it, although more work needs doing to confirm whether there are any inside the stomata or not.

More recently, a plastic resin has been used to obtain leaf peels. This is painted on the leaf surface, allowed to dry and then peeled off. If the organisms are stained on the leaf surface before the plastic is put on it, when the leaf peel is removed the organisms can be counted and identified under the microscope. So far this seems the best method of getting them without distortion of results, and as a result of this work Mr Stevens suggests that the traditional method of taking off the fungi and plating out on agar, letting them grow and then counting them may give the wrong impression and over-emphasise the importance of fungi.

There is no doubt that bacteria and yeasts predominate, and they are concentrated on the veins and around the stomata. Fungal spores do occur, but relatively few of them are able to develop a mycelium, either because the substrate in which they are living is unsuitable, or because they are inhibited after germination by the other organisms that are present.

Of course, all the media that are used for the growth of micro-organisms are selective to some extent or another. There is no one medium upon which you can grow these organisms to identify them, because they have different requirements. So many had to be examined.

The general conclusion that we have reached so far is that the microbial populations increase as the season progresses, and that there are big differences, not only between different plants but between different leaves on the plant. It was very soon apparent, in the first year, that Mr Stevens could spend the rest of his life—I won't say happily, but at any rate busily—trying to identify these organisms. So we had to do the only thing possible, which was to group them, count the totals and identify the most important.

For those of you who are pathologists, these were *Sporobolomyces* and other yeasts, *Cladosporium herbarium*, *Aureobasidium pullulans* and other fungi, *Erwinia* and *Pseudomonas* species and other bacteria. Somewhat surprisingly there were hardly any sporing *Bacillus* species.

Most of these studies have been done on rose cultivars known to be either resistant or susceptible to black spot and mildew. They have been grown under nutritionally controlled conditions in large polythene buckets.

Undoubtedly some phylloplane organisms are antagonistic to pathogens, but the differences in epiphytic populations of susceptible and resistant roses were very small, and it is most likely that the causes of resistance in rose will be found mainly in the metabolic processes of the plants themselves.

Nevertheless, this ecological study is continuing because we need to know much more about the environment in which the pathogen, and the pathogen spore especially, finds itself when it lands on the leaf surface. It is our aim ultimately to learn more so that we can hope to control black spot, mildew and rust and other pathogens, so we want to know if there are organisms that are antagonistic to these spores.

We want to do controlled experiments for which sterile plants would be very useful. Mr Stevens has constructed an apparatus for achieving sterile plants grown from seed. We have not had a chance yet to test it with rose seed, but we have grown sterile pea plants in it, so we are hopeful.

He is also studying the nutrients exuded from the plant on the surface of which these micro-organisms feed. This is very important, because the different nutrients will influence the different micro-organisms present. He hopes by chromatographic and other methods to identify these leaf exudates, and to find out if they are different in susceptible and resistant roses, and thus to determine the nutritional requirements of these epiphytes and the pathogens.

This work is being done in conjunction with Dr Duthie, who is studying the nutrition of the rose and the effects of major and minor elements on disease resistance. I am very sorry to tell you that Dr Duthie is not well, and therefore will not be able to come to talk to you to-morrow, but his paper will be read for him.

Now the other student, Mr Howden, is spending his first summer with us, studying rose rust—*Phragmidium mucronatum*. He worked last year at Exeter University for his M.Sc. on rose mildew, and he is an extremely keen rosarian. If anybody is mad on roses, it is Julian Howden, so we put him in charge of the rose species and cultivar collection that is being built up at Bath, and I would like here to thank The Royal National Rose Society for so gener-ously supplying us with most of the plants for this collection. We are trying to get cuttings from these plants on their own roots, using mist propagation, because we want to obtain standard plants for experi-ments and later to study the effects of root-stocks on disease resistance. This might be important, but before studying it we have to know how the plant reacts on its own roots, and I am sure many of you know how reluctant many species and cultivars are to root.

As in most parasitic fungi, several races of *Phragmidium mucronatum* are likely to exist and so we have established a spore bank, the spores being vacuum freeze dried for storage. Attempts to grow the fungus in culture have so far been frus-trated because it was swamped by con-taminants that were introduced with the uredospores.

Various antibiotics were successful in controlling bacterial contaminants, but the wide range of fungicides that we tested were not completely successful in con-trolling the fungal contaminants, and so further work is going to be done, using the sterile leaf technique in the hope that this fungus can ultimately be cultured.

Relatively little is known about the biology of rose rust fungus; that is why we decided to study it first, after consult-ing Mr Allen and The Royal National Rose Society. Over-wintering studies were begun last year, after a spore collection technique had been worked out. Leaves carrying teleutospores, the over-wintering spore, were placed under a variety of natural conditions, so that we could in-vestigate the effects of exposure, humidity, temperature and burial in the soil. These samples of leaves were tested at intervals during the winter, and again during the spring. In the laboratory parallel work was done, subjecting the teleutospores to freezing and to alternating temperatures and humidities. Only those spores that were fully exposed on leaves over-win-tered and germinated. None of those that were buried or treated under unexposed conditions survived.

It has been suggested that epiphytic microflora on the leaves gradually break down the walls of these spores during the winter, thus permitting them to take up water and germinate in the spring, but so far experiments with fungi and bacteria from Mr Stevens' collection have failed to substantiate this theory.

As relatively little was known about the incidence and importance of rust, it was decided to make a survey, with the sup-port of The Royal National Rose Society, of commercial, public and amateur rose growers. Many of the people approached have filled in and returned the question-naire which seeks information on past experience with rust.

Folklore can often be extremely valu-able to a research worker, who can obtain clues that might help him in his work. We want to know what opinions are held about rust and its control. Of course the returns have not yet been analysed, but it does appear that rust is usually rare in northern England and Scotland, which you already know, and, as also most people know, it is most prevalent in the south, which is another good reason why we should study it in Bath. Growers, both amateur and commercial, really have been most co-operative. They have described the cultural conditions on their holdings, and have given their opinions as to what conditions do discourage or encourage rust. However, I would appeal to anybody who has had a questionnaire form and not returned it: please send it in. The information we derive from this will be most valuable, and the wider the response, the more informative will be the conclusions reached.

We are going to organise a second survey in September, which will throw light on this year's rust and we hope also that growers will send in samples of rust from different parts of the country.

Unfortunately my colleague, Mr Firman, is off to Fiji for three years, which is going to delay the work to some extent, but I am sure we shall do our best to get more people involved in it and try to solve some of these problems which affect growers, not only of roses, but of all plants.

DR. ELDON W. LYLE
Plant Pathologist, The Texas Rose Research Foundation
Black Spot, Powdery Mildew and Crown Gall

The subject I have deals with black spot, mildew and crown gall. Now, the first two are caused by fungi; the last is associated with a bacterial spectrum.

Black Spot

You are all familiar with the damage and destruction where black spot is involved. The fungus is colourless in itself, but it does cause deterioration of tissue which becomes black. The actual damage is the defoliation from the fungus activity on the leaf. Scientific investigation has proved that the fungus can initiate infection on either the upper surface or the lower surface of the leaf. It is equally damaging, regardless of where it starts; by investigation, if the spore alights on the upper surface of tender tissue of leaves, it will germinate there and spread only on the upper surface, but if it alights on the lower surface it will go through rapidly to the upper surface and contaminate both sides and produce further sporulation from both sides.

This slide shows the black spot lesion as it occurred naturally on the lower side of the leaves, and you see an infection also on the midrib and down on to the petiole of that leaf. Black spot is damaging whether it occurs on one side of the leaf or the other. We also can tell you that a leaf lesion this size represents as infection of at least six weeks of time, because the spots increase at about the speed of 1 millimetre diameter of infection per week.

To examine the infection on the canes themselves, you will see that spots do occur on tender tissue. I have to go back 50 years to give credit to the first person to really emphasise the importance of these lesions on the rose canes. It was N. L. Alcock of England, a lady, who first published that the infections on canes were of great importance in perpetuating this disease over winter. Now the tie-in today is that you hear references or read of reports of the importance of fallen leaves on the ground as perpetuating the disease over winter. I think if it is this analysis on which Professor Broadbent and Dr Fletcher are working, they will find that it is difficult to get some of these fungi to exist in abnormal environment; the black spot fungus is one that will not live readily in the soil; it is not going to survive long with competing fungi in rotting tissue of the canes and leaves. So, Miss Alcock, in her presentation 50 years ago, has brought out something that is still very important today; the over-wintering of the black spot organism is primarily on the leaves and stems that are remaining above ground. In areas where the leaves are not shed, it is from the leaves. If it is in an area where the infected leaves are lost through frost in winter, then it would be from these cane lesions that the black spot would perpetuate.

Now, the spores themselves are peanut-shaped, and they are some 18 microns in length; if they are in water for 24 hours they will germinate and produce a germ tube as you see here. An atmosphere of less than 90 per cent relative humidity will not cause those spores to germinate, so we know that, in the case of black spot, it is particularly water that will cause germination and infection. The spores are hyaline, or colourless. When stained, so as to be photographed, they appear in this fashion. It would take 2,000 of these spores end to end to be an inch in length.

The control is the important thing to most growers, whether it is in the field or in the home garden, and here you see in the illustration the fungicidal control of black spot in preventing defoliation on the variety 'Floradora' which is very subject to black spot.

Eight weekly applications (10 June through 29 July) followed by six biweekly (12 August through 21 October) in field plots totalling about 6,000 bushes gave control of black spot and increased the weight of the plants as indicated in the table presented.* The plants from each plot actually were weighed at harvest time (28 January 1960), and the ones which received the best fungicide treatment, the No. 1, which was Dithane M-22 at only half normal concentration, produced plants 98 per cent heavier than the check plants listed in No. 12 position in the record.

Two so-called fungicides gave results even poorer than the checks, and on the list there is a number of commonly-known fungicides. Phaltan is excellent, Cyprex is just a relatively poor material. Fermate, you have heard about, but none of the last on the list can compare with Dithane M-22, Manzate and the Phaltan. We could put on Daconil, Difolatan and a number of other fungicides which now have appeared to give almost 90 or 95 per cent control of black spot, as you have seen in this particular slide.

Under field applications, the commercial growers are anxious to prevent black spot so that they can get good mature bushes that will over-winter nicely and do well in home gardens. This is an East Texas picture where the propagation is on sandy land soil condition. There is a spray machine that will take care of over 10,000 bushes in 15 minutes, and the pressure of that particular sprayer is up to 600 lbs., so that it can go along at rapid speed. All the

nozzles are projecting the fungicide in an upward direction, to control, to put the fungicide on the lower surface as well as the upper surface.

And here is a custom-built sprayer for garden use in a municipal garden at Tyler, Texas. This machine has been constructed with a boom that will swing, and it can have as many as four operators with hose nozzles so that, the nozzles being lowered to the ground, the spray can come up and project upward and cover the lower surface of the leaves as well as the upper.

Next, if we were to examine a cross section of the rose branch or the rose cane at the fall and winter months, and having made a section that can be examined with a microscope, and treating it with an iodine solution, it brings out the starch content, which is represented by those black areas. Those are the medullary rays, in particular, that accumulate the starch first. If we find the starch accumulating to this extent in the cool weather of the fall and winter, we know that those plants are mature to ship or to save budwood for future use. In this example, in the upper left-hand corner is the bark; the lower right-hand corner is the centre of the cane. The wood is the principal place where the starch will accumulate, and any time we see this degree of starch accumulation we know that those plants are suitably developed, that they will do well in home gardens. In other words we have exercised disease control, retaining the foliage on the plants, and have built maturity into the bushes.

We do not know what rust is in our particular area, but I know it can cause defoliation. Also red spider mite insect can cause defoliation. Were these to have affected the plants, they would not have the starch. It is similar to black spot causing defoliation and starch not being developed. So we are interested in this particular phase, to determine whether the bushes are of quality for use in storing and for selling.

Here is an illustration at the end of the season where many varieties are brought together. Although there are 52 inches between one row and the next, with

*Not reproduced. Ed.

proper fungicide care those bushes begin to overlap into the middle such as you see here, and into the fall season there is a production of good marketable bushes.

Powdery Mildew

The next topic is 'powdery mildew' caused by a fungus which is more difficult to culture in artificial media than black spot, but it is still another fungus disease. The fungus of mildew is growing exterior to the surface on which it develops, and you would think it would be easy to control, but I think it is just as hard to offset or prevent the mildew development as it is black spot. The effect you see is distortion of tissue, the unsightliness of the parts on which it grows.

Some degree of success has been achieved in preventing powdery mildew from developing. The illustration here is the result of three fungicides, starting very early in the season using Phaltan with Karathane, Phaltan with sulphur, and Phaltan with Acti-dione. These fungicides were applied at regular intervals through the growing season. They controlled and prevented the powdery mildew from developing on this very susceptible variety or cultivar, 'Christian Dior'.

More recently, materials are being produced which can control mildew even after it occurs, and this is one of the numbered compounds which is coming under trial and has appeared very suitable for two years of time, so I think we will find this being marketed by the Company which manufactures it. You can see 'Mirandy' in the test here, and to the left the smoothness of the new leaves as the mildew is prevented, whereas on the check only 52 inches away in the next row, the mildew thrived. So we do have encouragement in the controlling of some of our diseases, even some that have been very troublesome in the past.

And then another mildew control material, and this picture was taken just two weeks ago in one of the trials. The Phaltan-Parnon combination was preventing mildew developing on new growth, in contrast with the next picture which shows the spread of mildew which

was prevalent just 48 inches away from the preceding picture. So there is a degree of success and promise from these new fungicides. I am proud to say this Parnon is available today. It is made by Eli Lilly and Company in the United States—located near Indianapolis. They also have another fungicide for mildew which I am not illustrating; it is called Pipron, which also is very good. But here is Parnon, very successful for controlling powdery mildew. We are going to watch this compound, because weekly application is giving the degree of mildew control that you see in these pictures. Previously we relied on a material called Acti-dione with which the mildew was controlled only if the fungicide was applied twice a week. Now, we like to reduce the number of applications; we like to reduce the concentration of chemicals; we would like to get away from them entirely, but up to the present time we have to depend on some of these fungicides to give disease control.

Crown Gall

Next to the subject of crown gall. This is a typical example—I think some of you have seen it, but anyway it may occur on the shank of the understock, such as you see. If it were at the base where the roots develop, then we would say the crown gall originated probably in the nursery. If the gall occurs up on the branches or out on the roots, it would have developed probably due to a condition in the garden in which it is planted. We are sure of this because, in growing under field conditions, the places where we see these crown galls are almost entirely on that original cutting. The bacteria associated with the organism do not migrate through the tissue of the rose. They would migrate through some soft tissued plants, but so far there is no proof of migration of bacteria of the crown gall type through the rose tissue.

Hairy root is a related disease, and I am bringing it in, even though I am not to talk on it. Hairy root is associated with another bacteria very closely related to the crown gall, but the stubby roots coming from galls are indicative of that hairy root condition. The same environment is as apt to cause one as the other, but there is an association with *Agrobacterium rhizogenes* in this case, instead of *A. tumefaciens* in the preceding picture.

Crown gall can get very large in its growth and can even occur up on the branches under some abnormal conditions. In the upper parts on the left-hand side you can see the gall in the branch. So there is an environment in this location which is bringing out the gall. I get samples sent to me from various parts of the country. This one happened to come from near the Gulf Coast, nowhere near where the field propagation of roses is being done, but it did show that there was conducive environment that was very suitable for the crown gall or condition which caused that particular development.

Here we are testing ways to offset the gall on cuttings, and we have tested over 300 chemicals which can be used safely on rose cuttings, but none of them is consistent in preventing the gall formation. In the picture you can see that chemicals can allow nice callusing; even though No. 156 and 164 type of chemicals were applied the callusing goes on normally. I wish we could say we had a chemical which could completely prevent the gall initiation, but we haven't.

In view of study of the crown gall development, we asked one of our nurseries to save all of the plants with crown gall he could of one cultivar, so you see the 'Cavalcade' variety. Now at the left, every one of those plants had a crown gall originally, and there were 30 plants which were saved in this collection. Nearly all those plants in the bed at the left survived 12 years in the garden; so the galling condition had not deteriorated those plants a great deal. To the right those plants survived less than 12 years. They were the checks, or the healthy plants originally.

Now, I am not saying that crown gall is a help to the development of roses but we know, after examining the roots of the plants in both beds, that crown gall had deteriorated or had been inactivated in the bed at the left; the plants were growing

normally, very little active gall remaining, whereas, in the bed at the right it was root-knot nematodes which had come into the bed to cause harm. And we actually now fear the nematodes such as rootknot more than we would crown gall.

Next is the variety 'Calypso', and this picture was taken rather recently. After six years, all of those plants, whether they had hairy root or crown gall, have survived in spite of the fact that they did have galling condition on the roots originally. Perhaps the simplest explanation as to how those plants survived and why the galling condition went away, may have to do with the bed structure, the aeration and drainage, because there was good drainage in these beds and each time we examined the roots of these plants we set the plants back at 2–3 inches higher level than previously planted, so we were gaining in aeration and drainage.

I think perhaps one of the leading things that we can watch today is the position in which the rose is planted in our garden. At St Albans yesterday, it was a tremendous satisfaction to see that those beds were raised beds to guarantee drainage, and I daresay that it will help prevent the damage from crown gall type of organism.

Next is 'Floradora' cultivar, and here you can see even the roots are being exposed, and without any chemical, that gall, though untreated chemically, was dying down. We still have that plant growing in the garden today, so it is further evidence that if we can raise the planting level and gain more aeration and drainage, we are going to offset some of these problems without any chemical control whatever.

Next is an illustration of the rose garden in Houston, Texas, and I am very proud of their garden. A magnificent job of maintenance has been done, but I think the main success has come from that raised bed and the planting of those bushes with the bud being well above the surface of the ground.

Then recently, within the last two or three years, one of the research workers at the University of California, Dr Milton N. Schroth has worked with the crown gall organism. He has tested chemicals that can penetrate these gall structures, and he'has found an aromatic type of chemical called Bacticin. It is now available through the Upjohn Chemical Company, and Bacticin can be painted on those active galls.

This is a tomato stem, which has been subject to crown gall; this is an innoculation test, because tomatoes do not actually take crown gall naturally, but it is a good base for growing the organism for test because a fast response may be obtained. The gall at the right has been penetrated with this Bacticin and the penetration rate is just phenomenal. It will penetrate the gall in just two or three hours, whereas we still see the yellowish-amber colour of the untreated active gall in the specimen to the left in the cross-section.

This slide shows the quick penetration using Bacticin with a dye substance. The pink colouring shows the penetration of Bacticin into the gall structure.

Most of the work on crown gall has been done with peaches, with apples, with apricots, things like that. This picture is an apricot, but the galls are beginning to drop off around the base of the apricot tree. The grey on the gall is the excess chemical that had not penetrated into the gall tissues. It is not going to harm the healthy tissue, but if a large gall structure is treated with Bacticin, it is recommended to treat only part of that gall at one time, and then later—a few weeks later—to treat the rest of it. So we now have a means to use chemically, if we cannot get greater aeration for the plant, to offset the crown gall type of development.

Next is the rose under test. The whiteness of the untreated active gall is to the left; in the upper right there is the greying of the galls as the Bacticin is beginning to penetrate into those galling structures on the canes.

Now I do want to close with just a picture or two showing you that, under field conditions, black spot and mildew can be controlled.

Study Session on Rose Classification
Chairman: Brigadier C. E. Lucas Phillips

F. FAIRBROTHER
United Kingdom

The chairman asked us to consider the reason for rose classification—whether it was necessary to have a rose classification at all and, if so, what was its purpose. Well, simply, a rose classification has the same purpose as any other classification— as a library classification for example—to enable a reader to select his material quickly and effectively, and I think if we bear that in mind we shall see that there is something valuable in a classification of a rose system.

Now, I know it is a very difficult thing to get this accepted internationally. That is the ideal, and I think we should strive after that ideal, and I particularly liked the final paragraph of the American paper, which said, "It would seem that the time has arrived when an International Committee could profitably be formed under the leadership of the International Registration Authority for Roses, and composed of representatives of the national rose organizations of the world". It is only by getting together and discussing every point of view that we shall ever get an international classification.

We have been studying this problem— the Committee of the Royal National Rose Society—for the past year. We have had all manner of difficulties to contend with, but I think we have arrived at something which might be of interest and I hope of use.

Today there are no clear-cut races of roses, apart from the three main divisions —climbing, shrub roses and bedding roses. There are even certain cultivars which may not fit conveniently into these three divisions. Breeding proceeds apace, and roses of every conceivable variation in growth, shape of flower, form and colour are being raised. The range of variation will increase with every fresh species that is pressed into service for hybridising. Whilst it should not be necessary to abandon existing class names of roses already raised, such as the old shrub roses, the noisettes, hybrid musks, it cannot be assumed that new varieties will necessarily fit into these classes which are genealogical rather than functional.

After considering various suggested outlines of classification, preference was finally given to a method which (*a*) made provision for the retention of the present classifications (these to remain operative for all cultivars prior to 1970) and (*b*) provided a more flexible framework to cater for the new trends in hybridising and to be used for all cultivars from 1970 onwards.

As a basis for discussion it is suggested that roses be classified into three main groups:

1. Species (wild roses) and their mutants (double-flowered, and other sports).
2. Cultivars prior to 1970.
3. Cultivars from 1970 onwards.

These groups may be subdivided using a numerical code to indicate the groups and the sub-divisions. The first numeral would indicate Group, the second numeral the class, the third and subsequent numerals for variations within the class.

Group 1. Species

1.1. Climbing Species. 1.1.1. single-flowered Climbing Species; 1.1.2. double-flowered Climbing Species.

R.R. arvensis, brunonii, wichuraiana, filipes, would be examples of 1.1.1. and *R. moschata* and double-flowered sports of *R.R. multiflora* and *setigera* would be examples of 1.1.2.

1.2. Shrubby Species. 1.2.1. Single-flowered shrubby species; 1.2.2. double-flowered sports of shrubby species.

Examples of 1.2.1. *R.R. canina, rugosa, hugonis* and of 1.2.2. *R.R. roxburghii plena, fœtida, californica plena.*

Group 2 Cultivars prior to 1970

2.1. Climbing Cultivars. 2.1.1. would be ramblers, and 2.1.2. would be climbers, ramblers having lax habit of growth and climbers having stiff stems. Examples of 2.1.1. would be 'Dorothy Perkins' and 'Crimson Rambler'. Examples of 2.1.2.— that is the climbers with stiff stems— would be 'Gloire de Dijon', 'Madame Alfred Carrière', 'Maréchal Niel', 'Climbing Lady Hillingdon', 'Parade' and 'Easlea's Golden Rambler'.

Then we come to any further subdivisions. For instance 2.1.2.—that is the group I have just mentioned, the climbers with stiff stems of the climbing cultivars prior to 1970—could be further subdivided into 2.1.2.1. Climbing Bourbons; 2.1.2.2., those cultivars described as Noisette. An example of the first would be 'Zéphirine Drouhin' and of the second 'Blush Noisette'. 2.1.2.3. would be classed as Climbing Tea Noisette—'Gloire de Dijon'. 2.1.2.4., climbing hybrid tea— 'Climbing Ena Harkness', etc. And 2.1.2.5., Kordesii Climbers—'Hamburger Phoenix'. That is, dividing the bigger group of climbing cultivars, ramblers and climbers, into separate groups of those cultivars.

2.2. would be old shrub roses. That is roses without the influence of *Rosa chinensis* and *Rosa gigantea*. These may be subdivided into cultivars known as 2.2.1.— Gallica; example, the French rose 'Charles de Mills'; 2.2.2.—Damascena, the damask rose; example, 'York and Lancaster'. 2.2.3. —Alba, the white rose; example, 'Maiden's Blush'; 2.2.4., Centifolia, the cabbage rose, *Rosa centifolia*; 2.2.5., *Centifolia muscosa*, the moss rose; example, the 'Common Moss' or the hybrid 'Nuits de Young'; 2.2.6., the Autumn Damask, as an example, the Autumn Damask itself or the 'Perpetual White Moss'.

2.3. would be cultivars prior to 1970, and 2.3.1. would be bedding roses; 2.3.1.1. would be classed as the miniature bedding roses (less than 50 cm. in height and width) e.g. 'Sweet Fairy', 'Cinderella'. 2.3.1.2. would be poly. pompons and dwarf floribundas—those that have small flowers in medium to large clusters; example, 'Ellen Poulsen', 'Paul Crampel'. 2.3.1.3., floribundas—those that have medium-sized flowers in medium to large

'SUMMER HOLIDAY' (H.T.)
'Super Star' × unknown seedling
Raised by C. Gregory & Son Ltd
TRIAL GROUND CERTIFICATE 1968
See page 185

'SUMMER MEETING' (floribunda)
'Allgold' × *'Circus'*
Raised by R. Harkness & Co. Ltd
TRIAL GROUND CERTIFICATE 1968
See page 185

clusters like 'Dainty Maid' and 'Orange Triumph', 'Arthur Bell' and 'Pink Parfait'. 2.3.1.4. would be grandifloras; these have large flowers in small flattish clusters; for example 'Dearest', 'Queen Elizabeth', 'Sea Pearl', 'Paddy McGredy'. 2.3.1.5. would be hybrid tea roses, those with large terminal flowers, solitary or in small conical heads in the first flush; for example 'Super Star' and 'Fragrant Cloud'.

The next group would be modern shrub roses, 2.3.2. and that class would embrace cultivars of no uniform character. They are descended from a wide range of species and hybrids. Sub-divisions of the class would include, as 2.3.2.1. cultivars flowering only once in the season—'Constance Spry', 'Cerise Bouquet', 'Morlettii', 'Scarlet Fire', 'Refulgence', 'Gipsy Boy'. 2.3.2.2. would embrace recurrent flowering cultivars with at least two flushes per season—'Honorine de Brabant', 'Pink Grootendorst', 'Comte de Chambord', the Portland Rose.

An alternative to these sub-divisions could be based on the history of the cultivars. For example Portland, Bourbon, hybrid perpetual, hybrid rugosa, hybrid sweetbriar, hybrid musk, hybrid spinosissima. This would entail including cultivars, for example, 'Fritz Nobis', 'Scarlet Fire', 'Elmshorn', 'Kassel', which do not fit into the alternative sub-divisions.

Now we come to perhaps the most difficult of all—what are we going to call the roses from 1970 onwards? We suggest Group 3.1. for dwarf roses, varieties rarely exceeding 60 centimetres in height and spread, and, by the way, such measurements refer to roses in the first year after budding, because you can get any height and any spread in subsequent years by altering the method of pruning.

3.2., bedding roses of compact habit with stems rarely exceeding from 61 to 150 centimetres.

3.3., shrub roses, growth dense to lax, height 1·5 metres and over.

3.4., pillar roses, habit of growth narrow, up to 2·5 metres.

3.5., climbing roses, varieties with stems over 2·5 metres long.

Then, of course, those classes could be further sub-divided if required, according to the flower size. 3.1.1. for example, would be miniature, under 5 cm. across. 3.1.2. would be small, 5 to 8 cm. across. 3.1.3. medium, 8 to 11 cm. across. 3.1.4. large, over 11 cm. across.

Similarly with all the others, 3.2.1., 3.3.1. and so on.

A further possible sub-division would be an inflorescence sub-division, so we could get 3.1.1.1. where the terminal flowers are solitary or few, not forming a flattish head; 3.1.1.2. covering those flowering in flattish clusters. I mention that to show the elasticity of this method of classification. It can go on to meet any new type that is introduced.

An additional sub-division could include duration of flowering period by adding a further "1" for non-recurrent, that is one good flush only, and a further "2" for recurrent, with at least two good flushes per season.

Also in some sections it may be desirable and possible to have a further division for flower type, single, semi-double and double.

The numerical system used above will, in all probability, prove to be confusing, in that the same figures are used for more than one purpose. For example, the numeral "1" can mean group, class and several sub-divisions of classes, its connotation depending upon its position in the line of numerals. The first 1 would be the group, the second 1 the class, the third 1 one of the various divisions. It will probably be desirable to replace some of the numerals by internationally agreed letters. I may say we chose numerals deliberately because the numerals are more flexible than the English alphabet. Some of the letters of the English alphabet are not very useful letters to use in a code, but the numerals in any nation could go to any number we liked. That was why we finally decided on the numeral system, and at this point I would like to thank Mr Allen, our scientific adviser, who is largely responsible for the suggestion of this numeral system of classification and its expandability.

Certain recommendations were made

by the committee, and they are similar in a way to the American recommendations. For instance, we suggest that a Classification Committee shall be appointed and be responsible for recommending, in the case of the United Kingdom, to the Royal National Rose Society Council, on all matters relating to the classification of roses in this country. No rose shall be accorded the Royal National Rose Society's classification until the Classification Committee has recommended its proper classification. That might easily apply to an international classification.

Errors shall be amended by representation of any interested person through the secretary of this Classification Committee.

And then we suggest finally that the classification list shall be published either as an alternative to or as an addition to *Roses—A Selected List of Varieties* that The Royal National Rose Society issues periodically. Additions and amendments would be regularly published in *The Rose Annual*.

DR R. C. ALLEN
United States of America. Presented by O. Keister Evans Junr.

The horticultural classification of roses involves the grouping of cultivars into reasonably well-defined types with similar characteristics and uses. Such a classification is a handy tool for both the amateur and professional rosarian, because a rose belonging to a given class will be similar in habit of growth, method of flowering and use to all others in the same class.

During the past 150 years, the classification of rose cultivars has become increasingly complex and indefinite and now in retrospect we can see that the present-day system evolved in a most haphazard way. In some instances the class name is based on habit of growth such as Climber, and in other cases on heredity or species origin such as Hybrid Multiflora or Hybrid Rugosa. Some classes have pseudo-botanical names such as Polyantha, Grandiflora, Floribunda; and some are based on mere garden terms, such as Hybrid Perpetual, Moss, Rambler or on common names such as Hybrid Tea.

Because of the inconsistencies in the classification terms, the logical grouping of cultivars is difficult, especially on an international basis. New terms are applied for commercial or promotional purposes. Classification is frequently changed and is often indefinite and variable. Not all hybridisers, nurserymen or amateur gardeners internationally accept or use the same class terms, and the present system is not expandable except by the use of new terms that do not fit into any logical pattern.

In an effort to start a movement to develop a systematic classification plan, the American Rose Society, as the International Registration Authority for Roses, was asked by the Council of the International Horticultural Congress in 1966 to begin work on the problem. The project was immediately referred to the American Rose Society Classification Committee under the leadership of Dr Griffith Buck of the Department of Horticulture of the Iowa State University.

There are four salient features of the proposal prepared by this Committee: 1. Parentage of a rose is to be disregarded as a means of classification. 2. Classification is to be based only upon consistent horticultural characteristics. 3. Permanent classification of rose cultivars should be delayed until their correct placement can be assessed adequately. 4. A code system of classification embodying both plant and flower traits is adopted for the five major recurrent bedding rose groups.

Cultivars should be assigned to groups based as nearly as possible on consistent characteristics. Parentage is not a dependable means of classification except in those roses which are relatively close in their relationship to their species parent or parents. The pedigrees of many garden roses are either very involved, unknown, unreliable or unavailable. Characters used in the American Rose Society proposal, in their appropriate order are: 1. plant habit—shrub, bush or climber; 2. flowering habit—once-blooming, recurrent; 3.

manner in which the flowers are borne—inflorescence.

In comparing the plan proposed by the Royal National Rose Society with that proposed by the American Rose Society, there seems to be no difference in basic objectives, nor in the principle of the use of a digital or code system. There are differences, however, in the priority given the various horticultural characteristics. For example, the American proposal groups roses according to habit of growth, which is a fairly constant horticultural characteristic; although it must be recognised that manipulation by pruning, training and the like can alter the habit of growth in the garden. The British proposal begins its separation on the basis of botanical species, followed by cultivars prior to and after 1970.

While the American plan takes into account certain chronological relationships, it proposes that the Shrub roses, including Old Garden Roses—Shrub Type —be permitted to retain their current names such as Gallica, Damask, Alba, etc., although provision is made for them in the code system. This same principle is also to apply to the Old Garden Roses— Bedding Type—and to Climbers. In general, most of the pre-hybrid tea cultivars are comparatively static, having for all practical purposes reached the end of their development.

The emphasis of the American proposal is on the group of contemporary bush roses where the greatest confusion in classification lies. The plan here proposes to divide the group according to size of flowers and the type of inflorescence.

Determining the size of flowers is a problem because of the variability in different localities, even in the United States. But while the precise measurements may vary, the relative size of different cultivars remains constant. A means of determining the size of the flowers for classification purposes will have to be found. The British plan also has the problem of determining various measurements.

While it must be admitted that there are problems with the American proposal, the system is designed to be expandable.

The ordinary Hybrid Tea, as we are familiar with it, would be classed as IIIA and additional digits or symbols could be added if in future years distinct types of Hybrid Teas are developed. For instance, if a cultivar is produced which according to habit of growth and size of bloom is classed as IIIA, yet has a very mossy calyx which promises to be the forerunner of a distinct type of Hybrid Tea, it might be classed as IIIA 1.

The American plan also presupposes the addition of symbols for general colour and height to assist in classification for exhibiting and garden purposes. Thus, a rose like 'Queen Elizabeth', now classified as a Grandiflora, would be classed as IIIB, mp, t (IIIB, medium pink, tall). Such a designation immediately gives the exhibitor or gardener the most essential information he needs to grow or exhibit the cultivar.

It would appear that the British system is even more expandable and complete than that proposed by the American Rose Society. Likewise, it seems to be correspondingly more complicated and takes into account more characteristics than are essential and seems to contemplate a complete coding of descriptive material. Even if letters are substituted to indicate height, flower size, type of inflorescence, etc., it tends to destroy its practical usefulness. A cultivar classified as 3.1.1.2.1 is difficult to interpret quickly. Perhaps, however, it has special merit if such descriptive information is used in electronic data processing.

The American point of view is concerned only with a minimum of horticultural characteristics, namely, habit of growth, size of flower, type of inflorescence and, for exhibition and garden use, colour designation and relative height. As a starting point the American system is concerned only with the contemporary bush roses wherein the greatest development is likely to occur and where the greatest need for an expandable system lies. While the American proposal provides for the digital classification of the Old Garden rose types, the American Rose Society takes the position that these classes are well established in the literature and are no longer being actively developed.

The use of the digital or code system, according to either the British or American systems, should in no way complicate the commercial promotion of any rose type. Under the American system a rose classified as IIIC can be catalogued or sold as a Floribunda, Grandiflora, Hybrid Polyantha, Sweetheart or Love Token rose. As long as the code IIIC is attached the habit of growth, size of flower and type of inflorescence will be known, regardless of what it is called commercially. As for the help to the gardener and exhibitor, symbols for overall colour and relative height would be useful.

As far as the American proposal is concerned, it represents a starting point and will not be presented for international acceptance until it has been adequately

tested and undoubtedly altered to incorporate the thinking and the needs of the international rose community.

The American Rose Society, in acting on the request of the Council of the International Horticultural Congress, did so with the expectation of sharing the responsibility with all national rose organisations. It has been encouraging to learn that the Royal National Rose Society has also given consideration to the matter, and while its proposal differs in detail from the American, the plan has great merit. It would seem that the time has arrived when an International Committee could profitably be formed under the leadership of the International Registration Authority for Roses and composed of representatives of the other national rose organisations of the world.

D. S. BUTCHER
New Zealand

From my point of view, we do not want a telephone directory. What we want is something plain, simple and easy to look after. We do not want figures and figures and more figures.

In New Zealand—and I am not exaggerating—we have per head of population the highest membership in the world, but we have never heard anything or been asked to prepare any paper. We should have been asked to do something, because this is vital to our society. If this is going to be introduced, we are not going to get

tangled up in a whole lot of numbers. We will not agree to lists of figures, and we should be unanimous.

We will go along with anybody and everybody because the majority want it. We will go that far, provided it is something plain and simple, where you can put down say, B2 or B3 or A1. But if we are going to have about three or four numbers, nobody will ever know what they are going to buy or where they are going. I think that is the position as far as New Zealand is concerned.

LA BARONNE DE LA ROCHE
Belgium

Most Europeans are rather reluctant to break with a slowly evolved tradition. The groups of garden roses were named one by one in the course of at least four centuries; when a new group acquired importance, it was not a rule that gave it a name but the writings of several authors, slowly followed by the rosarians. Each group detached itself when necessary from the group or groups from which it derived.

Is there at the present time a necessity

to build a new system? I believe so, because the garden rose has become an international commercial product, bought by millions of people, who only care for a short and simple way of knowing what they order. Another reason is because rose shows and rose trials are becoming more numerous every year, and they must be judged by general and simple rules.

We thus need a new and easy international code. Thanks to such a code we shall know that all roses belonging to the same group will look alike and will be meant for the same purposes in the garden.

The new code proposed by the American Rose Society seems to fulfil this object. It divides all cultivated roses, whether species or cultivars, into four classes:

Class I, shrub roses, including the old Gallicanae roses.

Class II, Old Garden roses, bedding type, strangely including the climbing teas and the Noisettes. Despite several minor points which could be revised, these two first proposed new classes are in accordance with the traditional classification.

Class IV groups all the other climbing roses. It corresponds to a natural division for the ramblers which are derived from related Synstylae species. It is artificial, but certainly very useful for the climbers, which are of different origins and include many sports from bush roses.

Thus, we shall only examine in detail Class III which, strangely enough, is called contemporary bush roses, although it contains only bedding roses. This class is divided into five groups, and the division is perfect.

The groups are:

IIIA, large-flowered roses with sub-solitary flowers, often used for cutting and exhibition purposes. They are mostly hybrid teas, and I believe the term "hybrid tea" is easily understood in any language. Only the German appellation "Edelrosen" should be discarded.

IIIB are what the Americans call "Grandifloras", and the English "floribundas of hybrid tea type". They are mainly used for garden decoration.

IIIC includes bedding roses with medium flowers in rather flat-topped clusters or floribundas.

IIID includes roses which bear small flowers in large pyramidal panicles. They are mostly of polyantha type, although many of them are not true polyanthas.

IIIE includes dwarf plants bearing small flowers in few-flowered clusters, or miniatures.

These five groups can each be designated by a single word. The American proposition is to call them, not by name, but by their code number. One wonders if a single name would not be more easily remembered than a number, and one should try for several years to use both the name and the code number. Time alone will show which will survive.

On the whole, it seems that the proposed International Code, when more or less adapted, will certainly be useful for a superficial knowledge of the rose, but we feel it can never be called a classification. A real classification can only be based on the knowledge of the parentage or derivation of the roses and of their genetics. For instance, a division between climbers, shrubs and bedding roses has no deep scientific meaning. It has a practical meaning, but it has no botanical value.

We cannot agree with the first part of the new American text, saying "The parentage of the rose is to be disregarded as a means of classification". But we could admit, for instance, that: "The new horticultural code is not based on parentage". Happily there is no deep contradiction between the proposed code and a real classification. This is because the American Code—and excuse me if I do not call it a classification—is based mainly on the inflorescence, which is one of the main hereditary distinctive characters. But one character, however important, is not enough to classify a Genus. The invisible recessive characters, transmitted by many hybrids, must also be recorded. It is indispensable for breeders, for dedicated rosarians and for those botanists who do not disregard all horticultural plants that a classification resting not only upon all the important visible characters but also upon the derivation of the garden roses should be maintained.

The progress of the rose seems to be possible only on condition that the breeders will continue to know which crosses have been tried and what results were obtained. It is true that this knowledge of the parentage or derivation is not always possible. Many parentages are unknown; others are very intricate and some of the given parentages are unreliable. But I think to disregard what can be known would slow down the progress of the rose. Moreover, if roses were classified only on their appearance, they would soon become as uninteresting to botanists as are now dahlias or gladioli to which this method of classification has been applied. Few people take a botanical interest in these flowers.

Many of us feel that everything should be done to encourage the breeders to publish in specialised literature the real results of their crossings. This will enable future breeders to make new investigations and prevent their working in ways which have already been tried without results.

The botanical classification, taking most hybrids and some mutants into account, thus remains a necessity. It cannot be replaced by a horticultural code which, from another point of view, is also indispensable. The maintenance and progress of the rose classification is not only a matter of continuing a respectable tradition; it is the only way, it seems, to ensure as quickly as possible, the appearance of newer and better roses.

DR A. S. THOMAS
Australia

Quite frankly, I don't like this business of letters and numbers. I think this is quite satisfactory from the point of view of recording things in a library and an international registration centre. But when you are going to use classification like this to give out to the general public, the people we are trying to encourage to grow roses, you are only going to confuse them.

It is a different matter when it comes to growing daffodils. They have a system like this, but this relates only to the flower. And if you are going to start giving numbers and figures to not only the flower but the colour of the flower, the size of the flower, type of plant—whether it is a miniature, a floribunda, a hybrid tea, a climber (I am deliberately leaving out the word Grandiflora)—I think you are going to create tremendous confusion except for Mr Evans sitting in his office as official international registrar for the whole world or the likes of myself, sitting at my desk as registrar for the Australia/New Zealand area. I think beyond that it is completely wrong. I cannot think of anything more harmful to fostering rose growing.

I do not like this word Grandiflora, and I have been told that, if I do not like it, I should also not like floribunda. Well, I will go along with floribunda, because it does mean an abundance of florets. In the early days, an abundance of florets was interpreted as meaning an abundance of florets on one stem. In more recent days, we in Australia have taken it as meaning an abundance of florets on the plant. Now this takes in floribundas such as 'Paddy McGredy' and 'Pink Parfait'. I know 'Pink Parfait' is classed by the Americans as a Grandiflora, and so is 'Queen Elizabeth'. But I will go along with floribunda because it does mean an abundance of florets, an abundance of bloom.

As to Grandiflora I would suggest very strongly the dropping of this classification; the reclassifying of the larger roses classed under this heading such as 'Montezuma', 'Buccaneer', and 'Super Star', and including them with the hybrid teas. In fact, I cannot see why they have not been hybrid teas from the very beginning.*

Secondly, I would suggest that the Grandifloras with the smaller blooms be re-classified as floribundas. Drop the term Grandiflora altogether, and group them into hybrid teas or floribundas, whichever they fit better.

We in Australia sub-divide floribundas into three groups; this is quite new and it was started by the National Rose Society of South Australia. Group A we make the obvious original floribunda with large heads of many smallish florets such as 'Moulin Rouge', 'Europeana', 'Orange Triumph' and 'Masquerade'. Group B covers the floribundas with up to seven medium-sized florets such as 'Dearest', 'Orangeade', 'Violet Carson' and 'Circus'.

* They have always been so classified in the United Kingdom—Ed.

Group C relates to the floribundas with one to three fairly big florets.

I have seen these roses staged in this country. In a stand of 24 distinct or 12 distinct, I have seen 'Kordes' Sondermeldung' commonly called 'Independence'; I have seen it staged here as a specimen bloom. This is not a Grandiflora, or a type of floribunda in the strict meaning of the word, but it does produce an abundance of flowers on the plant. These are the so-called floribundas of hybrid tea type, for example 'Queen Elizabeth', 'Pink Parfait', 'Kordes' Sondermeldung', 'Sea Pearl' and 'Red Dandy'.

I can see no virtue whatever in this numbering business. The term Floribunda of Hybrid Tea Type is clumsy. It is too long, and for this reason I am not enthusiastic about it at all. This would be for our Class C—the one to three blooms per stem. However, it does imply what it means. Let us try to devise a shorter term than Floribunda of Hybrid Tea Type, and let us leave the roses alone. We have got our old-fashioned roses, but an old-fashioned rose need not be old. 'Blue Boy' was somewhere about 1958 I think; 'Lotte Gunthart' I would even put in as an old-fashioned rose, and that is much more recent. It is an old-fashioned type, and there is no age limit on type.

As to starting a new scheme in 1970, I think this is only going to create more and more confusion. It is like trying to re-classify 'Ophelia' and 'Spek's Yellow' today as Grandifloras.

But if we can only leave roses as roses, and not care whether they are hybrid perpetuals, which after all have almost ceased to exist except in old-fashioned gardens. Have roses, and they can be sub-divided into roses as bushes or as climbers. You can have that sub-division, but after all it does not matter much once you have cut the bloom, whether it came from a climber or a bush. Then we can have the floribundas; we can have the miniatures. That means four classes; old-fashioned; roses; floribundas and miniatures.

GRAHAM THOMAS
United Kingdom

Our own classification is the united effort of several of us, and as Mr Fairbrother said, it was very much polished up by Mr Allen. It is therefore our joint recommendation, but I think there are one or two little points that should be specially considered, or perhaps you have already thought of them.

Our chairman asked whether we really need a classification. I would pose the question, "how many classifications do we want"? There are the keen amateur gardeners, the professional gardeners and nurserymen, who want some means of knowing, when they plant a tree or select a flower, what kind of a plant it is going to make and what sort of treatment it wants. I think something quite basic and managed with letters or numerals would help them enormously, providing the whole matter is put over carefully in the first place, so that in every catalogue there is a synopsis of the classification. Without that, these numerals of course would be completely useless.

Then there is the international aspect where, of course, like the use of Latin for botanical names, some sort of code can be understood by people who speak all manners of languages, and I think in this sense this scientific classification is admirable.

But there is also the man in the street, the "common or garden" man, who perhaps will not want to be bothered with numbers, and I am sure he would rather call them hybrid teas or floribundas or hybrid musks or what you will. If we can have the two schemes married, I think we shall be suiting everybody.

I was delighted to hear that the term Grandiflora was going to be stamped on by some people, if not by everybody. The great danger in selecting a term like Grandiflora is that there might at some time be raised roses with flowers a foot across, and what are you going to call them? It is like a botanist who called a plant that he discovered, for instance, *Rosa gigantea*. It is a very large grower, but the man who named it did not know that he was not going to find an even bigger one, and, of course, when that crops up, as it does in many genera, you have the anomaly of a tiny-flowered plant being called Gigantea or Grandiflora, and something much bigger being called Scott Thompsonii or something of that kind.

H. C. SWIM
United States of America

I have no prepared paper either, but I do have a few random thoughts that I would like to express.

First I would like to endorse what Mr Graham Thomas has said, because to me—I think this is pretty much what Mr Butcher was saying—the real purpose of classification is to inform the public. We in the industry feel that we are not doing the job if we do not tell the people who buy roses what they are buying.

My toes have been trodden on today because I was involved in the original description of the Grandiflora rose. I must agree that this term is poorly chosen but I had nothing to do with that. I would be glad to see it tossed in the ashcan. On the other hand, the intention here was to set aside a group of roses which we felt was sufficiently different to be set apart from the Hybrid Teas, in order to inform the public. There is a large mass of people who are not sophisticated enough to know what a Hybrid Tea is, I grant that. They do not know what a Hybrid Tea is; they do not know what a Grandiflora is; they do not know what a Floribunda is.

I think that what I would like to see, and I believe I have some support in this, is eventually to have coined names. I notice that Dr Thomas approved of the word Floribunda, and I think I go along with that. That is a coined name. It is reasonably descriptive of the varieties which we know to belong to that class, and I really see nothing wrong with this. In fact, this is what I personally would like to see—some coined names without any pretence of

I will also comment upon the last speaker's wish to include varieties such as 'Blue Boy' among the old-fashioned roses. I do feel that we should make a very clear-cut issue for that race of roses which was raised many years ago and is quite distinct, and this is surely a case where we do need to know and to retain the parentage. Once we start getting these old roses mixed up with the Chinas and the hybrid teas, we come into more modern groups.

belonging to a generic group, or even to a botanic group, but which, in the course of time, through support from the nursery industry and the Rose Societies, would be useful terms to associate with these groups for the general public.

I might say further that I do not mean to give the impression that I frown on the system that is proposed by either the American Rose Society or the Royal National Rose Society. I think they have merit from a permanency standpoint. The All America Rose Selections, of course, was originally responsible for the term Grandiflora—I think the intention was good here. They came up against the variety 'Queen Elizabeth', and they saw this differently from what Dr Thomas does down in Australia. It was so different from what we were accustomed to think of as Hybrid Teas that they felt it would not be right to foist it on the public as a Hybrid Tea without some qualification.

Well, this started out, as I say, with good enough intentions, but what happened was that then they decided that the Grandifloras were not going to sell well, although in the beginning, as near as I could tell, there was no thought that this particular class would sell better or worse than the Hybrid Tea or the Floribunda. But along came 'Super Star' as you call it, and it was switched. It was originally thought of as a Grandiflora and then, because they thought Grandifloras would not sell, they decided it should be a Hybrid Tea. This is where we really went wrong, and the industry has to take its share of the blame.

David E. Gilad

B. E. Humphrey

Ralph S. Moore

Ena Harkness (*Mrs Ena Jeffries*)

Prof. L. Broadbent

Dr E. W. Lyle

Dr C. H. Cadman

Prof. J. Colhoun

Prof. S. C. Harland, F.R.S.

Mrs Vera Klimenko

Reimer Kordes

Herbert C. Swim

E. B. Le Grice

David Ruston

Mrs Jadwiga Grabczewska

Graham Thomas

O. Keister Evans Jr.

Flower Photography
Chairman: H. N. Raban

DR J. D. MCPIKE
United States of America

My remarks are going to be directed to the novice photographer or rank amateur as we call him, and I am going to speak briefly on the fundamentals of photography.

In rose photography, or in any type of flower photography, one of the most common faults is getting too much into the picture. What do we have here? Nothing but a blob of colour. Entirely too much. Your eye jumps from place to place. This is one of the most common faults of an amateur photographer. He tries to get too much into the picture. He does the same at a rose show.

Here again, look what you have—your eye jumps all over the picture. Let us talk a little about close-up photography, because when we use close-up photography we eliminate much of the extraneous material that tends to distract from our picture.

For instance, here we see the winning roses at a certain rose show, but what do you look at? Your eye jumps from one to the other. You do not know which one to look at. So let us just take one rose and bring it in close. See how much we have improved this picture? We have only one rose now so we can focus all our attention on it. But let us look at it a little closer—and still a little closer. When you go to a rose show do you see people stand back eight, ten or twelve feet looking at roses? No, they have their noses right up into the rose, so let us get our nose into the rose. See what close-up photography can do for you? We can even go a little closer if you wish. This is what I consider the ultimate in rose photography. To be able to get up close to the rose.

Take again a garden. Here is a garden scene; what do you see? Again, just a blob of colour. But let us pick out that one rose right in the centre. See how much better it is to photograph just one rose. So re-member, remove the extraneous material —do not get everything into your picture, and do utilise close-up photography.

Here is another example. You have two roses. Your eye jumps from one to the other. Which one does your eye rest on? Well, the one that may be the prettier of the two. Then why not just take that one? See how much better it is? See how much you have improved the slide by just taking one rose instead of two. So remember by close-up photography you remove the extraneous material.

I have often been asked "What kind of camera is best for an amateur?" I would say without question a single-lens reflex 35 mm. camera. There are hundreds of them on the market. They range anywhere from maybe 30 or 40 pounds upwards, and you can go as high as you like.

The big advantage of the single-lens reflex is that you see through the eyepiece exactly what the camera takes. You do not have this problem called parallax which can be quite confusing. In many cameras where the viewfinder and the lens are separate, what you see is not what the film sees. Where the viewfinder and lens are separated, you see this through the viewfinder; but, lo and behold, when that film comes back from the processor, this is what you have. Now you can eliminate all of this with a single-lens reflex because you can compose your picture and you get just what you see.

Now, how do we get these close-up photographs? We have three basic methods—the telephoto lens, extension tubes and supplemental lenses.

Your telephoto lens is just as it is described; it is a telephoto; it brings things up closer. Unfortunately, it has several drawbacks. Firstly, it is quite expensive. Secondly, you must use a tripod—you cannot have the slightest motion of your camera using a telephoto lens. It does have one advantage—when you cannot get up close to a rose you can bring the rose up close to you. For instance, here is a group of roses. I could not get any closer to this particular bed, but here is what I have with a telephoto lens. See how that is improved? You can bring things up close with your telephoto.

I think for the average amateur supplemental lenses are by far the simplest, the easiest to use and the cheapest. They come in different diopters, $+1$, $+2$, $+3$, $+4$, $+6$ and $+10$ on up. All they are is little magnifying glasses that tend to bring the image closer and make it larger.

You can bring them up as close as you want to, depending on the size of your lens, or the number of the diopter. In the last year or two there has come on to our market a lens known as a Proxovar. This is a sort of zoom diopter lens. You do not need to use the separate lenses. This will go anywhere from 3 feet, which will give you a picture like this, up to that one in the centre at 3 inches, and any place in between. This eliminates the various supplemental lenses and acts as one—a regular zoom supplemental lens.

Suppose you cannot afford a single lens reflex; are there any other cameras? Here is the old common Startech. Surprising as it seems, it will take fairly good pictures. It uses 127 film, so the slides are slightly larger than 35 mm. It comes as a kit, with two supplemental lenses and a wire frame, because you do have parallax problems with it. Here it is all set-up to take the picture. All you do is hold that frame in front of the rose and you will photograph what is within the frame. It is very simple. This gives an idea—I am sighting through the camera, but as long as the rose is within the wire frame I will get a picture of the rose.

There is another camera which has only recently come out on the market. I know you are all familiar with the American Instamatic Camera. It was developed by Eastman and uses 126 film. They do have a close-up camera, made especially for close-up work. It again comes in a kit, with flash bulbs, supplemental lens and framing device. This is a picture taken with the Instamatic Camera. Again the same rose taken at various distances with the Instamatic.

Lighting

As many of our pictures are taken inside, we must resort to artificial light. I much prefer sunlight, but nevertheless when you do not have sun, you have to use artificial light. I feel the best artificial light is strob or electronic flash, for our outdoor colour film. This is a ring light that was developed specifically for medical and dental photography, that I have used for a good many years. I have adapted it to flower photography. The only drawback is that it gives a rather flat or shadowless light.

Here is the equipment as it is set-up. You see the supplemental lens, your holder, your ring light and your condenser. On the camera mounted, it looks like this. The light completely surrounds the lens, and it does give you a very flat light. For black and white it is worthless, but, because the various colours tend to stand out, it does give a fairly good colour slide. This is rose 'Columbus Queen' with a flat lighting.

Now if you want to increase the contrast, you can mount the light to the side of the lens as I have on this set-up of the camera, and you will get this type of picture, which seems to make the rose stand out just a little bit better. This is a ring light mounted to the side of a camera.

Backgrounds

Now backgrounds are another very important factor in photography that many amateurs overlook. Here is a slide I borrowed from a friend. Look at the plate and other various objects that are distracting attention from that rose. Here is another background—very distracting. They took a flash picture and forgot that the trophy would bounce back the light of the flash. So watch your background. The best background, I feel, is the sky, but it is very hard to look down on a rose and still get the sky in the picture, so we have to do other things. A normal, natural green background such as evergreens is also very good.

If you want to make the rose stand out a little bit better, you can throw the background out of focus. This can all be done beautifully with single lens reflex. There is the same rose with the background thrown out of focus, making the rose stand out just a little more prominently.

Here again you can use a coloured card if you want to—a gold card, a blue card or green or black—and place it behind the rose to eliminate any distracting background. Often you can, by moving to a different position, also improve your background. You will notice here are three roses. At the top you have a distracting blob of colour. So just move your position, and see how much you have improved that picture. You have removed part of the background. You can even go farther than that, if conditions will permit. For instance, here are a few roses, a house and a few other things that tend to distract in the background. Remove one of these roses, and move your position, and this is what you get.

One technique that we use to emphasise or focus on a single rose is to employ sequence shots. All of you are familiar with the cinema and television. You see the man and woman come in, you see a whole scene of the room. Then they bring a close-up of them sitting on the couch, and then the third is them kissing—quite close together. And you can do the same with roses.

Another good method of documentary photography for the amateur is to take an overall picture of a bush. Always get the name of the rose in the picture so you know what it is. Most people cannot remember. And then take that one rose, right in the centre, above the sign, and then the close-up. See what a nice sequence that makes. You also have a little diversion—you do not have the same thing all the time. So get a little diversion into your slide photography.

Now I am going to tell you a little about special effects for lighting outdoors. I know this is going to be covered by the subsequent speakers much better than I can cover it, but I am going to show you how you can utilise outdoor light for some special effects. For instance, here is a bloom of 'Garden Party' taken in my own yard about high noon, with the sun directly on it. The next morning I rose bright and early and, with the light coming through the other direction, I have a much more beautiful rose. There it is in indirect light, light coming through the back of the rose. You notice how that has improved it. Go back to the first one—this is just a flat rose. Now let us see it in indirect light. You can use your sunlight a lot to help enhance your picture.

Here again is a rose with the light coming from the top—this is 'Pink Princess'—and notice how that tends to model, or make your rose stand out better. Here is side lighting—the light coming from the side on 'Apricot Nectar'; see how it also models the rose. All these effects, used extensively by the professional, top lighting, back lighting, side lighting can produce beautiful results.

If you want to get a picture of lavender or purple and similar colours, the best way you can pick those up with Kodachrome is with indirect light. With indirect light there is no direct sunlight—it is simply light reflected with white cardboard. This helps to bring out the blues and creates what we know as a cool picture.

Likewise, late afternoon sun is warm. There are a lot of red rays in it, and it can bring out the reds and make your picture very warm. Here is 'Kiss of Fire'; just notice how beautiful it is in the afternoon sunlight. Warm reds tend to make the rose more photogenic. Let us just see what you can do. Here is 'Garden State', taken at high noon on Kodachrome II film. Kodachrome II is a rather cold film. Now let us wait until about four or five o'clock in the afternoon, and take a picture of this same rose, same film—you notice a change in colour. You have that warmth, that added warmth coming from the afternoon sun. Now this is particularly effective with red roses. Here again is 'Chrysler Imperial', a dark red rose, taken at high noon in bright sunlight. This is the same rose taken five hours later. Note how the added warmth of the late afternoon sun has enhanced the colour.

In closing let us emphasise the following points:

1. Remove unwanted or extraneous material from your slides by utilising close-up photography and a judicious choice of backgrounds.

2. Enhance the beauty of the rose by utilising special lighting effects, side light and back light, etc.

3. Improve your slide presentation by utilising sequence slides.

HARRY SMITH
United Kingdom

I now feel like describing what I want to say to you in the next twenty minutes as "Rose Photography Simplified". Anyhow, I will spend two or three minutes just showing you the equipment that I use, and I don't think it is overall so expensive as the marvellous array that Dr McPike has shown us. Then I will show you some of the pictures that this set-up has taken.

He never uses a tripod, whereas I never take a picture without a tripod. He uses a single lens reflex which he holds to his eye. I use a Rollei type twin lens camera because, by looking down on to the ground glass screen, I can see exactly what I am taking. I spend a lot of time composing my picture on the screen—that is where the time goes—and once I am satisfied with the composition of the picture, I can then forget all about that and concentrate on the other important points—whether the sun is shining, whether the wind is blowing and so on. If there is a branch in the way when I have been setting up I can pull it away with one hand and click the shutter with the other. If I have got to hold the camera to my eye at the same time, well I ask you!

And the other point is this, with regard to eye-level cameras. Until you press the trigger you really have to concentrate on what you see through the eye-level camera. With the slightest distraction the composition of your picture can go completely awry, even by the unconscious movement of an eighth of an inch or so of the camera. There is nothing like that about the twin reflex camera on its tripod stand!

The stand is also fitted, as you see, with a ball and socket joint—a most important accessory because, if you are photographing a flower on the bush, the flower may

be in such a position that, if you are taking it with an eye-level camera, you have either got to bend over like this or you may have to get down to ground level; whereas, with a ball and socket joint, you can turn the camera round in all directions in order to accommodate it to the awkward flower on the bush. And, you see, it doesn't matter whereabouts on the bush the flower may be, because you can borrow a chair, and achieve a height with the tripod which I don't think you can with an eye-level camera. You can also go right down to ground level and, if the flower is obstinately only a few inches above the soil, you can still get down to photograph it. If you are working with an eye-level camera this is hardly possible.

Think of all the marvellous lenses of which we saw pictures on the screen just now for when you want to get a few inches away—6 inches and so forth. I have but two sets of twin lenses—supplementary lenses. The camera itself will take me down to as near as 3 feet; one set of lenses fitted to the camera takes me down then to 18 inches while the second set of lenses takes me down to about 10 inches. The pairs of lenses that I have also eliminate any trouble due to parallax.

That briefly is the equipment, with the exception of just one or two other items. We saw a picture just now of a bush with two flowers on it, one up here, one out there, as so often happens. That's where the odd bit of wire comes in, because if it is long enough you can, in a hidden sort of way, use the wire to bring them both together. This is a most essential part of the equipment. Can the camera lie? Yes, with the help of this sort of thing!

Dr McPike takes practically every picture with flash. I never use it—never. All my work is done in daylight, whether it is out in the open air in bright sunlight or in the light of a well-lighted room, but certainly without flash. I am not decrying the commercial studios—far from it—in which many of the coloured plates you see in the Rose Society's Annual are taken. Where you have proper lighting equipment with floods all over the place you can turn off those not required to illuminate the bloom, eliminate unnecessary shadows and so forth. I am talking now to the chap in the garden with a camera, who wants to carry around as limited an amount of equipment as possible and I recommend daylight every time. With flash, if this is the flower, and this is the camera and the flash is behind it, you are getting frontal lighting and the overall result looks flatter than if you had, for example, half back-lighting—I am in agreement here with Dr McPike. Side lighting, or back lighting, is trickier but you get wonderful results.

On the other hand, if you have sunlight coming down sideways on to the rose, then, if the light is at all strong, you will have one side of the flower in deep shadow and a reflector of some sort is very useful to lighten that shadow. All the books on colour photography tell you: "Avoid utmost contrasts if you can". Reduce the contrast between the highest light and the darkest shadow with the reflector. And here is my reflector, you see, just a bit of stainless steel folded in two; one side is bright, the other dull.

Now, if the sky is overcast, I use the bright side to lighten up the shady side of the flower, if I feel it is necessary. On the other hand, if it is bright sunlight I use the duller side of the reflector in order to illuminate the shady side of the flower. It is a very, very useful piece of equipment, and I wouldn't be without it. If you haven't anything like that, a bit of that silvery foil you wrap meat in for roasting will do just as well.

Well, I think I will leave the equipment now and show you a few pictures, all taken with that equipment and nothing more.

If you are photographing roses in front of an artificial background the question arises as to which colour are you going to put behind the particular rose you are photographing? I think it is much easier to take the pinholder, on which the stems of of the blooms may be impaled, into the garden and find a natural background. You see what I have done here. The blooms are on a pinholder and I have taken them out into the garden, and stuck them in front of a part of a border of 'Lilli Marlene'.

Over the years I have used Ferrania and Kodak film. Two years or so ago I went over to Agfa C.T.P. which I now use, and almost the only reason why I did so was because of the wonderful way in which it records shades of red. I don't know, from my experience, of any other film that would get as near recording the real colour of 'Lilli Marlene', which I am now showing, as Agfa film.

There is 'Roseraie de l' Haÿ.' I am quite pleased with the recording of the colour. This illustrates a great problem in rose photography—finding the colour film which will record as accurately as possible the actual colour of the rose itself.

Here now is a picture of the modern floribunda shrub rose, 'Fred Loads' taken at Bone Hill, last year, with blue sky as background. You will appreciate that to achieve this the camera was tilted up at an angle of 45° to throw the truss against the sky.

Here is 'Canary Bird', and one of which I am very fond now, 'Charles de Mills'. I always look upon these very dark red roses as a challenge to both colour film and the photographer, and, although I took this picture several years ago, I still have a warm regard for it.

I have shown this slide in honour of the President of the Society, General Naylor. It is 'Maigold' raised by Kordes and taken some two weeks ago in the President's garden—a really magnificent specimen.

Whilst at Kew, I spent a lot of time surveying the pergolas, clothed with climbing roses. These are most difficult subjects to photograph because you are standing underneath, looking up; and what you mostly see is the wood, of which the pergolas are constructed. All the flowers sensibly are on the top facing the sun. Here are a couple of attempts to try and show what two of the climbers at Kew can do and were like a fortnight ago. The first is 'Albertine', and the next one 'Chaplin's Pink Climber'. The latter slide does indicate how profusely this climber was flowering, but I would very much have loved to be up on top looking down, rather than being underneath looking up.

I was lucky with this one in Oxford Botanic Garden two or three weeks ago. It was a very dull afternoon, but I thought it made a very pleasing picture and regardless of the very gloomy conditions I tried that shot, and it came off. And there is

another point I would make, don't be deterred by the weather. It may be a gloomy day but, if you have got your tripod steady and are patient, you may be successful. If I had the choice of blazing sun like yesterday or an overcast sky, it would be for the overcast sky every time.

The last slides I want to show you now are a few years old, and they relate to three wonderful flowers of the hybrid tea 'Anne Letts'. There they are stuck up on a pinholder against an artificial background. I took the pinholder out into the garden, where the sun was shining, set it against a natural background and here is the same set of blooms. Of all the hundreds of rose portraits I have taken in the last few years, this is my favourite.

ANTHONY HUXLEY
United Kingdom

Now, I am odd man out today because, as I told the organisers, I am not really a rose photographer. I take the odd rose; I take garden flowers; I take garden scenes also. My favourite occupation, though, with the camera is to take wild flowers, and Mr Balfour said "Well, why don't you come along and show some wild flowers, because a lot of the audience will undoubtedly be taking other plants as well as roses?". And there are certain problems with wild flowers which do not exist with roses.

First of all, the rose is a shape which is more or less consistent. It is a round or flat object of approximately the same size and shape, and although, as you have seen, there are all sorts of ways of handling the shapes and the problems they cause and the way they are staged, the basic thing is the same.

Now, with the wild flower, you very often have to take it as you find it, and the background produces a problem. It may produce a challenge, and very often a very pleasing result, but it's there; you can't really shift it around. You can do some "gardening", as I call it—you can clear away extraneous grass, and that sort of thing. You can perhaps do a bit of wiring, as Harry has suggested, or fiddling

with the flowers. With a small wild flower, you can sometimes pull the odd stem out to put in the middle of a group. As Harry said, the camera can lie, but you must get a pleasing result which still looks natural.

I would also like to show you my equipment. Being a wild flower photogrpaher, one has to carry it around, lumber it up and down mountain sides and so on. Therefore, I use a sort of bag which is in fact a fisherman's bag. I sometimes take three cameras in here, plus other things. And it is the only bag I have found which does this without being hard, angular and heavy.

Now my camera is a big single lens reflex. Like Harry, I use 120 roll film. I prefer the format; for reproduction it is superior to the 35 mm., and I also think it gives you a slightly better result on the screen. This is an East German affair called a Praktisix. Like Dr McPike's camera, you see through the lens, but it is not an eye-level machine. Like Harry's, you look down at your ground glass screen. You compose exactly what you want as you see it.

For close-ups up to about five inches, I use auxiliary lenses which you screw on the front. These are larger than the lens itself, so you do not have any trouble with cutting off the corners, which sometimes happens with some of the other cameras.

If I want to take a real close-up, I use a tube or a bellows. The bellows is heavy and cumbersome, so these tubes are convenient—you have different sizes—and this is a very simple camera with a bayonet fitting. You just take the lens out, you push your tube in, and with this you can get right down to multiply the image of a flower about three times on the ground glass screen.

The trouble with this is that you need an exposure eight or ten times normal. Therefore, for close-ups, I always use a flash. Now my flash is a bit cumbersome. I have had it a number of years, and when it was new there was nothing smaller. But as it continues to work so well, I cannot bear to get rid of it, although really one could probably do with a smaller one. On the other hand, its big handle has its advantages.

I use a flash not only for these super-close-ups, these macro-photographs, but also if the wind is blowing, if it is raining or if the flower is in a dark corner. You need a flashgun, simply because you cannot get an exposure otherwise. And again, if you are walking about and you do not want to waste a lot of time, you often cannot wait. In the mountains you practically always get a wind; everything is moving around and a flash will allow you to stop the thing within limits. And if you provide a bit of exterior light as well, you can obtain an exposure which has the advantage of stopping the movement and yet gives a certain amount of natural appearance.

I do all my photography in the hand. I never use a tripod because, when you are out in the field, frankly, you do not have time for this sort of thing. In a garden you probably do, but when I am in the mountains or the middle of Greece I am usually in a hurry. Therefore I take my flower as I find it. I do a little bit of "gardening". Like Harry, I will walk around it and make sure I am getting the best position. Basically I am a snapshotter, and I take my pictures very rapidly.

Now, I think my next job is to come down to the projector and show you some of the results, usually with natural light.

Mr. Huxley then showed a number of slides of wild flowers, taken in various countries, which included straightforward plant portraits, a number demonstrating the plants' habitat, and one acting as record of a new discovery in conjunction with a pressed herbarium specimen. Other photographs were in much-magnified close-up, revealing unexpected textures and colourings as well as features of botanical interest, which included such common British plants as yarrow, white dead nettle, bog asphodel and old man's beard —each of them unexpectedly beautiful. He ended with three rose species, just to show that he did not eschew them.—Editor

Feeding Roses
Chairman: F. Fairbrother

DR D. W. DUTHIE
Bath University of Technology, presented by Adrian C. Stevens
Organic Matter in Rose Beds

Dr Duthie's talk is by way of throwing out an idea for discussion, and here we have a problem, because if discussion arises from this, my colleague, Julian Howden and I are not soil scientists, as Dr Duthie is, and I am sure that many of the other people here today, especially our other speakers, will be better qualified to answer the questions than I am. However, we have been primed by Dr Duthie, so we will do out best.

In back numbers of *The Rose Annual*, some of the leading rose growers have described their methods of cultivation and feeding roses, and they have in common the application of very large dressings of organic manures. This may be necessary for the production of show blooms, but many small scale rose gardeners wish to spend only the minimum of labour and expense on their rose beds. Most "front garden" rosarians must be deterred by the apparent necessity of incorporating very large organic dressings in the rose bed, and they wonder if there is an easier way to produce reasonable blooms with less effort.

The great popularity of the rose in small gardens is partly due to its tolerance of a wide range of soil types, from sandy soils to heavy clays, and from acid soils to those which are high in lime, but its greatest attraction is probably the fact that a rose bed requires less work than that needed to grow any other flower. And with modern methods of weed control, the work involved in maintaining a rose bed becomes virtually negligible compared with any other part of the garden. Even pests and diseases may be accepted by the lazy gardener as temporary bad luck, in the hope that next season may be better, although of course serious rose growers and commercial growers cannot accept this philosophical attitude.

Most garden soils are reasonably well drained and do not dry out too rapidly, but where the soil is light sand or sticky clay, it is essential to incorporate farmyard manure, compost or peat in preparing the rose bed. Roses do not tolerate bad drainage; if the soil is badly drained they may suffer, and also if it dries out too rapidly.

There seems to be little doubt that any rose bed will benefit from large dressings of organic manure, but most small-scale rose gardeners prefer to plant their twenty or thirty roses in the soil as it is, and hope for the best. The next step is to buy a packet of rose fertiliser and scatter this around the plants, sometimes with the mistaken idea that the more you apply, the better the roses will be. This method of feeding roses is so easy that quite heavy dressings of chemicals may be applied, year after year, leading to a decline in the vigour of the roses. The soil is often blamed for this, but the real trouble may be due to the excess of fertiliser and not to the soil itself.

One function of organic matter in the soil is to act as a sponge for plant nutrients, and to release these slowly but readily to plant roots. This is of particular significance in rose beds, which are often given heavy applications of fertilisers, as much as four ounces per square yard repeated year after year, perhaps even twice a year. This is equivalent to nearly 12 cwts per acre per application and it is almost certain that, without the sponge effect of organic matter, the soil solution will become too concentrated in places and prevent the roots from functioning normally.

Dr Dick stressed the "salt-effect" in *The Rose Annual* of 1963, pointing out that, if the concentration is too great, it may lead to water passing from the plant to the soil instead of from the soil to the plant. In a soil which is very high in organic matter, this salt-effect will be damped down, whereas in a soil with normal or low organic content, heavy applications of fertiliser may produce harmful concentrations of salts.

Thus, heavy applications of fertilisers are safe only when the soil is very rich in organic matter. With the ordinary garden soil, only light dressings of fertilisers are safe; about half an ounce to one ounce per square yard once a year. One ounce per square yard is nearly 3 cwts per acre, which will supply more plant food than the rose plants need for vigorous growth.

One important point is that fertilisers should not be applied regularly in a ring around the plants. Plant nutrients do not easily move sideways in the soil; they only move down. So frequent band applications may produce pockets of high fertiliser concentrations, separated by areas of relatively low fertility, thus causing a restricted root system. Of course, it is dangerous to apply fertilisers on the plant or very near to the stem, as this is likely to cause cankers.

The heavy dressings of organic manures used by some rose growers provide far

'PHARAOH' (H.T.)
('*Happiness*' × '*Independence*') × '*Suspense*'
Raised by Meilland, France
TRIAL GROUND CERTIFICATE 1967

An arrangement of red
roses at The International
Rose Conference, 1968

First Prize Arrangement—
1968 Autumn Show—
Mrs E. M. Woodcock
Class 52—An arrangement
of roses with any rose
foliage and/or heps, in a
box or basket with a lid

more organic matter than is needed to improve or maintain the drainage, water retention and general tilth of the average soil, and probably more than is needed to damp down the salt-effect that has been described. Yet these dressings must be beneficial; otherwise experienced rose growers would not use them. This suggests that organic manure contains small quantities of plant foods which are not normally supplied in fertilisers. These may include magnesium, boron and iron, since the work on mineral deficiencies of roses, reported in *The Rose Annual* by Professor Wallace in 1954, and Miss Aphra Wilson in 1961, indicates the importance of these elements in rose feeding. As they occur in very small quantities in farmyard manure and compost, heavy dressings may be required to provide a good supply of these micro-nutrients to the plant. Although magnesium and boron can be applied as Epsom salts and household borax, it is obviously more convenient for the small-scale rose grower to buy a packet of rose fertiliser which contains all the elements known to be required by roses. At least one firm markets a complete fertiliser of this kind, but only light dressings should be applied unless the soil is rich in organic matter.

The danger of applying too much inorganic fertiliser is illustrated by the instructions on the packet of one well-known rose fertiliser mixture. This advises applying 4 ozs per square yard in early spring, followed by a second application of 2 ozs per square yard as soon as the flower buds develop. The rose grower is then advised to make further applications every two or three weeks during the flowering period. These dressings of a chemical fertiliser could easily add up to a ton and a half per acre per annum. In a few years an extremely high level of inorganic salts may build up in a heavy soil, resulting in a shortened life for an otherwise healthy rose.

JADWIGA GRABCZEWSKA
The representative of Polish Engineers and Technicians of Horticulture Association, Warsaw
Roses in Peat Moss

Spontaneous development of rose nurseries, and especially the greenhouse culture of roses, after the last war on the one hand, and the permanent increase of mechanisation on the other hand, have made it very difficult to obtain adequate supplies of farm manure and have aggravated the problem of preparing good garden soil for roses.

Looking for alternative sources of organic matter, we must consider peat, which in Poland is readily available. Speaking about peat, and particularly about the coarse type, named in Poland high peat moss, we must always remember that it is not a fertiliser in the strict sense, but only a source of humus and an ideal soil conditioner.

We have in Poland about 1,700,000 hectares of peat land, consisting of high (or coarse) peat moss, which is exported from Poland to different countries in Europe and America; middle; low and surface peat. Low and middle peat occupy 90 per cent of the peat land, and high peat moss only 10 per cent.

High Peat Moss

High peat moss is very uniform in its structure, because it contains nearly 90 per cent sphagnum moss, has very low pH, 2·5 to 4·0, which is very convenient because we can easily obtain pH optimum for roses. We must remember that roses prefer and grow best in soil with pH about 6·0 to 6·5, that is slightly acid. If the soil is alkaline, we may see yellowing of the upper foliage between the veins, chlorosis due to the inability of the plant to obtain sufficient iron or manganese for its needs. But this alkalinity may be reduced to some extent by working acid— that means coarse peat moss—into the ground, or by application of sulphur. Also, the use of Chelated iron, for example Fetrilon, gives quick recovery from iron deficiency.

High peat moss is very poor in nutrient

elements, and it decays very slowly. You can even say that it is quite resistant to decomposition. So that after two years it loses only 7 per cent of its organic substance, which consequently yields so small a quantity of mineral matter that we can ignore it. Therefore we have precise control of fertilisation, and we can give all micro and macro elements according to the special nutrient requirements of roses, as in hydroponic culture.

High peat moss is sterile, free from pests and diseases, especially bacteria and fungi. It has great capacity to accumulate air and water, as well as to absorb nutrient solutions, so that there is no danger of fertiliser excess. It improves the crumb structure when worked into the soil, and gives it proper aeration and drainage for as long as ten years. It contains many growth substances and hormones that help the rooting of young seedlings and encourage the development of excellent rich healthy roots of rose bushes. In addition high peat moss is easy to handle; it is very light and odour-free.

We must remember also that peat moss should be thoroughly saturated with water just before planting, and that we can never permit it to dry completely because humus will coagulate and it will be impossible to saturate it again.

How to prepare peat moss for roses

When we wish to use peat moss instead of soil for roses, we must specially prepare it. First we must lime it. According to the curve of neutralisation, we can easily find what amount of calcium carbonate we must add to our peat moss in order to obtain the pH necessary for roses. Secondly, in accordance with the requirements of roses, we must fertilise our limed peat moss.

In Poland, we now have different ready-for-use complete fertilisers, but with peat moss we generally use special mineral fertilisers formulated by Professor Starck from the High School of Horticulture in Warsaw, that are called MIS 1 and MIS 2. For roses we use MIS 2. It contains more potash, in two parts; Part A with major elements, nitrogen, phosphorus, potash,

magnesium, and Part B with minor or trace elements, iron, manganese, copper, zinc, boron and molybdenum.

During the growth of roses, a special programme of fertilisation and control must be followed, but it would take too long here to give details.

In order to avoid trouble with the preparation of peat moss, we now make special sub-strata with peat moss in different combinations with fertilisers and composts, ready for use by gardeners.

Culture of roses in peat moss— experiments

Now in Poland, peat is Theme No. 1. We speak, we write, we have national and international symposia about peat, and we are beginning to use peat in the culture of vegetables in the open air, and in greenhouses and frames for flowers. Under the direction of Professor Starck and his fellows, Master of Science Adamiecki cultivated roses, variety 'Montezuma', in greenhouses with different combinations of high peat moss. About the results of this experiment, we can say as follows:

The best combination for roses in our conditions is high peat moss plus 5 grammes per litre of MIS 2. It gives 30 per cent higher crop in extra grade than in soil. The worst was that of peat moss with clay. We can expect the best results when we use small but more frequent quantities of fertilisers. The application of high rates of fertilisers was not satisfactory because the roses grew too quickly, were weak and delicate and consequently not very frost-resistant.

The preparation of peat sub-stratum is easier than the preparation and changing of the soil. It is also less troublesome and cheaper. There was, of course, no need for steaming, weeding, hoeing and applying manure to peat moss. We avoid fertiliser excess, due to the high absorbing quality in peat moss. It is easier to maintain in peat moss constant moisture and aeration, and the roses are healthier.

To summarise the results of the experiments, we can say that the production of roses in high peat moss is 25 to 30 per cent cheaper than when grown in garden soil.

I must add that other gardeners, encouraged by the experiments of Mr Adamiecki, have begun to plant roses in high peat moss. For example, small private gardener Szafranski, as well as the large greenhouse establishment of the municipality of Warsaw.

Culture of roses in surface peat— experiments

As was mentioned above, we have very small quantities of high peat moss; it is expensive, and some of it is exported. So we try now to use in gardening the surface peat that lies half a metre thick on high and middle peat land. It is the youngest part of peat land. Until today it was thrown out during the process of excavation, but now we use special machines that gather this surface peat.

Surface peat has pH 4·2 to 4·9, but it breaks down more quickly and is not sterile; therefore its structure and quality are inferior to those of peat moss. Consequently, it is about 30 times cheaper than peat moss, but it cannot be packed in bales and its transport is troublesome, so it ought to be used chiefly in the country.

Last year, in the High School of Horticulture in Posnan, Masters of Science Haber and Oszkinisowa planted eight varieties of roses in the greenhouse in surface peat with high peat moss. It was mixed with 5 kilograms of calcium carbonate and 1 kilogram of special fertiliser, "Azofoska" N.P.K. as 1 to 1 to 1·5, plus 10 grammes of copper sulphate and 2 grammes molybdate of ammonium for every cubic metre of this peat mixture. The first great advantage that was observed consisted in the two weeks earlier blooming of roses in the peat mixture than those in garden soil. The best variety was 'Eiffel Tower', and especially on *R. inermis* and Heinsohn's Rekord under-stocks, with an average of 19·4 flowers per year and an average length of 62·5 cm. The shortest was 'Dr Verhage' averaging 46·4 cm. The bunch type root system was very well developed and healthy and after washing was a creamy-white colour. Hence the growth was vigorous and flowering abundant. This was also true of the second year of cultivation.

In conclusion, we can say that surface peat with the addition of high peat moss, limed and fertilised according to the requirements of roses, can also be a good sub-stratum for their growth.

Low peat

This is organic matter highly decomposed. It has a structure like soil, with pH 5·5 to 6·5; it is not sterile like high peat moss, and is used for mulching, composts, etc. Professor Starck has now begun experiments concerned with the culture of roses in beds fed with low peat, which in greenhouses ought to be sterilised.

Mulching

We all know that mulches are used for a number of purposes in rose houses and in rose beds outside. As a mulch we can use high peat moss, of course limed, which is expensive but sterile. We can also use surface and low peat.

Peat for some gardeners seems quite satisfactory because it gives the rose beds a neat and tidy appearance, but generally there is another opinion about mulching with peat. Many gardeners say that peat is not good as a surface mulch, since it has not as effective a moisture retention potential as other mulches. Mr Allen wrote in his book that "Peat moss forms a crust when it becomes dry that induces rain or water to run off, instead of soaking into the bed. Also, if the peat is stirred up and loose, a strong wind will blow it away". But against this wind erosion, around the fields with peat culture in U.S.A., for example, they plant high quickly-growing trees as a protection. In conclusion, we can say that undoubtedly peat is best used under the surface as a soil conditioner, and it is wasteful to use it as a mulch.

Roses in peat moss rings

In order to economise precious high peat moss Professor Starck is trying now to plant roses in plastic rings. On raised benches of wood or concrete, on a 7 to 10 cm. high layer of high peat moss, he puts roses planted in rings of polyethylene filled with high peat moss. If we wish to have roses in rings on ground beds, we must isolate the ground from the peat moss by a layer of concrete or with thick polyethylene in order to avoid infection from soil with pests and diseases.

According to this method, we can save large quantities of peat moss. We obtain a higher temperature for the root growth, and we can remove and transplant our roses at any time of the year and at every stage of growth. Of course, high peat moss must, as usual, be limed and fertilised before use, and during the growing period watering and fertilising must be done very thoroughly.

We have not yet the results of this experiment, repeated also this year in low peat, but we hope that they will be promising for future culture in rings with peat moss and low peat.

Rose Breeding
Chairman: Professor S. C. Harland, F.R.S.

A. P. C. DICKSON
A. Dickson & Sons Ltd, N. Ireland
Selection of Breeding Material

I have the pleasure of leading, rather than following, this afternoon, which I feel is usually much easier to do.

The first thing I would like to mention is that I believe that a successful rose breeder should first of all have patience, a good eye for the rose, money of course, good luck and above all a love for the rose. One breeder did say—a very famous breeder at one time—that you should also be a little mad. Well, if I don't qualify for the other points, I certainly qualify for the last.

However, to get down to the serious business, as I only have a few minutes, what I want to talk to you about this afternoon is the selection of breeding material. Now obviously, if you are going to be a success in breeding, the selection of breeding material is of prime importance.

Perhaps I can best illustrate through my own experience how I have learned to select varieties suitable for producing something which we call "commercial"— an awful word, meaning that it will sell to people who want to grow roses. I have been breeding roses for a very short time, and am only beginning to learn about it, but fourteen years or so ago we knocked the top off two pig-sties and set a little greenhouse on the top.

I thought, "Well, it's very small, and the best I can do is to gather together all the yellow hybrid teas I can find and just mix them all up and see what happens". Certainly I learned a lot from this, and I think the first thing I learned—and it is a rule I have tried to abide by since—is that the mother parent which you select must be strong, a vigorous grower with good foliage, stout stem and a good neck. From that you can work in your colours, probably from the second generation, but more about that later.

Of course, from my first year's experiments I was not very successful, as I have said. I decided that the essence of doing anything really well is to go into it thoroughly, to find out as much as you can, and I must thank people like Wilhelm Kordes, Reimer Kordes, Eugene Boerner, Francis Meilland, Sam McGredy and above all my father for passing on to me the knowledge that they had gained through the years. This knowledge, of course, is absolutely invaluable.

The second year was planned, and I began to learn a little bit, but I tried to follow on what others were doing and in particular what my father had been doing in the past. This, I have discovered, is not the way to go about rose breeding; sooner or later you have got to think for yourself. It is all very well to produce, and you will produce some good seedlings, obviously, if you do what others have been doing, but sooner or later the lines will run out and you will have to find something with which to work on yourself. And if you are going to learn anything about it, then you must work on your own.

You cannot picture, and I don't think anybody in this room would give the same points of an ideal rose; every one of you would differ in some respects. So that the image you wish to create in your own eye of what you want to breed—the perfect rose, or near perfect rose that you want to produce—will differ in some respects. One of my objectives is the production of a really good crimson hybrid tea.

Obviously, if you are thinking of plant breeding, you have to think of the commercial aspects. You have to think of the short cuts that you can take so that you can make your programme pay, because it must pay. So you look to the type of market in which you want to sell; whether it is the United Kingdom or if it is the American market, because the type of market which you are going to sell to will in certain cases indicate to you the type of breeding material you will require. For instance, a thin rose, like 'Anne Watkins', will probably not do well in a hot climate, whereas a rose like 'Montezuma' will do well under strong sunlight but won't open in Northern Ireland where we get more than our share of rain. So you will understand that the type of flower in any case has a bearing on the type of material which you use.

Now I said to you earlier that one of the rules which I have learned in my short time as a breeder is to choose as a mother parent a strong plant. If I may illustrate this, there is a rose outside in the seedlings there which I thought might be breeding material. It is a rose called 'Duke of Windsor'. Now that, to me, looks as if it has the basis of a good plant. It has large foliage, a good stem and it has got colour which is again important. I cannot pass on to you really all the things which I see in a rose because these cannot be put into

words; but I look at something which creates a picture, and from that I work.

Now 'Duke of Windsor', if I may say so, is a little short in the petal. It also probably could be a little freer in flowering. But at least it has the plant there, and without a strong plant, in my opinion it is not worth producing a rose which may perhaps only grow in certain gardens. We get too many letters from customers complaining that the trees have died.

Then I start, if possible, to look for the parentage of that plant. This is where it is very difficult for somebody beginning because all breeders, for certain reasons, do not give the complete parentage of the varieties which they are introducing. So that if you are relying on somebody else's material, probably it is best to experiment for a little while. In fact, you nearly always should experiment annually with new varieties, bringing them in; you cannot rely on just looking at something and believing that it will fit into a particular line on which you are working.

But I try to find, on the father's side, the colours, and this very often does not come in the first generation—that is to say, that I will use 'Duke of Windsor' for one year, and from the seedlings may be able to find one which could be brought into the hybridising house again and used to further the aims at which I am working —in other words that search for the red hybrid tea. And I am not pretending here that 'Duke of Windsor' is going to produce a red hybrid tea—I am only using it to illustrate my point.

So that, in the second year, we may be able, through the father parent plant, to produce the length of petal, and of course the number of petals is very important. We look upon the American market as a very valuable market. Also, roses are becoming more and more popular in New Zealand and Australia. So there again, we want our varieties not only to be good in this country but good all over the world. I think a fellow breeder on the platform once said, not so long ago, that a good rose is a good rose anywhere. That may not be completely true, but I believe that certainly a good rose seems to turn up practically anywhere where roses are grown.

You may say, "Well, if I try to produce a rose with fragrance, what should I do? Should I gather together breeding material which is strong with perfume?" In my experience this does not often work. If I may quote an example again here; 'Peace' has no fragrance, 'Karl Herbst' has no fragrance, and yet in the second and third generations from 'Peace', many of the seedlings are found to have fragrance. So I would say that probably in this case it is a question of selection from the seed beds— not selecting parents to produce fragrance.

Another experiment in my early days of breeding was to gather together about four floribunda varieties which were not commercial; they were not very good as far as the flower and so on was concerned, but they were exceptionally free from disease, and to muddle these all up in the same way as I did with the yellow hybrid teas, to see what would happen. I was disappointed to find that the resistance which the parents had shown was not borne out in the children which they produced. So that again I cannot give any hard and fast ruling in this respect.

Remember that, if you are starting, it is difficult to find this material from which to start; you should follow the rule which I have suggested of strong plants, and should be prepared to exercise patience— and I really mean patience. Because a certain variety does not bear a lot of heps in one particular year, this does not necessarily mean that it is a bad variety for breeding—you must keep to what you have set out to do and try to follow it through, so that you get to the second generation and have these seedlings from which to select. Then bring them back into the house again with the strong plants, you hope, and somewhere near the colour which you are working towards, and I think the colour will follow in subsequent generations.

HERBERT C. SWIM
Armstrong Nurseries Inc., California
The Limitations of Rose Breeding

I am a little embarrassed because Pat Dickson has stolen some of my thunder. He emphasised a point which I wanted to bring out a little later, but really I am grateful for your support, Pat.

I wish to make clear at the outset that I make no claim to original discovery with respect to any of the experiences I shall relate. I deal with them because they seem, from my point of view, to have been the more useful of the observations I have made over the years, and they have come to my mind now.

In looking back, it seems to me that, among the more significant of my early discoveries was one that made itself apparent after a series of frustrating experiences associated with failure. My first experiences in making exploratory rose crosses were not entirely failures, but were sufficiently so to make it appear expedient to evaluate the factors involved in the failures and further try to give them a rating as to their relative importance.

In casting about for some apt title for this procedure, entirely for my own use, I have found a phrase which is meaningful to me, "a priority of limiting factors". I shall try to illustrate what I mean by using some actual experiences and telling of them in their approximate order of importance and their influence on the success or failure of a given objective. It seems to me that the clearest way to do this is to name a subject problem and to follow with a discussion of the problem and this I shall be doing.

Vigour

I noticed in my first years of crossing that many of the families of seedlings—we call them populations—were disappointingly lacking in vigour, to the extent that often as few as 10 per cent of a family were vigorous enough to be acceptable on this basis alone. Since in the early stages of any plant breeding programme, one must do some close in-breeding in order to explore the inheritance traits of the prospective parents, it naturally follows that there were a number of such populations, or families if you prefer, in my early crossings. I noted that, almost without exception, these populations displayed a major regression in vigour. I discovered soon also that this result could be predicted from such crossings with a high degree of accuracy. Beyond this, however, I discovered that, unless I was very careful to use parents that were not only distantly removed from one another in origin but in themselves having more than ordinary vigour, I could again expect no more than a small proportion of the resulting offspring to be acceptable for vigour.

My second subject problem was **flower petalage**—quantity, that is. As the result of selfing, that is, using the same cultivar for both seed and pollen parent, we early discovered that the single-petalled cultivars bred completely true to this trait. In other words, all singles when crossed with singles, gave single-petalled cultivars only, as offspring. Since there are, of course, a great many petalage levels in rose cultivars, it would seem probable that the inheritance of petalage quantity may be due to a complex of factors. Be that as it may, it became apparent that a generality in this area could be made with a reasonable degree of assurance. If the breeder were expecting or desiring rose progeny with double flowers, he had best make sure that any semi-double cultivar he uses as a parent be completely complemented by another parent that has a good degree of doubleness—not necessarily fully double, but at least adequately so. I discovered that, if one fails to do this, very few of the progeny will be acceptable in quantity of petals—again, a limiting factor.

My third subject problem was **mildew resistance**. I think I might say that this particular point is becoming of more and more importance to us in the United States because of the rather unfavourable comparisons that we make of our seedlings with those of European origin. I think your breeders in Europe are ahead of us. This quality, together with the next two,

rank about equally in the degree to which they limit the breeder to selecting offspring with an acceptable level of each given quality. It is generally thought among rose breeders with whom I have talked that this quality is a dominant one—that is covering up its alternative quality, mildew susceptibility, when both genic qualities are present in a given cultivar or seedling.

Unfortunately, the wild roses that formed the basis for much of the early breeding work of the past 150 years, particularly in the larger-flowered cultivars, have a fairly substantial degree of susceptibility to mildew. As a result, we have very few garden cultivars today that can be considered immune, or nearly immune, to mildew. This inevitably means that, in our eager search for advance or novelty with respect to the flower qualities of our larger-flowered garden roses, we are working with parents on both sides with at least some degree of susceptibility to mildew. This inevitably means that we will have very little resulting that is better than the better parent, and with most of the seedlings being not only no better but somewhat worse than the better parent with respect to this quality. Here again, if we find it expedient to use a parent cultivar with some susceptibility to mildew, which of course we are often forced to do, then we should also find it expedient to use a mate for it that has a corresponding resistance to the same disease. Otherwise, our resulting offspring will be useless because of their susceptibility to that disease. I am glad to report that in this field some very fine progress is being made by various breeders; unfortunately most of them are in Europe, and we are confident that it is only reasonable to expect that, in the next decade or so, we shall see some substantial progress, especially in resistance to powdery mildew, and I hope that we can see some more of these coming from the United States.

Flower form

I would incorporate in this category the form of the bud also. The rosarian of today seems to like most of his flowers to be regular in form. We have, in the last generation or so, tended towards a stereotype. This is in spite of the fact that the classic rose is very informal in the arrangement of the petals, and to me very beautiful. Nevertheless, be that as it may, our present pattern is of more formal nature. Perhaps the rather globular buds and informal open blooms of yesteryear's rose is the more natural form pattern for the flowers of this great plant. Today's rose public seem to prefer larger quantities of the cultivars that have long, slender, pointed or urn-shaped buds, opening to perfectly formed flowers of not less than semi-double petalage, and preferably double or very double in this respect. I suppose I might say, as an aside, that I have often wondered if the form of the first hybrid tea, 'La France', could have set the style for the roses of today. The bud form popular today is not greatly difficult to achieve, particularly since we have prospective parent cultivars today that have this characteristic. The form of the open bloom, however, seems ever to tend to this informal trait that we associate with the old roses, irregular, and unfortunately some of our seedlings now are even messy and lop-sided. This is so to the extent that, if one does not have both parents with fine form in the open flower, then one had better have one of them with such form, or the breeder will preclude the possibility of having a meaningful quantity of progeny plants with acceptable open flower form.

My next subject problem—size and shape of foliage. As far as I can determine, most rosarians prefer foliage that is more or less flat in character; large, heavy, leathery and perhaps glossy. All these qualities except the last seem to be difficult to attain, and in combination this is particularly so. Experience has shown that it is very difficult to obtain foliage of medium to large size from a cross where even one parent is afflicted with small foliage. Some growers contend that this is not such a handicap in the floribunda class, but most would concede that it is a handicap in a popularity contest among hybrid tea varieties. I should point out, before leaving this subject, that it is not my intention to imply that the foregoing topics, either singly or in combination, may be considered total objectives in breeding roses. I would like to emphasise again that the form, colour, substance and so forth of the flower itself must be the final measuring stick of a rose cultivar's value. The foregoing qualities are merely mentioned as the principal road blocks to reaching that final destination.

A most important experience, from my point of view, is fairly frequent contact with buyers of rose plants, particularly those sufficiently interested to show them at flower shows, or to judge them. Some such experience is for me an essential, not only for inspiration but for education. To know what my fellow rose lovers see as beautiful in a rose sets the pattern for my own effort. It is satisfying to see some of the cultivars from one's own effort appear in a rose show accompanied by a Blue Ribbon.

SAM MCGREDY
Samuel McGredy & Son Ltd, N. Ireland
Field Selection of Seedlings

I have chosen for my subject Selecting in the Field, because it is probably something that I know a little about, and I am assuming first that breeders have selected their roses in the greenhouse and have decided to propagate certain varieties in the field. In this respect might I say that my experience has been that anything less than five plants of a variety in the field makes it rather difficult to recognise a good variety quickly. I am continually amazed by the ability of our American rose breeders, particularly Herb (H. C. Swim), to select seedlings on their own roots, as they do so quite extensively, where they have one plant of a variety and many hundreds of thousands of varieties. To me this is almost an impossible task; in fact, the only time I have own-root seedlings in the field, taking them straight from the seed benches and planting them out on their own roots, is when I am testing climbing roses. Here I am principally interested in whether they will repeat flower or not, and the quality of the plant and the quality of the flower is secondary.

From my point of view one of the most important things one can do in selecting seedlings is to inspect them regularly. I try myself in Ireland to do this in the mornings, because our blooms are then fresher and by the end of the day they are becoming rather tired. When the sun does shine, which is rarely in Ireland but frequently in California, it is rather important to inspect them frequently. In other words, in our climate where it rains a lot, it is not necessary to see them quite so often as in sunnier climes.

When I walk through the seedlings I try to have some very distinct objectives. I try to walk with one other person, because I find that when I walk alone it is very much more difficult. On the other hand, if there is someone with whom I can keep up a constant stream of chatter and who can talk to me of what he sees and what he doesn't see, it makes life much easier. First of all we look at the parentage of anything in the field that looks promising. I think this parent checking is very important from the point of view of looking for roses to breed from. Very often I turn to my foreman, Harry McKeown, when we go over the fields and I say, "I wish we had some of these in the houses to breed from, and not the roses we have in the houses"; we very often come to the conclusion that we are not going to make any progress until we get the latest and the best into the breeding houses. We also look for garden roses, and apart from the usual qualities of colour, flower form and so on, one of the points we consider most important is to look for a repeat flowering habit. Very often you can see roses that look wonderful in the field, but there is no sign of any second growth from the base and they are going to be a long time in blooming again; in some cases there is no second flush. So even if a garden rose is very good, if it doesn't have the repeat

flowering habit, I don't think it is worth a great deal.

One of the most difficult tasks, and probably one of those I am least qualified to discuss, is trying to pick forcing roses. Those like Meilland who have large forcing houses, do all their selection under glass, but we try and make our preliminary selections out doors. All we can do is look for long stems, perhaps not too much foliage and a quick repeat-flowering habit, but the real problem is to try to look at roses in the fields and visualise what they would be like if they were disbudded, particularly in the case of floribundas, because most forcing floribundas are disbudded. Further, it is almost impossible to discover whether a rose is long-lasting under glass or whether, in fact, it will winter-crop under glass, but you can at least make some preliminary selections.

By far one of the most important points we watch and probably one of the reasons why we have had some success, is the health of the plants. In the autumn we go over every variety, and these may number some 50,000, and we place against them whether they are clean or if they get mildew or black spot. Every single variety that has any black spot or any mildew is noted accordingly, and it is amazing really how few do come out with a fairly clean record.

I try, although I fear not very successfully, to check on the roses that might be suitable for hot weather. It is something that Herb. Swim and I have been doing, trying to see the difference between roses in California and roses in Northern Ireland; this is really a most perplexing problem and I would not like to comment on it. For it is one thing to try and breed roses in one climate and quite another to pick them for successful propagation in another climate.

We also do quite a lot of selection on climbing roses. Here again, I think it is very important to see that the rose repeat flowers, and the only way I think you can really do this is to plant the variety outside. You can test garden roses in the field nursery line, but it is just impossible to select a climbing rose unless you go to the lengths of planting it out on a pillar or against a wall. As Pat Dickson said, rose breeding can be very expensive, and we keep on saying to ourselves, as we walk up and down, could this possibly be one of the three or four roses that we can sell? If you keep on doing this and saying to yourself, is it—could it possibly be—and if you come to the conclusion that it isn't possible, that it wouldn't be commercial, that is the time to stop—when you have 5 plants and not 500.

Another maxim we follow is "Wait and see". Very often if we wait for a year, leaving the plants alone and letting them flower into the autumn and come back and see them as two year old plants, we decide "No". It is well worth holding back a variety for a year to give it a chance to settle down.

Our own plan of progression is to increase them from 5 plants the first year to 25 plants the second, and then from 25 to 250. Most of you will have been to or intend visiting the Bone Hill trial grounds. I am somewhat perplexed by some of the varieties that are planted there. It does seem to me that if breeders would wait a little longer before sending varieties to the trials, and perhaps not send them when they have only a few plants, but propagate them more, looking at them under their own conditions for one more year, they might send somewhat fewer.

My plan is to stake anything that looks promising. We stake 6 trees, nobody cuts any budding eyes from them, so that we send the strongest plants possible to the trials. At the beginning of the year we might stake anything up to 40 or 50 varieties, but by the time we get around to the autumn they have been discarded for so many reasons that we end up with 15 or 20. But I do feel it is worth while staking a fair number of varieties at the beginning of the year and starting to weed them out thereafter. We transplant our varieties into beds just as the Royal National Rose Society do. I am somewhat doubtful as to the value of this from our point of view, because we have never really picked a variety out of our trial beds, planted out, that hasn't been successful in the nursery rows. The only thing I would say, is that where you get a variety which is somewhat prone to die-back, then it is worth while putting it out to see if the variety will over-winter.

One of my great aids is my Seedling Book. It is one of the few jobs I really do myself; I draw it up from one end to the other and I write every single word. I find even making out a seedling book refreshes my memory as to what has happened the year before, and I wouldn't delegate that to anyone. The more basic details of the number of the varieties, the row, quantity and parentage, go without saying, but when you are trying to look at a lot of varieties it is sometimes difficult to give a detailed description in writing to each of them, to refer to later. What I would say is this: if a variety is early flowering please make a note of it, because that is a real bonus as far as a rose goes. If it is repeat-flowering, also make a note of it. If it has health, make a note of it. It isn't so important to say what colour it is and what the flower form is in your notes, because if you cannot remember that, the variety wasn't worth propagating in the first place. Another important point—whenever you send the buds of one of your new pets to somebody, do remember to note the fact in your seedling book, because sometimes you find you cannot remember.

Finally, I would just reiterate the most important point when you are looking at your seedlings and selecting in the field. Ask yourself if it could be one of the roses that you are going to sell. If the answer is in the negative, discard it at the outset.

VERA KLIMENKO
The Botanical Garden of Nikita, Yalta, U.S.S.R.
Rose Breeding in the South of the U.S.S.R.
summarised by Professor S. C. Harland

Mrs Klimenko is a Senior Scientific Worker in the State Nikita Botanical Garden in the Crimea—that is a sort of Riviera of the Soviet Union, where the comrades go down to relax. Now, in this garden a large amount of scientific work is being carried on, as I said in a climate somewhat like the Riviera but hotter in summer and I think cooler in winter.

This garden was founded in the year 1812, and the beginning of the rose collection dates from that period. They began breeding work very early on, in 1828, and then there was a period from 1860 to 1938 in which nothing was done except to maintain the collection. Now during the second World War a considerable part of the collection was destroyed, so that in 1950 it had only 370 cultivars left. In 1955, just 13 years ago, rose work was resumed, both in the area of plant introduction and on the breeding side.

They began with very definite objectives. These objectives were to produce roses suitable especially for the southern parts of the country and, more specifically, cultivars resistant to great heat with disease resistance and with a long and abundant flowering period. In the period from 1955 to 1967, 210 cultivars were selected for large-scale propagation, and altogether 55 new hybrids were produced. Of these, 12 have been approved by the Testing Department of the Ministry of Agriculture, and Certificates of ownership awarded.

Of course, the Soviet Union being what it is, a breeder cannot put his new variety on the market; only the State can do that. But I think, from my own experience of the Soviet Union, that the testing is quite adequate and pretty complicated. The new variety is submitted to rigorous testing over a wide range of conditions, and until it passes the test it cannot be released.

Mrs Klimenko goes on to say something about her methodology. Now at first she says they sowed seeds from open pollinated material, and they got no positive results, and only when control of pollination was practised between more recent cultivars were valuable seedlings produced. For example, she made very extensive use of 'Peace' and of the floribunda 'Kordes Sondermeldung' ('Independence'), which is rechristened 'Nezhenka'. 'Peace' is rechristened 'Rassvet'. I suppose they felt like some of us when we see names like 'Souvenir of Head Gardener Smith' coming from certain quarters.

In addition to these they found effective and worthwhile combinations using 'Tassin', 'Karl Herbst', 'Ena Harkness', 'Floradora', 'Spek's Yellow', 'Frühlingsgold', 'Tantau's Surprise', 'Hens Verschuren' and 'Red Favourite'—those are some of the principal varieties mentioned as taking part in their hybridisation programme.

Later, she received from Dr Lammerts of the United States 'Charlotte Armstrong', 'Chrysler Imperial', 'Nocturne' and 'Mirandy', and she found 'Charlotte Armstrong' especially valuable for imparting heat resistance and a long flowering period.

One of the most important objectives was to prolong the flowering period into late autumn, which is of course far more difficult in the Soviet Union than it is in this country, and in this she mentions specifically 'Floradora' as a very promising parent.

Now, one of the favourite ploys of the Russian plant breeders in general is to make what they call Echo Geographical Crosses—that is, they would prefer to cross a French rose with a United States rose, a Dutch rose with a Scandinavian rose, an Italian rose with an English rose, on the grounds that by this means it should be possible to produce new types of adaptation by re-combination of factors from both sides. That is, if you have on the one hand the Italian climate, on the other the Scottish climate, you ought to get in the offspring a range of climates that you could work on. Now, I do not think myself that there is very much in this story, but at any rate they got this from Mr Lisyenko, who I think is now not in the scientific world.

In breeding they have been rather original minded. They have gone over to various species belonging to—she specifies that they used species of the Irani Group, from Section Lutea Pimpinellifolia, and she mentions also *Rosa fedtschenkoana*,

Rosa laxa and then she finally lays great stress on work with *Rosa moyesii*, which has a high chromosome number and has been very little used, and another high chromosome species called *Rosa acicularis*. She says, of course, as we all know, that inter-species hybrids very seldom give valuable novelties, and she used the species hybrids in making further crosses, using them principally as male parents.

From this point she goes on to say something about inheritance. She does not say very much—I don't think she says anything that we don't know already—but she did a study intensively of a cross between 'Peace' and 'Kordes Sondermeldung', and she made the cross both ways. She says that in these crosses the male parent imposed the characteristics of leaf glossiness, vigour and flower colour. This view, of course, is in line with the views of many breeders of the present day although I personally do not happen to subscribe to it.

And then she discusses the transmission of fragrance from this point of view, and she says that the scent of the male parent is the most important factor. That is, if the female parent is fragrant and the male non-fragrant, most of the progeny were without fragrance, the only exception being a seedling of 'Crimson Glory' by a non-fragrant male parent. I may say *en passant* that this subject is extremely interesting and also extremely controversial, and I am very sorry that we do not have Mrs Klimenko here today, because we might have had quite a warm discussion in which more heat than light would have been generated.

Mrs Klimenko does make one mention of a technique which is applied in other materia but so far as I know it has not reached the rose world, although of course my friends on the platform have a lot of secrets which they do not tell us about. You know, in the Lancashire textile industry, there are only three secrets in the whole industry but everybody knows two of them. This technique mentioned by Mrs Klimenko is, if you want to make a very difficult cross, you put a few pollen grains of your parent on the stigma and then you flood it with the pollen that you want the cross from. Now this results in a few seeds being set as a result of its own pollen, and that gives a chance for the foreign pollen to pollinate when otherwise it might not be successful.

To sum up, Mrs Klimenko has created heat resistant cultivars with dense, non-fading petals, glossy leaves, resistant to mildew and with a long, almost continuous flowering period prolonged into late autumn.

In this work—I was quite astonished at the magnitude of it—they have raised one and a half million seedlings, and they have propagated the most successful to the extent of, she says, two million cuttings.

This concludes Mrs Klimenko's paper, and I am sure you will share my regret that she has not been able to be present today to give it in person.

E. B. LE GRICE
E. B. Le Grice (Roses) Ltd
Breeding Blue and Brown Roses

In ten minutes I must leave far more unsaid than spoken and I can assure you that many fruitless sorties were made before the final field of discussion was settled. For those who wish to pursue the more technical side, a few of the books and papers which I read are listed as being considered the more useful.

In "Colour Technology" F. A. Taylor asks what is colour? A property of light rather than of bodies. "Lightwaves", differing in lengths according to the colour, reacting on the brain. To seek to build the colours of a rose from the artist's palette is not possible and no satisfactory solution can be found by applying a general rule to colour in a particular form.

Professor J. B. Harborne, now of Liverpool University, in a reprint from "Colour and Life" speaking on chemical colours in plants states "that the colours of plants are due to the presence in the plastids or cell vacuoles of pigments which are capable of absorbing, transmitting and reflecting white light" ... "A relatively small number of pigments account for the majority of plant colours but these may be modified in a number of ways, such as mixtures of pigments occurring together, resulting in the brown and purple colours of certain primulas and wallflowers. Trace metals in petals may alter flower colours—the blue of the cornflower begins with cyanin, a substance found in most roses—but a magnesium and iron complex turns the magenta to blue. Other ways in which variations in the pigments occur is in their concentration or in the variation of the pH of the cell sap."

I continue to quote from Professor Harborne on "Chemical Colours in Plants"— "It is important to bear these colour modifying factors in mind when considering the production of new flower colour varieties. Many attempts have been made to breed a blue rose. The chemical evidence indicates that one source of blueness —the purple pigment, delphinidin—is absent from the Rosaceae, so that there is no chance of raising a blue petalled rose by this means. Blueness, however, can also be produced by either metal-complexing or co-pigmentation and breeders might consider using varieties with this metal ion or high flavone concentrations in their petals. Co-pigmentation of the crimson rose pigment, cyanin, by unidentified flavone materials is certainly responsible for the mauve and purple shades now available (in, for example, the variety 'Reine des Violettes')." Again to summarise it can be said that our knowledge of plant colours is fairly complete. By contrast, our knowledge of the form in which pigments occur in living cells is still very superficial and much remains to be learnt about the distribution and function of plant pigments. In other words we know the chemical constitution of the colours but we don't know what makes them "tick".

For these reasons alone it would be useless for a layman to enter this field with any anticipation of progress along these lines, but one may tackle this question from the experimental side and, by analysing the measure of success already obtained, seek to follow the paths indicated.

One finds at least four strains of the magenta—lavender—brown roses and one will find that they all appear to have common factors. The first and most important strain more frequently used than any other is the 'Grey Pearl'–'Pinocchio' cross by Boerner, who perceived the possibilities of an unusual colour break. The resulting 'Lavender Pinocchio' released a wave of experiment. Of over 30 cultivars listed in these colours 13 owe their existence to 'Lavender Pinocchio' and its parent 'Grey Pearl'.

'Grey Pearl' reveals a remarkable diversity within parentage, both in colour and variety. 'Mrs Charles Lamplough' white: 'Sir David Davis' red, 'Southport' which in its parentage varies from the purple red of 'George Dickson' to bi-colour from Rosa foetida persiana, a parent of 'Soleil d'Or'. For reasons which I will refer to later I think the chain might well be completed by the unnamed seedling in its pedigree being 'Charles P. Kilham' or a similar derivative of McGredy's breeding. In other words we find a complete admixture of colour, with a considerable bias towards bicolours which derive originally from Rosa foetida persiana as employed by Pernet-Ducher.

Then there is what I would call the 'Meilland' strain based on 'Charles P. Kilham' and R. foetida bicolor. Unfortunately the McGredy rose 'Charles P. Kilham' has no declared parentage; but we find the key in 'Prelude', a cross between 'Fantastique' × ['Ampère' × ('Charles P. Kilham' × 'Capucine Chambard')]. Here 'Ampère' has 'Charles P. Kilham' × 'Condesa de Sastago' and 'Fantastique' contains 'Ampère' × ['Charles P. Kilham' × ('Charles P. Kilham' × 'Capucine Chambard')]. Again we find this strong admixture of colours with bicolours and Rosa foetida persiana playing an important part.

The third strain again deriving through Meilland I would call the 'Peace' strain where a cross with 'Peace' has resulted in the violent purple violet of 'Purpurine'. Here we have ('Peace' × Seedling) × 'Fashion' which is 'Pinocchio' × 'Crimson Glory'. In 'Peace' we find 'Joanna Hill' × [('Charles P. Kilham' × *R. foetida bicolor* seedling) × ('Charles P. Kilham' × 'Margaret McGredy')]. Here we have the same pattern of parents bringing the same results. This same result through 'Peace' has been experienced by other raisers.

Even when some unlikely stray appears, a little detective work brings the same results and in 'Lilac Time' ('Golden Dawn' × 'Luis Brinas') we find the strong admixture with white and the *R. foetida persiana* background.

In my own case a cross between 'Tantau's Surprise' and 'Marjorie Le Grice' resulted in a mauve seedling, the ancestry giving the same results.

The major part of this paper is largely the history of the mauves, lilacs and purples, but the brown shades are intimately related although much more loosely held together. Let me explain: Blue × Blue, say 'Blue Moon' × 'Heure Mauve' gives many selfs in this colour. Purple crosses largely give reds. Browns intercrossed with salmons give wide variations in red, pink, yellow and white. In other words, building up of colours to their peak give the so-called blues and purples, but browns are caused by the partial break-up of those same colours. In conclusion I would give the results of a few experiments for which you may find some explanation. 'Rosenresli' crossed 'Blue Moon' gives whites, in some cases heavily greyed like 'Grey Pearl'. 'Blue Moon' crossed with yellow gives whites with pink tints. *R. californica* crossed with whites gave light browns and mauves and further crosses with lavenders gave bicolour browns, with characteristic dominant slender but short growth and frequent bunched flowerings. This cross appears to give some stability in the browns. My latest break has come by crossing 'Lilac Charm' with 'Tuscany', which has resulted in purple floribundas but an earlier unnamed seedling × 'Lavender Pinoc-

chio' cross with 'Marcel Bourgouin' gave the Egyptian buff 'Amberlight'.

Here we must leave this fascinating subject, which owes its possibility to those wizards of hybridising McGredy II and Pernet-Ducher, who leave us to perfect that which they so ably began.

APPENDIX

Early ancestors of 'Lavender Pinocchio' (taken from *Modern Roses* 6). ('Grey Pearl' × 'Pinocchio').

Grey Pearl (H.T.) McGredy intro. J. & P. 1945. ('Mrs Charles Lamplough' × seedling) × ('Sir David Davis' × 'Southport').

Southport—('George Dickson' × 'Crimson Queen') × 'Souv. de George Beckwith'.

George Dickson (parents unknown).

Crimson Queen ('Liberty' × 'Richmond') × 'General MacArthur'.

'Souv. de George Beckwith' unnamed variety × 'Lyon Rose'.

Lyon Rose—'Mme Mélanie Soupert' × direct descendant of 'Soleil d'Or'.

Soleil d'Or—'Antoine Ducher' × *R. foetida persiana*.

Above contain a mixture of colours, red, yellow, white, pink with *R. foetida persiana*. True in all 'Blues' and lavenders.

Pinocchio—'Eva' × 'Golden Rapture'.

One parent being 'Grey Pearl' giving lavender, brown and lilac: 'Simone' '57: 'Lavender Garnette' '58: 'Lila Tan' '61: 'Heure Mauve' '62: 'Intermezzo' '63.

One parent being 'Lavender Pinocchio': 'Lavender Lady' '56: 'Cafe' '56: 'Brown Eyes' '59: 'Lavender Princess' '59: 'Overture' '60: 'Lilac Charm' '62: 'Pigmy Lavender' '61: 'Lavender Charm' '64: 'Lilac Dawn' '64.

Foundation and other parents of Meilland Strain:

'Ampère' '37 ('Charles P. Kilham' × 'Condesa de Sastago')—scarlet red, yellow reverse.

Fantastique H.T. '43 (brownish yellow, flushed carmine). 'Ampère' × ['Charles P. Kilham' × ('Charles P. Kilham' × 'Capucine Chambard')]. N.B. 'Capucine Chambard'—unissued seedling of *R. foetida bicolor*.

'Pigalle' '51; 'Prelude' '54; 'Lavender Girl' '58; 'Lila Vidri' '58.
'Fantan' '59; Violette Dot' '60; 'Heure Mauve' '62.

Other 'Blues' and 'Browns' owing their colour to 'Peace', 'Mrs S. McGredy' or similar parentage:

'Royal Tan' 55; 'Purpurine'; 'Sterling Silver' '57; 'Blue Diamond' '63; 'Blue Moon' ('Mainzer Fastnacht' or 'Sissi') '64. 'Amberlight' '61 (seedling × 'Lavender Pinocchio') × 'Marcel Bourgouin'.
'Tom Brown' '66 (unnamed seedling (from *R. californica*) × 'Amberlight'); 'News' 69 ('Lilac Charm' × 'Tuscany').

Books, etc., for further information.

"Colour Technology" F. A. Taylor, Oxford Press.
"Journal of Genetics" 32 pp. 117–170 "A bio-chemical survey of Mendelian factors for flower colour". Scott-Montcrieff.
"The Genetics of Garden Plants" by M.

B. Crane and W. J. C. Lawrence, especially Chapter 3, Main Floral pigmentation due to anthocyanins which may be

(1) Pelargonidin in new vivid orange—no blue.
(2) Cyanidin, usual in roses: some purple red can be made blue under some mineral complexes.
(3) Delphinidin, not present in roses, producing vivid blues and purples.

These three may be modified by anthoxanthins; yellow and ivory will influence the other pigments or by insoluble plastid pigments making a background producing greater depth of colour.

Also "The Anthocyanins of Roses, Occurrence of Peonin" by J. B. Harborne and reprint from "Colour and Life" (The Institute of Biology, 41 Queens Gate, London, S.W.7).
"Chemical Colours in Plants" by J. B. Harborne.

RENÉ ROYON
Universal Rose Selection, France
Rose Breeding in the South of France

Unfortunately M. Meilland could not come over due to a recent death in his family and neither could he prepare the text of the paper he had to read to this Conference, which was entitled "Breeding in the South of France". I will try to present to you the Meilland family and their work and to enlarge upon the three main characteristics of the Meilland breeding programme.

First of all I have to stress the fact that the Meilland family have two breeding departments: the "Cut Flower Department", that is breeding roses for the commercial growers, and then the outdoor Rose Department, that is breeding roses for amateurs. I will concentrate mainly on the breeding for outdoor roses.

The three main characteristics of this work, which I will afterwards illustrate with some colour slides which I have brought over, are, firstly, that the hybridising and selection is on a team work basis. It is done both by Papa Meilland, who represents the first generation of the Meilland family, Louisette Meilland who is the

second generation and widow of the late Francis Meilland, who was the breeder of 'Peace', and Alain Meilland, who represents the third generation. They always prepare their breeding plan together and then share their job among the roses, the result being that every year over 20,000 crosses are made, yielding an average of approximately 80,000 seedlings. These 20,000 crosses represent approximately 1,000 combinations. The germination of the seeds takes place between 15 January and 30 March.

The second characteristic of the Meilland's breeding work is the use of a hydroponic system, by which all the seedlings are planted in benches of sand, through which there flows a nutrient solution. This hydroponic system covers a ground surface of approximately 2,600 sq. metres, and we use every week some 30 cubic metres of nutrient solution which goes through the system. I will not go into too many details of the hydroponic solution, but if I've mentioned this characteristic it is to indicate to you that it presents very great advantages for our work of breeding, because first of all, we can observe quite a lot of new seedlings in a very restricted area. We plant between 90 and 120 seedlings per square metre, so this gives you some idea of the tremendous capacity we have for observing the seedlings. I will indicate to you the way the selection of these seedlings is made, but they are all planted in this hydroponic solution, which provides a homogeneous medium which helps us to see the real genetical differences between the roses.

If the roses were planted in ordinary soil, there might be differences which would stem from variations in the soil and not differences in the roses, which is very important in our opinion. Then this hydroponic solution, of course, helps us to do quicker work, because when you have 80,000 seedlings a year coming on, it means digging out the bad roses all the time, as they are rejected, and you know that to dig out a two or three year old plant from soil takes some time. When you have 80,000 seedlings multiplied by the three years of the first selection this is a formidable task, whereas with the hydroponic system you can just go along the benches and pull out the roses by hand, as they come away very easily.

Now the last advantage of the hydroponic system is that, of course, we do not need the so-called soil rotation, and when you think that in Cap D'Antibes in the French Riviera a patch of earth costs about £20 to £30 per square yard, you will realise that is something very important for us too.

Now I have to come to the third main characteristic of the Meilland breeding work. This is the organisation of selection. I think that our colleagues here have spoken very thoroughly about the scientific approach to breeding, and M. Meilland follows more or less the same lines with perhaps some variations, as there must be between all the breeders. But we think it is most important to have a set routine for selection, if we are to obtain good and quick results. The selection we thus have in mind comprises two main characteristics amongst perhaps the ten characteristics of a good rose. These are, first, to find new colour breaks in roses, and second to have plants which are free from disease. The other characteristics, which are weather resistance, keeping qualities, repeat-flowering, free blooming and so on, are secondary to the first two in our present set-up.

As I told you the 80,000 seedlings are observed in this hydroponic solution over a period of three years. We eliminate approximately 78,000 seedlings after these three years, and the 2,000 which are left are transplanted and budded in the open, notably in a trial ground which we have in the South of France, where we study them for another two years. After these two years have elapsed we have approximately between 150 and 200 varieties left. It is at that time that we send these 150 varieties to four trial grounds which we have distributed in several countries. One is in the U.S.A. in Pennsylvania, one is in Denmark, south of Copenhagen, the third one is in England in Ruddington at Wheatcroft Bros. and the fourth one is in France in Lyon which has a very continental climate. We have tried with these four trial grounds to cover most of the climatic conditions we could meet.

So these 150 varieties are studied in these four trial grounds, plus the original trial ground in the South of France for another period of two years, where we cut down the number of varieties to 30 on an average. These 30 varieties are then sent to all the agents of Meilland all over the world, which means 22 countries, including Canada, South Africa, Japan, Australia, New Zealand and all the main European countries. All our agents, including those having the first four trial grounds, study all these varieties for another period of three years, and give us systematic reports on the varieties. They also regularly attend yearly meetings at our headquarters in Antibes, where we discuss the value of the roses under the various climatic conditions, and where we finally decide upon the roses to be commercialised. It is only after this lengthy procedure of selection and reports has taken place that we finally decide upon the release

'ELIZABETH HARKNESS' (H.T.)
'Red Dandy' × *'Piccadilly'*
Raised by R. Harkness & Co. Ltd
TRIAL GROUND CERTIFICATE 1968
See page 184

'LIEBESTRAUM' (H.T.)
'Colour Wonder' × *'Liberty Bell'*
Raised by W. Kordes, Germany
TRIAL GROUND CERTIFICATE 1968
See page 185

of the varieties. We then have an international distribution through these same agents, which means that whereas we breed roses in the South of France, these are intended for a world-wide distribution.

As time is short, I will now very briefly show you some pictures to illustrate what I have just been explaining to you.

JACK HARKNESS
R. Harkness & Co. Ltd
Observations of a New Breeder

I am a new breeder, the newest of all these experts sitting up here, and I feel a little diffident at being in such exalted company. I am looking forward in ten years time to coming back and blinding you with all the science which I have now learnt from them, and shall shortly apply.

We started off knowing nothing about hybridising roses, nothing even about growing under glass, and we embarked on this venture in conjunction with Mr Alex. Cocker of Aberdeen. It has been a very happy partnership, and the first thing I would like to say to anybody who is thinking about starting breeding is, that if you can do it in conjunction with a good friend, you get a lot more pleasure out of it and you get along about four times as fast, the two of you, as you would otherwise have done.

Also we got some very good advice in Aberdeen from a Scottish farmer who is a friend of Mr Cocker's. This chap was interested in breeding cattle, and as we were interested in breeding plants we compared notes; and the remark from this Scottish farmer, which pleased me very much, and which I often bear in mind when selecting rose parents, is 'Choose a guid bull and a reasonable coo".

We were in a hurry to get started and would not wait to put any heat in the seed house. We were glad we didn't, because we saved our money and it would have been a waste. You don't need heat in the south of England. I am not going to speak for other parts of the country, but if you should have the idea of hybridising, you should be very careful about using heat, because you can bring your parent plants into flower too soon. Pollination naturally takes place when there is a lot of sunshine, and consequently I can see no advantage in having your plants forced into early bloom.

Far better to let them flower naturally which they do in a cold greenhouse in our district round about the early part or middle of May. We then get all our hybridising done from about that time on to about mid-June, when we just stop.

The next important thing, having got your seed to set, is to keep a look out for Botrytis. Fellow breeders have told me that you can expect to lose anything up to about one-third of your pods with botrytis, and rather than spend an awful lot of money, and getting worried about keeping it away, we have a terribly easy solution. We just hybridise a third more of everything than we need. This is the insurance cover and, with a little bit of common sense, you realise that botrytis is going to take place in conditions of a fair amount of humidity. Therefore, we always try to keep plenty of air in the seed-house, and also to keep the air moving. We notice that botrytis nearly always forms where the sepals are curled back over the seedpod; therefore, we remove the sepals at the time we are preparing the flower. Thus, two jobs are done in one operation. This doesn't seem to affect the set of the seed or the quantity of it in any way. Botrytis starts in that place because that is just where humidity can hang around and encourage it.

We made several experiments with botrytis. We thought originally it came from damage done to the seed-pod when we preparing the flowers, from finger nails and so forth; but we purposely damaged pods, and we even rubbed botrytis into them, but we were never able to infect a pod. We think it may be coming from unfertilised ovules in the centre of the pod, and working its way out. I may be wrong, but something like this very often does happen, and to guard against it, we give the stigmas about 55 times as much pollen as they really need in the hope that we'll get all the ovules fertile.

The second big problem that one comes across is in the germination of the seed. Many people are resigned, I think, to finding germination rather uncertain. We are very happy now with the rate of germination that we attain and the method that we found to be the first effective break through, as far as we are concerned, was to let the pods ripen on the plants until that time when we thought no more ripening was likely to take place; this is normally some time in November. You just get a hunch one day that it is time you had those seed-pods off (see how scientific we are) so we take them off with about 2 inches of stalk and then we put them upside down into seed trays in a mixture of sand and peat. We keep them moist at all stages, keeping them at 60° F. for about three or four weeks, and then we put them outside into the open—not quite into the open, but into a cold frame with a bit of wire netting around—anything to keep the birds and the mice away. We like to leave them there while the temperature goes up and down a few times; the Hitchin climate is very obliging in this way—you nearly always get several frosts, then several fine days in between, and I think this fluctuating temperature is very good for the seed. But if we get a very hard spell we bring the seed pods into the cold house and leave them in there until sowing time.

Growing the seedlings isn't scientific at all, it is purely practical. I felt that these practical things were the vital lessons I had learnt in our early efforts, things which perhaps you might find interesting if any of you are wanting to make a start. We think it is vital to keep the seedlings growing once they do start; you don't want any checks. We use a sand and peat seed and potting medium; actually the one we use is J. Arthur Bower's compost. We have always been very pleased with it, and we sow the seeds directly into it on the bench and keep the house pretty cool until they start germinating. In fact, we don't really like the temperature to get

much above 50° F. until we have so many seeds germinated, that you start thinking of looking after those that are up, and you are not quite so interested in those that are not up. When that stage is reached we give them a little more temperature— 55° or 60° F. is a perfectly adequate growing temperature for rose seeds. You see we have heat in the seedling house, but not in the parent house.

In these artificial media—although sand and peat are not really artificial—you have to pay very careful attention to watering; seedlings are very easily under- or over-watered. This again is a thing one judges by eye and the look of the plant, the great thing being to keep them steadily on the move and, with rose seedlings, to ensure that the humidity within the house isn't too high. Then later on when they are growing pretty well, if you are lucky with the germination you will find they are far too thick on the benches. I'm glad to say that this has been our experience anyway, and this is when you get danger from mildew, whether the black or the white variety. There is no colour bar in mildew, we dislike all races equally, and at this stage it is most important to be very watchful of the ventilation in the house and particularly to keep the air moving. We have a very handy method of heating to do this; it is air blowing through poly-thene tubes, and we can have cold or warm air, and by putting this on we have currents of air blowing in the house. We avoid nasty cold draughts, but the move-ment of the atmosphere does do a great deal to keep mildew away. The other thing we do to stop mildew is to have sulphur burners, which are very efficient. You just switch the thing on over night and that deals with the mildew.

Now about feeding. I think one can very easily over-feed seedlings, and we don't like to over-feed ours. We like to see them growing reasonably tough and smallish, because we think that we then see a good deal of their true character. If you grow the whole lot looking lush with big leaves and big flowers you can very easily be misled as to their true character. So we go very easy on feeding them.

We would like to have a lot more experience. We have had only a few years at it, and have just completed I think our seventh lot of crosses. We would like to have a lot more experience of selecting roses from the bench and making comparisons between our observations under glass on the seed bench and then next year out of doors. You never get time to do this properly, but you get an awful lot of impressions and memories and guides and hunches; and selection is very important.

We find that we are most apt to save rubbish by being carried away by some pretty little flower and not looking at the foliage or the vigour of the seedling. It is surprising, in my estimation, how truly the seedlings show in their seedling stage on the bench the type of foliage, the type of vigour and some indication of the sort of plant that they are going to make. These are the things we are always naturally looking for—lovely flowers and colours, but however wonderful the flower is, if the plant is weedy and won't grow, you might as well not have had it in the first place. If the plant is good and the foliage is good, even if the flower just doesn't look as good as you had hoped, it is surprising how many improve out of doors. We think very often that those looking best in the greenhouse are not necessarily the ones that we should have budded at all, and one of my own personal hunches is that if you were to point them in the greenhouse and give this one 9 out of 10 and that one 10 out of 10, and if you were to bud all those, you would bud nearly all duds; the winners always seem to be the sixes and the sevens and perhaps the eights.

As far as selection of parents goes, I'm not really well qualified to deal with that. It has already been discussed. We do notice strains that we would rather have had nothing to do with. For instance, we thought what a marvellous thing to breed with 'Ophelia' and 'Madame Butterfly'. Surely you would get fragrant floribundas from these. But it seems that from 'Ophelia', 'Madame Butterfly' and 'Lady Sylvia' there is failure all along the line. I wouldn't touch them any more—but some others may have different experiences. By the next Conference we ought to have several volumes of notes on this topic and should a marathon session be arranged it will be a pleasure to read them all out to you.

Views of Representative Users

BRIGADIER C. E. LUCAS PHILLIPS
Amateur Gardener

This is rather a false description of myself, because I am not merely an amateur gardener; I am also a non-exhibiting gardener. Therefore, I speak from the point of view of a person who grows roses for the love of them in his garden, and not primarily for exhibiting. So I am not speaking now for the exhibitor.

In one single sentence, what we as week-end gardeners want are roses that will give us the longest possible display with the least possible fuss. To that there are several riders. The first is the question of disease, which has been talked of this afternoon earlier, almost *ad nauseam*. One of the things we look for first of all is something which will relieve us of this awful, constant business of spraying. I have to spray and spray and spray all the time, and sometimes I think: Is it worth it? Or shall I let the black spot have a bit of fun? I don't know if anyone has got on to a systemic fungicide yet or not. There are people working on the idea, but we want something of that sort or else we want the breeders to produce for us roses that are resistant to mildew, black spot and rust. That is a big order for you gentlemen to start on.

The next thing that we want, as ordinary week-end gardeners, is not sufficiently rammed home, and that is a rose that will be beautiful from its bud to its full bloom. There are so many roses that are beautiful in the bud or at the half-stage, but when fully open they are wretched things and we haven't got time to go round every day and take off the dead blooms. We want a rose which, like 'Ophelia', 'Pink Parfait', 'Dearest' and 'Anna Wheatcroft', will remain beautiful until the last possible moment, until you see the stamens gleaming in the centre. To my mind few flowers are really complete and perfect unless you see the stamens at some time. That is a very old-fashioned view, which no chrysanthemum or dahlia grower would agree with. In fact, we ought to be able to make roses grow as easily as dahlias, which are probably the most easily grown of all plants.

Also we want roses that are resistant both to sun and to rain. We don't want varieties that are going to be sodden masses of pulp after a few hours rain, and we don't want those that will shatter and go to bits after a day's hot sun, as we had on Tuesday. Those are the main requirements.

There is one final requirement, which I don't think you will ever get over, unless you have really scientific minds, and that is the other awful business of suckers. Nowadays I do not find it so easy to get down to the ground as I used to—and you always have to get down in an attitude of prayer to deal with suckers—so that they are one of the banes of my existence.

There is a lot more work that needs to be done on rose stocks, and we want those rose stocks that will not produce suckers. We all know, of course, that certain roses can be grown from cuttings, and that if you get shoots from the ground they would be the true thing, but that is no answer for a great many cultivars or varieties of roses, and so sucker-free stocks are really our final requirement.

F. A. GIBSON
Exhibitor

As an ex-exhibitor, but still with a great love of roses, I can endorse a lot of Brigadier Lucas Phillips' remarks. From an exhibitor's point of view, we want a rose with a long stem, sufficient petals so that it will last, and long petals, but not so many that it will rot and fall off in the rain.

Let me cite a case. I'm not on the B.B.C. and I hope I am not advertising. On Sunday afternoon I cut a 'Silver Lining', brought it down here in my buttonhole, 200 miles, in the heat of all Monday and I was wearing it until yesterday noon. Now that, I think, is the perfect example of an exhibitor's rose.

As far as floribundas are concerned I can go to Ireland again. One of my favourites is 'Evelyn Fison', with a lovely round compact head. Then there is 'Orange Sensation', and in a single one 'Olala', and possibly 'Paprika'. Going back to a hybrid tea there is 'Royal Highness' which unfortunately doesn't stand the rain, but is a long laster. These are the roses that we want. We want to be able to cut them say today, take them 200 miles and exhibit them tomorrow. We want a rose that we can cut and which will last 24 hours before it is on the show bench, and finally I endorse all the remarks about disease and suckers made by previous speakers, and if scent can be provided as well we will have the ideal.

JULIA CLEMENTS
Flower Arranger

I think really today I ought to take a back-seat because there are so many eminent people here, especially concerned with breeding. Rose decorations are really the end product of all that the breeders do, but as I represent about 600,000 Flower

Arrangers, who are very keen on using roses, and as I suppose all home lovers and garden owners bring their roses into the house, perhaps what we who arrange them need may have some little bearing.

I cannot easily say exactly what we want, because it depends very much on the occasion. For instance, for a large party, or for a Church arrangement or for a wedding, we want very long arching sprays, rather like the Banksia Rose or a very fine polyantha. We would love it in a pale colour, because pale colours will show up from a distance, very necessary if you are making a very large arrangement for a wedding, and of course we would like it to flower all the summer. But I don't see why you couldn't get a rose that is pointed at the ends, a spray and roses all down, rather like philadelphus, or something like that. I know it is asking an awful lot, but since you all seem to be full of knowledge of chromosomes and genes, I don't see why you can't find these things.

At the same time we do love the hybrid teas, and I think when we say what we want of a hybrid tea we like them because we can graduate the sizes. All flower arrangers know that you want points on the outside and larger roses at the centre as focal interest; therefore, with a hybrid tea we can pick them in gradation. But as to colour, the rose arranger is really looking for something off-beat. There is a great fight to be one up on the other person, and this challenge of "one-up-manship" among flower arrangers is almost a fetish.

The interest today, I would say, is veering towards peach, brown and tan, and the parchment shades in roses. Now I am not saying that these are good garden roses, or colours for roses, but my goodness, they are absolutely stunning when you see them in an arrangement and when you are judging them. I have used 'Brownie' and 'Fantan' and 'Café' but they do seem rather hard to come by, although I have used these in the past with tremendous success. Placed with lime green items, you find that this gives a very unusual colouring, and the exhibitor and the judges at all these shows are looking

really for the unusual. I saw last week some colours rather on these lines; I think it was 'Tom Brown' I saw, which was in two-toned brown. 'Valencia', too, seems to have a good future in this colour. I like the apricot yellow of 'Sir Lancelot', and only today I've seen 'Fairy Dancer'. It isn't exactly brown, but a pinky peach, and I think this has a great future also for flower arrangers.

'Grey Pearl', I think anyone would admit is not a terribly good grower, and is not a garden rose; it has an awfully dirty look, like unwashed washing, and crumpled up parchment paper, but if you put this with flame colour and browns and add green grapes with this you have really got an arrangement that is out of this world, and this is what everyone is looking for.

'Lavender Pinocchio', which I heard mentioned today by Mr Le Grice, is a nice browny-mauve colouring and this has a tremendous success and great rarity on a table with tall lime green candles and *Alchemilla major* and funkia leaves with it. In this way 'Lavender Pinocchio' will command attention from everyone who sees it and it really is a tremendous success; we want some more of this type.

Of course, we like the old-fashioned roses very much and they are now coming back into favour with us. I find apart from the things which we like ourselves, it is this colour break that we are really wanting. It is always the search for something that is different, and apart from these tans and browns and parchment colourings, I think as a parting word, having mentioned lime green candles now, if only a breeder could produce a lime green rose, wouldn't this be something? All the flower club women would just rush to anyone who finds a lime green rose. It could be an acid green, a chartreuse, whatever you like to call it, but we want a lime green rose and if any of the breeders, when they are doing their selections, would like to send for me, especially if they live in California, I shall see what they are throwing out. I am sure that I could find a lovely colour break from those that they are really discarding.

C. PAWSEY
A Nurseryman

Coming in third wicket down with a lot of runs on the board, it behoves me to make what few runs I can quickly, or retire with another wicket down.

I represent a firm which is itself a seedling, as it were. It is the child of a merger between Ben and Frank Cant, two firms which before the war brought out many roses of worthwhile and established merit. Unfortunately, the Management of the day, after the war, discontinued the rose breeding programme, but this has been recently re-started and it is on the programme that we are embarking upon that we have looked for the things which we ourselves ask the established breeders to produce.

Now these have already been mentioned in some detail by previous speakers, so I would pass on two points which I think vitally concern the commercial grower. We do not want a rose which has a ten-dency to throw single-shooted plants, which no matter how often you stop them, will only produce single-shooted and therefore second quality trees. We want roses with which, budding-wise, an average budder can produce a good take of buds. That is very essential to the commercial aspect of rose growing.

Finally I would make one point on the relationship which exists between the licensee and the breeders, and that is I must say, a very friendly and workable basis. I would make one plea to them, and that is that the licensee be supplied earlier with buds of a novelty, perhaps two or three years in advance of introduction, so that, before we hop on to the band-wagon, we have the opportunity of finding out how it buds, cuts back and plants up, so that we can recommend it to our customers with absolute confidence.

N. R. DUNCAN
Wholesale Florist

I should perhaps explain that my immediate interest in roses, other than growing many of them in my garden at Wimbledon, is that I am with a wholesale firm in Covent Garden who sell great quantities of cut roses throughout the year. I would just mention to the organisers of this Conference that it seems to have coincided with the worst trade in roses in Covent Garden for many years, and I trust if you have another Conference that this will not apply then.

I would like first of all to draw the attention of breeders of roses to the size of the commercial market, because I feel today a bit of an interloper, in that so much emphasis has been placed on the amateur; whereas I am now really dealing with the commercial grower. I don't think his demands should be overlooked, and I am sure they are not by many breeders, but I would just like to mention that at the moment, in the British Isles, we probably have 100 acres or so of glass under which roses are grown commercially. But if we take an example like Holland, where ten years ago they also had about 100 acres, now they have about 600 acres. With the way the demand for cut roses is increasing in this country, I think we are on the verge of a revolution here, too. We shall see, in my view, a tremendous surge in demand for cut roses; that means that the outlet for our breeders of roses for commercial use, will increase tremendously over the next few years. It is very interesting to see that in Europe, where hitherto roses were of minor importance compared with carnations as a cut flower, roses have now overtaken carnations as a cut flower in many of these countries today, and more roses are being grown under glass than carnations. Here at present we have 200 odd acres of carnations being grown under glass, so the same trend may be seen here as well.

It is very difficult to put over this story in a few minutes, but I will be as brief as

I can. So far as the commercial side is concerned, the breeder has to satisfy two parties; the grower and the consumer. It is no earthly good the grower growing roses he likes unless the consumer is prepared to pay economic prices for them, and the Chairman when he talked to me just before this session, said "I suppose like many, you will be wanting the impossible". I realise, like many, that we do want the impossible. We have to satisfy two classes of people.

Of course the wholesaler, as the man in between, you can ignore. Nobody cares about what the wholesaler wants! But the grower must make a profit out of growing these roses, and the retailer must make a profit out of selling them, otherwise the whole thing is a "dead duck". Now to satisfy the grower, very briefly, there are various requirements. Firstly, it must be a variety of rose that sells easily. It must be a variety that is easy to grow and to grade; it must, if possible, not require peeling or taking off the outside petals. I know some varieties today where this has to be done and as this is an added job, at peak times it can become an absolute curse. A rose must also, as far as possible, be easy to grow from a disease point of view. There are many roses which are very beautiful commercially, but they have disease problems.

When they are new varieties they must not be so expensive that the grower cannot grow a sufficiently large block. Commercial varieties, really to get established on the markets of this country, must be grown in quantity, otherwise one never gets a true public reaction. Therefore, the breeder must, as far as possible, be able to offer these roses to the growers at a reasonably low price, and here, I know I am on very dangerous ground. But we have the patent rights today on many varieties of roses, and if these rights, these fees, are too high it will stop growers buying new varieties that are perhaps well worth trying out. The average gross yield from an acre of roses per year should be in excess of ten thousand pounds, and if a grower is going into production in the winter months, when his costs of produc-

tion of course rise considerably, these roses must yield from ten to fourteen thousand pounds per acre gross, otherwise they are just not economic.

The variety must stand up to rough treatment and this is where it differs so greatly from the garden rose. I grow roses in the garden; my wife and I cut them and take them into the house and put them in a vase and it is all done in five minutes. But a commercial rose has to stand up to an amazing number of rough handlings. Briefly, it is cut in the nursery, taken to the packing shed and graded. It's probably put in a cooler to take the heat out of it, brought back, put in a box and the box is placed on the floor. Then it is loaded on a lorry, placed in a railway van; then it comes off the railway van on to the floor, then into a truck into the market, on the floor, then up on shelves. Down to the florist, into the florist's van and over to the florist's shop. I'm not exaggerating, this is every-day practice with commercial roses. So you must have a rose which is tough; otherwise it has no commercial value whatever.

If possible, one would want commercial roses to be able to flourish under our winter conditions. In this country we do make comparatively high prices in the winter. I have some grower friends here, so I mustn't say very high prices—comparatively high prices, and it is this market we want to supply. We in the British Flower Industry Association send out a questionnaire once a year to florists all over the country to obtain their reactions about various flowers, and time and time again florists are telling us that they cannot get as many roses in the winter as they want. There is a tremendous demand then for roses at reasonable prices. So again a rose that flourishes under summer conditions and doesn't grow in the winter is almost valueless.

In view of this talk this afternoon, I have asked many florists when they buy flowers, what they really look for in order to meet public demand. As is so often the case, commercially of course, they all look for something quite different. The first one I asked was a man who sold a lot of roses in the street, and he said "Well of course Guv. the first thing I want is scent", so I said "Well, you make more money, do you, with roses that have a good scent?". He said "Oh! no, but they all want scent, and they think that if it has got good scent it will last longer". I don't know if there is any truth in this, there may well be, but he then said "If it ain't got scent we can soon put some on it, you know"!

The next thing they want is colour, and today, especially this season somehow, we are seeing so many new varieties of roses coming onto the market it just isn't true. In a way we can have too many colours, I think, for commercial roses. For the garden we can't have enough, but commercially we can overdo it, and I'm told by one of the leading West End florists that one of the main colours required is red. Apparently this colour has a tremendous demand, I'm sorry to say from mostly male buyers, who have either been naughty or who have guilt complexes! I can only tell our breeder friends that there are apparently enough male buyers about to make red roses really worth while breeding. It must have stem length; up to a point the stem length is a good point in selling, but you can overdo it. So often we have lovely long rose stems that are taken straight back to the florist's shop and chopped in half, but to a certain extent price does depend on stem length, assuming of course, that the bud at the end of the stem is in proportion. In addition the rose must have a strong neck. Weak neck roses—you know, the rose that just falls over—cause endless complaints, and are very bad for the relationship between the florist and the buyer. So roses with strong necks are commercially absolutely essential.

Long life, of course, is so obvious that it is almost stupid mentioning it, but the whole business of commercial selling of flowers is basically dependent on satisfaction by the buyer. It is no earthly good, in the market, being able to sell to the florist a beautiful-looking rose, which he takes home and sells to the public, if within 24 hours it is dead. Some people might think that's good business, as they then have to come back and buy some more the next day, but of course they don't. They have got to have complete satisfaction with their purchase, so that long life is probably more important than all the rest put together. The rose must take up water easily, so that if it looks a little limp when the housewife gets it, then she can give it some water without any complications and it should take it up and quickly become reinvigorated.

It should, if possible, be available all the year round, because it is so important to keep people buying roses once they have started, and it must, as I explained earlier, be tough; it must stand up to the commercial rough handling, which unfortunately it gets. Another florist told me that what it must stand up to is the ignorance of the great British public on how to look after roses. I don't think our public are any more ignorant than in any other part of the world, but it is a fact that one hears the most amazing stories of what people expect of the flowers they buy, so we must produce varieties which are commercially tough. I know, as your Chairman said earlier, we are probably asking the impossible, but at least we can ask.

S. M. GAULT
Parks Superintendent

My guess is that the breeders on the platform will have to get their computers to work out all the various combinations that have already been suggested. I work for an organisation which uses computers, and we find they give us far more work than we had before we got them.

Now I am speaking entirely on behalf of myself, as parks, like gardens, vary very much according to the part of the country where they are located. I grow roses in Regent's Park, and you can't grow roses in Regent's Park like you do in Glasgow or Aberdeen. The climate is quite different, so I am just going to say what I think we should have in Regent's Park.

The perfection of the "quartered" bloom in 'KÖNIGIN VON DÄNEMARK'

The beauty of a single bloom in 'COMPLICATA', a rose suitable for covering banks, tree stumps or climbing into small trees
(see page 146)

'CONSTANCE SPRY'
a delightful modern introduction with the form of the
Old Garden Roses (*see page* 142)

'SCINTILLATION', a vigorous sprawler for covering banks

R. *paulii rosea*
suitable for ground cover (*see page* 148)

'SCARLET FIRE' ('SCHARLACHGLUT')
(*see page* 144)

'BOBBIE JAMES'
a vigorous creamy-white climber, but not so rampant as
R. filipes 'KIFTSGATE' (see page 148)

R. chinensis mutabilis (see page 149)

I think we all agree that we want strong healthy roses. We all want winter-hardy roses and roses that won't suffer from die-back. We all want roses that won't get black spot, mildew—even worse than black spot in London—or rust. I would like to see a rose with the colour of 'Western Sun', the formation of 'Silver Lining', the foliage of 'Pink Favourite', the ability of breaking from the base of 'Perfecta', and that will grow and flower into late October and will carry its foliage into November as a hybrid tea. As a floribunda I would like a rose with the habit of 'Lili Marlene' or 'Marlena'; that would shatter its petals like 'Paprika', have the glossy foliage of 'Paprika' and would be mildew resistant and resistant to all other diseases. This is the type of rose that we want for parks—a rose that we can use as a substitute for bedding plants. We haven't got the staff, the young people that are coming along don't have the training to grow bedding plants as we used to do in the old days. A lot of these plants will have to be replaced, I hope, by roses, and we want roses that will cover the ground so that you can't see weeds and won't encourage any weeds to have room to grow.

Roses in public parks, especially in this part of the country in Regent's Park, I think serve two functions. We have an educational function to serve. Very many people come into the park to see the roses growing and they want to see what would be suitable for growing in their own garden as garden plants. Quite a number of these varieties, of course, are also suitable for exhibition, but there are a lot of people who walk around with their note books and make notes of the roses of the colours that they like. They can see how they grow and I think this is of great value to the producers of roses, to the breeders, that people can come in, and they do this in various parks and they go round and

particularly look at new roses. There is tremendous interest in new varieties or cultivars, whichever term you like to use.

Another thing, of course, from an educational point of view, is how you can use roses in the parks. You can show the people how they can use them in their own garden. Some of the rose exhibitors don't like the way we use roses, but I like to see mixed borders of shrub roses under-planted, as nobody wants the chore of bending down and pulling out weeds. You can under-plant with hardy plants, hardy geraniums, ground cover plants; this is very useful and people like to come along and see this sort of thing. Another thing that I do, and I know that this isn't very commercial, I like to see roses grown up trees. Many people have old apple trees and other old trees in their garden; when you get over 65, or round about 65 as I am, nobody wants the job of cutting out old trees. It's hard work, and they may as well use them as a hat stand and put climbing roses on them. I would like to see roses like *R. filipes* and *R. longicuspis* with colour bred into them that will flower again in the autumn, and get away from the one flowering season of these roses, charming and beautiful as they are. I would like to see another flush in the autumn, and some to have heps, something like 'Francis E. Lester' but even larger and brighter, a cascade in fact of *Rosa moyesii* heps.

I don't know that I have very much more to add. I would just like to say to Brigadier Lucas Phillips that I grow dahlias as well, and hope we never see roses get virus in them like we have in dahlias. I know there is virus in some roses, but the weeding out we have to do every year with dahlias, the reselection we have to do—in three years time some of the new varieties are absolutely hopeless—and I hope we will never have to do this on the same scale with roses.

GRAHAM THOMAS
Garden Designer

I wonder whether we are being sufficiently venturesome in our rose breeding. It seems

to me that enormous efforts are being put into the creation of roses similar to those which have been raised in the last 20 or 30 years or more. Are we not being obsessed with the accepted style of rose? Earlier speakers have stressed certain points, such as strange colours, and ramblers which would flower later. Do we not want the rose to develop in many other different directions from what is taking place at the moment? May I make a few suggestions, not as a rose breeder, but as one who has studied the genus for a long time, and may perhaps by throwing out a few crumbs, sow the seeds—to use mixed metaphors—of future roses in many different styles from what we are having today? **Foliage** is a very important matter; it has been stressed several times today. In addition to dark green foliage and coppery tints, I should like to see roses with grey foliage and mauve-grey foliage. This may sound very extraordinary, but Mrs Klimenko's Paper mentioned *Rosa fedtschenkoana*, a rose with silver-grey foliage which produces single white flowers continuously from May until the autumn. Isn't this a possibility? Another is *Rosa rubrifolia*, which has foliage of mauve-grey. With plants of those colours, and I am perhaps speaking more about shrub roses than about the bedding roses, I should like to see flowers of white, or purple or pink particularly appropriate with a shrub of grey foliage.

When it comes to **flower colour** I should like to endorse what has been said earlier that we do need a really good purple rose. We have striven after light blue-tinted or mauve roses, but so far I think nothing superior in colour has been raised to 'Reine des Violettes' which was bred around 1860. This still remains the bluest rose that I know. Many of the modern ones are of cool lavender but they are no more blue than the old; whether we shall ever have a blue rose is beside the point, but in our formal designs we do need, I think, something in dark colour to balance the richness of the dark red roses, and I would suggest that a purple rose—purple in its own right and not a crimson fading to purple—would be valuable. Likewise a welcome modern rose would be one of the colour of 'Tuscany', which

Mr Le Grice mentioned that he had been using, which is maroon.

Like Mr Gault I should welcome **ramblers which would flower again later**. We have a slight beginning of this with 'Crimson Shower'. *Rosa wichuraiana*, its parent and the parent of many other ramblers, doesn't flower until August in this country. Surely this is a pointer that we could at least have ramblers which if they didn't flower twice, could flower in August instead of in July? By hybridising perhaps 'Crimson Shower' again with *Rosa wichuraiana* and adding that invaluable rose, *Rosa moschata*, which also doesn't flower until August and goes on until the autumn, should we not be helping ourselves towards perpetual or repeat-flowering ramblers and climbers? *Rosa moschata* is scarcely known; most people grow *R. brunonii* under its name, which is a summer flowering rambler, but *R. moschata* is a rare plant recently rediscovered; it was the parent of the Noisettes, which I venture to say are the most perpetual of all climbers today. Many of them are old but they go on from mid-summer to the autumn. I would just mention such varieties as 'Alister Stella Gray', 'Gloire de Dijon', 'Madame Alfred Carrière' and the almost original Noisette-type 'Blush Noisette'. If something could be infused from these roses into our moderns I think we should have far more perpetual climbers.

Roses for shade: have we ever thought about that? *Rosa arvensis* is a British native, which actually thrives in the shade, and in years past gave rise to two or three varieties one of which was 'Ayrshire Splendens'. I came across this hanging down from trees in dense shade in Sussex a few years ago, with trails ten feet long with a flower at every six inches, in full bloom. 'Ayrshire Splendens', in addition to thriving and even loving shade, has a scent which is not found in many other roses; in the old days it was called the Myrrh-Scented Rose, and that strange scent crops up in one or two roses such as 'Belle Amour', 'Constance Spry' and slightly in 'Magenta'.

Ground cover: nobody has mentioned

that. I should welcome roses which would grow so densely that no weeding was necessary under them and they should be so dense that they would also stop hooligans. I can visualise a plant about 3 ft high, sprawling on the ground, being in full flower for a very long time in the summer months. We have an approach to this in *Rosa wichuraiana* itself; it is nearly evergreen, completely prostrate, utter ground cover, together with its one or two hybrids, *R. paulii* and 'Max Graf'.

Finally, may we consider **thornlessness**? How much more popular a rose would be if it were thornless! Many roses have been raised which are thornless, the Boursaults and several isolated varieties, and I think in addition to our garden roses we need stocks without thorns too, and some little effort has been made in that direction

The Value of Shrub Roses in the Garden
Chairman: Gordon Edwards

GRAHAM THOMAS

It is important at a talk like this, when, I imagine, some of you will be shall I say addicts of shrub roses, and others may be starting to take an interest in them, to have a little explanation of what we are going to consider. You must begin with an open mind. It is no good approaching them through modern roses. If you do, you will find that the bulk of the shrub roses assume in some peculiar way a kind of background value, that they are grown on sufferance in the garden, just a few around the fringe of the modern rose garden. I am quite sure that is the wrong approach, however much one may love a modern rose.

And here I think it would be a good plan just to say that I very much admire the hybrid tea roses, their beautiful shapes and colours, and the floribundas for their brilliance and continuity. I mention this in passing because once or twice I have seen it stated in periodicals that I only appreciate old fashioned roses and think growers of modern roses are—well, the word "barmy" was used in one periodical! I can assure you this is very far from the truth. I have a love for all sorts of roses, but it has been my particular pleasure to delve deeply into the genus and to discover what its many merits are from an unprejudiced standpoint. There again I may be called over the coals. "Am I unprejudiced, do you think, Mr Edwards?" "No." Right, well now you know, but at any rate I *try* to be unprejudiced!

We have to consider roses which are shrubs. Now if you refer to a dictionary to find the difference between a shrub and a bush, you will see that they mean the same thing, but during the last twenty years, ever since I wrote a little pamphlet called "Roses as Flowering Shrubs", the shrub rose has been looked upon as a different thing from a bush rose, by which we usually mean the bedding or modern roses. So we have to consider flowering shrubs, that is the first point. The next point is we must look at shrub roses as plants and not as flowers. That is a little phrase I rather like using; you can divide your gardening friends into those who like flowers and those who like plants. They are quite distinct; they may seem at first sight to be the same thing, but it really means whether you are keen to appreciate the plant as a whole or merely to look at a flower and enjoy it cut or as an individual bloom. People who like flowers very often like plants as well, but there are two distinct categories. One can appreciate a flowering shrub as a whole because it has distinctiveness in its foliage and growth; it is valued as a whole and not just as an individual bloom.

Another point which always crops up, especially among those who primarily like modern roses, is whether the rose is perpetual or recurrent-flowering. This is a bone of contention, but if you love the plant as opposed to the flower, recurrence assumes much less importance, and every now and again comes the thought that we are being too greedy over roses. Why should the poor things have to flower right through the season? They don't in the wild, with the exception of one or two species. One happily plants a forsythia, a lilac, a philadelphus, azalea or rhododendron, and one enjoys them for their beauty over a period of a few weeks and then they slide gently into the background; some may be host plants for clematis which could be cut to the ground every year and would grow up and flower in August. Or they will provide, alternatively, welcome shade for plants which will grow underneath them and flower in the spring. So that even with roses that flower only once there is no reason to have six or eight foot square of your garden simply devoted to the rose itself. This is why I think it a little greedy to expect shrub roses to go on flowering. They may be recurrent, or have a second crop, and it is perhaps dangerous to say there never will be a shrub rose that will be as perpetual as the floribunda. But I think that if we ever achieve such a hybrid, it will automatically lose much of its grace, because in order to get a flowering shrub covered with bloom, the bloom more or less has to be produced on last season's growth, and if it is not produced on last season's growth it will automatically, as a rule, be less graceful. The shrubs which do this and flower along the branches obviously have to produce another of those branches in order to produce the same effect. We do get a certain amount of recurrence among shrub roses, but they are more of the breed between a modern bedding rose and a shrub rose with erect branches, such as we find in the very strong floribundas.

It is possible that we might think of shrub roses as a whole, the species and the hybrids, as a kind of splendid backcloth to all the modern roses. If you can think of a stage with a magnificent piece of scenery at the back which develops in different ways through the season, and that the principal actors come and go in the shape of the modern roses, I think you will have a fair simile.

Another point that I think is important is the floral shape. This is going back slightly upon what I said—that we should appreciate the plants as a whole—but the floral shape is very important. In modern roses the main attraction is from the bud to the half-open bloom, although I was delighted to hear one of the speakers say that he felt that it was highly important that we should have flowers that remain double and full of petals to the end. Well now, in the species and the old shrub roses and a few of the moderns, the beauty is not usually revealed *until* the flower is half opened and will continue as a rule until it is full-blown; so, compared with most moderns, we must look at the flower quite differently. In fact in old-fashioned roses the beauty lies in the fully expanded bloom, and it was not in the old days considered necessary for the bud to look beautiful. Very few of the old-fashioned hybrids are really beautiful in bud, apart from the Mosses and 'Celeste' and one or two more, but they hold their tremendous beauty right through until the petals actually fall. So there are all sorts of new assessments to be made in considering shrub roses.

Fortunately, they will grow pretty well anywhere. Apart from a bog or an ill-drained piece of land, I can think of no garden in this country where a number of shrub roses could not be grown successfully; even on chalk or extremely limy soil, many kinds will do well and on poor acid sands there are certain kinds again which are highly successful. They range from plants one foot in height to thirty feet.

There are shrub roses for every possible garden position, not only in height but in width. A natural garden of gentle, informal design, is perhaps more appropriate to a wild species—a single-flowered rose—than perhaps a great modern shrub rose such as 'Constance Spry'. There are others which will suit more formal designs. Collectively, they give an effect, I'm sure you will all agree, second to none in flowering shrubs. Our most brilliant shrub roses can give as much colour value in the garden as an azalea, philadelphus, rhododendron or any other flowering shrub. One is often told, "Oh, I cannot grow shrub roses in my garden, it isn't big enough". This depends upon whether you are looking at the plant or the bloom. There is undoubtedly infinite variety, and I thought we would now go through some slides, in which I shall seek to point out the different merits of different groups and how they can perhaps best be used in the garden, so would you kindly put on the first slide, sir?

Although I have been at pains to stress the importance of looking at the plants as a whole, I don't want you to feel that I think the flowers themselves are in any way to be underestimated. Some shrub roses have the beauty of the single bloom, such as this *Rosa spinosissima altaica*. I was so delighted to hear Brigadier Lucas Phillips yesterday expressing what he called his old-fashioned idea, that stamens should be somewhere in a flower. Here they are again in a semi-double bloom, a Spinosissima hybrid, 'Stanwell Perpetual', which I'm showing you specially because it is a perfect specimen of a semi-double bloom, with stamens, and also it has the greyish foliage about which I spoke for a brief moment yesterday afternoon.

Then we come to the fully double flower. In this we find perfection among the older and some of the newer roses. This is 'Madame Lauriol de Barny', a Bourbon which is of somewhat procumbent habit, needing support. It looks marvellous when trained into and hanging out of a cypress, and it gives me a chance to say that we should not eschew all nodding roses; they have a charm of their own, particularly when they are climbers and their flowers are borne above our heads; a nodding flower is then an asset. 'Madame Lauriol de Barny' as you see is nodding and it has the wonderful perfection of the old-fashioned shape. Another style of perfection is found in the quartered bloom of 'Madame Isaac Pereire'. So with those four slides I think we can

say that the shrub roses have considerable beauty of individual bloom.

Now a few slides of the old-fashioned roses. First of all the Red Rose of Lancaster—*Rosa gallica officinalis*, a very ancient plant, which gives as much effect in the garden as any. I show it growing in extremely sandy soil in my own garden and making what I consider a good show. It not only brings home at once the floral display, but also the fact that the Gallicas will grow on sandy soil, though mark you, they will be far better on a rich Sussex loam, and this applies not only to the Gallicas but the Damascenas. This is 'Ispahan', a brilliant rose that is used, I am told, for the extraction of attar in the Caspian provinces of Persia; it is one of the first to come out and one of the last to go over, and is an extremely strong growing Damascena. Another, 'Celsiana', provides an equally good effect. I think one can forgive a plant for not doing more during the season if it produces over a hundred blooms in a space of three weeks.

Here is a collection of old-fashioned roses, which was planted at the John Innes Institute at Bayfordbury some 18 years ago; this picture is of their second season of flowering. It is proof, if need be, that they provide a great spectacle of bloom pretty quickly. In the foreground is *R. gallica* 'Complicata' and there are beds of Gallicas, Damasks and so on, and the older climbers on the walls.

Now a garden in Essex on rich loam. These plants are three years old. As you see, there is a lot of underplanting. This soil was extremely heavy clay, impossible to walk on in the winter, impossible to dig, impossible to hoe, cracking badly in periods of drought, and the only thing to do was to give it a thick mulch of fallen leaves and rotted straw and to cover all the foreground with ground-cover plants, avoiding all work on the beds during the year. Truly a labour-saving garden. The pale yellow *Alchemilla mollis*, *Stachys lanata* and hardy geraniums fill the fronts of the borders in between the bushes; they do them no harm and help with the display.

This picture, in the same garden, shows

the value of *Rosa rubrifolia*. I'm not going to enlarge upon this now, but this purplish-leafed rose will appear in later slides. Yet another view; this time the bed on the left is mainly of Alba varieties. In grouping old-fashioned roses plenty of whites should be included. The bulk of varieties are pink, pinky mauve, mauvy crimson and mauvy purple, and one does need the white and grey-leafed plants to give a lightening effect to these and also to the darkest maroon varieties such as 'Tuscany'. This white one is 'Madame Plantier', something between a Damask and an Alba, a thornless rose. It will train up into trees. At Sissinghurst Castle in Kent they had climbed into pear trees some 15 feet and hung down in a crinoline of pure white blooms.

At Sissinghurst Castle a different style of culture of these older roses is adopted. The last slides have shown them being allowed to grow completely freely, with very little pruning and displaying naturally their graceful charm. At Sissinghurst they are trained onto wooden frameworks and are pruned and thinned out after flowering and tied in so that the blooms create an absolute mass of colour over each support. I wish I had some more slides of Sissinghurst because that is the one garden which I have seen where they are trained in this very splendid way. They create great tea-cosies of blossom, solid with colour, and in that rich soil they do particularly well. Another way of growing them is in what a friend of mine calls her "pulpits". Those of you who find the old-fashioned roses rather floppy can put in three stakes and three supporting bars at about a yard from the ground around each rose; these will provide a resting place for the arching branches and saves them from trailing on the ground. They will still be full of grace.

We can go still farther into formality and adopt the French method of growing them, which is hard pruning and disbudding and keeping the plants down to two or three feet in height. This is a view at Bagatelle; it doesn't actually show many old-fashioned roses, but you can see the remarkable exactness of the French culture.

So there are the several ways of growing the old-fashioned roses.

As you know, the old-fashioned roses are looked down upon today because they only flower once, but we can have the best of both worlds if we grow the Portland roses of which the best is 'Comte de Chambord'. They are old-fashioned roses which do flower a second or third time during the summer. 'Comte de Chambord' is almost always in flower. Its true old Gallica-type flower is soft pink in colour. It is certainly the best of them, but 'Jacques Cartier' and two or three more are well worth growing.

One that assorts very well with old roses is 'Constance Spry'. Though it has as a parent a floribunda, 'Dainty Maid', it is also bred from one of the Gallicas and it shows little modern blood in it. It is a very large bush, better on a support or trained over a stump or hedge, but it has the true Centifolia bloom with a deep centre, so much beloved by Redouté in his portraits, and it was named in honour of one who did so very much to preserve these roses. I am glad that the raiser is with us in the hall and I hope he will feel that the photograph does justice to his rose, but when you see a bloom of 'Constance Spry' about 6 inches across, fully open, it is an experience, the experience of the season.

Now I want to show you some slides of the early flowering shrub roses. The old-fashioned roses come out in June and give their great display from about 15 June until the middle of July, according to season and district, but there are also many shrub roses which flower earlier. Here we have a native of these shores growing in the sand in Devon, *Rosa spinosissima*. It is an extremely hardy rose and has been used to breed very hardy roses for the centre of Germany; it grows in Greenland, Scotland and all round our shores and other parts of the Northern Hemisphere and it has two or three special attributes. One is that it thrives in a sandy soil; its running roots extend in every direction, making quite a thicket. It is ideal for binding sand dunes and for colonising waste spaces, and grows so thickly that weeds as a rule don't grow through it. It flowers very early in the season, very often by 20 May, and has an exquisite perfume, but it has only one season of flowering. It does though, usher in the beginning of the rose season and later on it has heps which are quite unusual, like black-currants.

During the last century a very enterprising Scottish nurseryman listed about 200 forms and hybrids of *Rosa spinosissima* and he described them all with simply eleven adjectives. I don't mean that every rose was described with eleven adjectives, but that the whole 200 were described using only eleven adjectives between them. They were whitish-pink, or pinkish-white, or white with pink or pink with white and so on, and I always think that this was a record in nurserymen's economy, because you know how verbose we usually are! But the roses showed only slight variations. Here is 'Andrewsü', quite a famous old pink variety, and they vary from creamy white through pink and mauve and also show yellowish colours when they are hybridised with *Rosa foetida*. The double white is one of the most famous and often seen in old gardens. As you see they have an astonishing number of blooms and they smell as fresh as lily of the valley.

Here is 'Frühlingsgold', one of Kordes' hybrids of *R. spinosissima*, growing in extremely sandy soil in the shade under a pine tree, at Sunningdale Nurseries. It is an amazingly tolerant plant.

Apart from *R. spinosissima*, there are a few other roses which grow well in sand, among which is this extraordinary rose called the Gooseberry-leaved rose, *Rosa stellata* and its close variety R.s. 'Mirifica'. It comes from Mexico; it is absolutely hardy, and flowers for a very long time from the middle of June onwards. Its flowers are silky like those of a Cistus and it makes a good bush up to about 3 to 4 feet, and will colonise the ground fairly rapidly.

Among other roses which will flower early and will do on lightish soil are the Hugonis hybrids; I will not say *R. hugonis* itself, because it seems to suffer so much "die-back". But its hybrids—*R. canta-*

brigiensis, 'Hidcote Gold' and *R. headleyensis* which you will see in a moment, are thoroughly reliable plants, and far easier garden shrubs than *R. hugonis* itself and 'Canary Bird', both of which I find die back badly. 'Hidcote Gold' is a hybrid with *R. sericea* as many of these are, and with *R. hugonis* and all its clan will create this wonderful display of yellow just at the time when laburnum and the irises are in flower. There is no doubt that this clear yellow is one of the very best things you can have to display the purple and lavender coloured iris. *R. headleyensis* is very little known, but I must say I think it is one of the supreme hybrids of Hugonis; it is somewhat paler, but it is a far more graceful bush than any of the others and well worthy of inclusion in any collection.

Among other early flowering roses are the Boursaults. Hybrids between *R. pendulina* or something near it and the old-fashioned roses, they are thornless. The one I am just showing you now is 'Madame Sancy de Parabère' with this lovely floral shape of wide outer petals and a sort of hollyhock-centre. It is best for trailing over other bushes, but once again it gives early bloom and comes in the lilac and iris period. Here are some blooms close-up, revealing this unusual shape of flower. In spite of the numerous different shapes found in new varieties today, I haven't seen any like it so far.

Other early flowering roses for our late May and June period are the *R. moyesii* breed, which you know well. Here is 'Geranium', I think the most satisfactory of the Moyesii forms for the garden. It has a lighter green leaf, is more bushy and even more brilliant in flower; a better shrub than the ordinary *R. moyesii*. Their blooms are fleeting but their heps are long-lasting. *R. sweginzowii* is a close relative of *R. moyesii*, and the whole group have these wonderfully valuable, long flagon-shaped scarlet heps in August and September. This makes them useful in herbaceous border schemes, as at that time of the year there is a super-abundance of yellow and orange daisy-flowers in herbaceous borders. We all know the trouble, don't we—the heleniums, the gaillardias, the solidagos, rudbeckias and all the rest —and these roses are superb for planting behind them. *R. sweginzowii* has this glossy hep, whereas *R. moyesii* has a dull but even larger hep, and there are many others in the same group.

The heps last well into September, and here you see *Rosa highdownensis*, a hybrid of *R. moyesii*, being used in the "red" borders at the National Trust Garden at Hidcote in Gloucestershire. These borders are devoted to red, orange and purple flowers augmented with many shrubs and plants with coppery-purple leaves, and the whole scheme of the borders is rich and glorious in sunshine, somewhat heavy in dull weather, but you see how the orange red of these heps will build up into this sort of colour scheme and add a great deal of grace. I think this picture was taken in the middle of September, which shows how long they last. In the border also are floribunda roses and scarlet dahlias.

'Scarlet Fire' ('Scharlachglut') is brilliant in flower, but these heps will last through the winter until severe frost turns them into brown pulp. This photograph shows it at Sunningdale, in a somewhat daring colour scheme with *Alchemilla mollis*, grey santolinas and in the foreground *Geranium psilostemon* (*G. armenum*). The dazzling red is scarcely surpassed by any rose today and it retains the superb single form.

Now we return to *Rosa rubrifolia*. Having looked at a good many flowers and heps we can now spare just a few minutes for leaves. *R. rubrifolia* in sunshine develops this rich purple colour in foliage. In the shade it will be greyish or silvery greyish, and there are other species like *R.R. fedtschenkoana*, *beggeriana* and *murielae*, all of which have grey foliage, but *R. rubrifolia* is the only one with this coppery leaf. The single pink flowers are followed in August and September by red-brown heps, quite distinct from any of the others, and once again it assorts well with the yellow of the herbaceous borders, but it is equally good if you have a scheme for mid-summer of soft colours. This picture of *R. rubrifolia* was taken from my study window the other day showing the value of the cooler tinted young foliage, some-

what in the shade, with the dark green of a yew hedge in the background. Again my old friend alchemilla is in the foreground. It is one of the very best plants for associating with any of the summer-flowering shrub roses.

Then there are some late-flowering shrub roses which are extremely valuable as they prolong the season to quite two months. *R. multibracteata* is only just coming into flower with me, and will go on for two or three weeks. It is a very important plant these days because it is the parent of an extremely good hybrid, 'Cerise Bouquet'. You can see in that middle truss of buds how the character of *R. multibracteata*, with its multitudes of bracts, has been transmitted to the footstalks of the flowers and has given vigour to the hybrid, which has derived its flower size and colouring from 'Crimson Glory'. This is another of Kordes' hybrids which opens up all sorts of possibilities in hybrids among the shrub roses. 'Cerise Bouquet' is one of the strongest growing of all roses. We have had annual growth as much as nine feet in length, and the next year the whole length—well, at least the top six feet of it—has flowers the whole way along. It is graceful, and ideal in almost every way. I have yet to find any faults, except the oft-repeated one that it flowers only once, but can we not again forgive it with two or three hundred blooms from one bush which is, after all, a fair return.[*] I find it ideal for planting with *Buddleia alternifolia* and various philadelphus. They flower together, and are the perfect complement to each other.

Rosa virginiana is not only late flowering, with single pink blooms in July and into August, but is followed by scarlet heps in late autumn, which last through the winter, and it is also renowned for autumn colour. If you are planting a garden for autumn colour, you would not automatically think of roses. The Rugosas go bright yellow, but *R. virginiana* can hold its own with any autumn colouring shrub. The leaves first turn to maroon with

[*]October 1968. I have just seen established plants of 'Cerise Bouquet' with a fine second crop of bloom. G. T.

'ESCAPADE' (floribunda)
'Pink Parfait' × *'Baby Faurax'*
Raised by R. Harkness & Co. Ltd
CERTIFICATE OF MERIT 1967

'GLENGARRY' (floribunda—H.T. type)
'Evelyn Fison' × *'Wendy Cussons'*
Raised by J. Cocker & Sons Ltd
CERTIFICATE OF MERIT 1968
See page 184

crimson and yellow inside the bush, and later turn to flame.

Now to return to one or two hybrids. I have shown you a lot of pink and bright clear yellow colouring. In 'Maigold' we have a semi-climber, or a bush which needs some support, another of Kordes' hybrids, with ravishing fragrance and these splendid apricot-yellow blooms early in the season. It does need support, unless you have plenty of room when it will make a sprawling bush, such as that in the picture.

'Golden Wings' was classed originally as a hybrid tea, but I have seen it making bushes some 5 or 6 feet high and five feet through, and it is in flower constantly through the season, until autumn, with a most lovely fragrance; a perfect bloom with soft green leaves. It needs a strong soil to grow well, and is not much good in sandy soil.

I wanted you to see this slide particularly, because it shows *Rosa chinensis mutabilis*, producing a mass of bloom, which it does all through the season. It is, I believe, something which might be highly useful in breeding for bedding plants, or as a really large shrub, but I will go into that further later on. There you can get the effect of it in the landscape.

These hybrid Musks are some of the finest of shrub roses, not only for their June/July display, but for their secondary growths that bloom later. These two or three slides were taken at Sunningdale Nurseries; here is 'Felicia' with a foreground of *Geranium* 'Johnson's Blue'. Behind 'Johnson's Blue' is 'Golden Wings'; the yellow and the mauve and the salmon pink are an ideal combination.

'Buff Beauty' here is associated with helianthemums in the foreground and 'Frensham' roses and cardoons behind. The value in the garden of these shrub roses is partly that they will stand competition from near neighbours. They are so vigorous that one can plant really big things amongst them and make quite a grand effect.

Among these hybrid Musks I find 'Cornelia' to be most free of its fragrance. You can walk twelve yards away from it

and have the scent wafted towards you. It is strawberry-pink in summer and coral-pink in the autumn. Again there is complete underplanting here of santolinas and *Tellima grandiflora* and no weeds can be seen. Most of the roses in the long borders at Sunningdale are hybrid Musks and as you see a great variety of foliage plants is with them. Roses being of an arching and somewhat spotty nature in flower, with multitudes of small flowers, need the contrast of grassy foliage and large round leaves such as one finds in hostas and bergenias to give contrast and connect the groups together with quiet leafage.

'Vanity' is not so popular as the others, but strangely enough I have twice shown this rose before the Royal Horticultural Society and two awards have been given, both of them in October. 'Vanity' is growing as a bedding plant in the rose garden just outside the Oxford Botanic Garden; with hard pruning it is constantly in flower. It is equally good on a north wall; I found it growing in the north forecourt at Cliveden, another National Trust garden, where absolutely no sun reaches it after 9 o'clock in the morning, and it never stops flowering. Here you see it with late October autumn colour and these huge late trusses of blooms, sometimes two or three feet across, bear many flowers like a cloud of butterflies. The pink in the autumn is much more delicate than in the summer and it has a most refreshing scent; it is an excellent autumnal rose of a clear enough pink to associate with autumn colouring shrubs and trees. Another picture is of 'Felicia' which I rank very highly among the hybrid Musks, with 'Will Scarlet' nearby. These are unpruned bushes 7 years old. Though I stress that they are unpruned they flower well at midsummer. But of course with winter pruning a better second crop would mature.

Hybrid Musks have been used considerably for hedges; this is 'Penelope' at Kew, a very old hedge which every year provides this wonderful display and sheds its scent around. Many of the shrub roses from the old-fashioned group are suitable for hedging. This famous hedge at Kiftsgate Court, Gloucestershire, just below

Hidcote National Trust Garden, is clipped over with shears every January or February, and in that good soil throws this amazing amount of bloom, although I am sad to see that it is reverting to *R. gallica officinalis*. It started life as the striped 'Rosa Mundi'. However, they are both equally free-flowering, equally vigorous, although 'Rosa Mundi' is more spectacular. All the Gallicas will respond to this clipping; there is no need to prune them. You must take your clippers to them in mid-winter and give them a good hard shearing over. All the flowers, as you know, are borne at the tips of the upright shoots so a level effect is obtained.

Among the modern shrub roses are some very good tall hedging roses. I think very highly of the rich pink 'Aloha'; this has sweetly scented, large excellent flowers, continuously borne among splendid foliage, and it will get up to something like 6 feet, but it builds itself up slowly. It is very dense and impenetrable. Very few people today, I think, grow 'Laughter'. This is a rose which I singled out some years ago as being worthy in several ways. It is late flowering; if pruned, it doesn't give its first flush until about 10 July with us, which is very useful, because a lot of other kinds are then going over. Its rich scent is like that of sweet peas, it has good foliage, and flowers after its first crop on and off until its second crop comes in September. It will easily attain 6 or 7 feet. The day before yesterday, when some of us were at the discussion on classification, it struck me that the term "background roses" might be a useful one for such things as 'Aloha', 'Laughter' and some of the big upright shrub roses and 'Queen Elizabeth' which, if allowed to grow, have no flowers under 4 feet from the ground. They are ideal for the backs of borders, whether they be shrub, herbaceous or rose borders. They are background roses in the very best sense and their flowers will be displayed at the right height.

'Sarah van Fleet', a hybrid Rugosa, is also an ideal background rose. If allowed to grow freely we should see no flowers under 5 feet from the ground, but above that up to 9 feet it would be a shower of

blossom, and is one of the most famous American hardy hybrid shrub roses. It brings in the Rugosas, and I expect several of you have been wondering why I am leaving them so late, but they don't fit into other groups. They are early flowering, which is an important matter, and their first flush brings them into our lilac and *R. hugonis* period. This is a picture of 'Frau Dagmar Hastrup' and is an example of the large well-filled bush that is produced by the true Rugosas. 'Sarah van Fleet' is a hybrid and very stalky, but the true Rugosas are dense and bushy. The single white, the single mauve-pink and the single crimson-purple and 'Frau Dagmar Hastrup' all have the most wonderful heps later on, whereas the doubles, 'Roseraie de l'Haÿ', 'Blanc Double de Coubert' and so on, are not so good in hep, but they have large double flowers. They are free with their fragrance too; you can smell them as you walk past. They give you this great flush of bloom in May and June, and the doubles are seldom without a flower. Those which go on developing heps push their goodness towards the heps and not so much towards the flowers, but I find that by hard pruning in mid-winter a very long flowering period is ensured. There is no *need* to prune them, they are disease proof, they are insect proof seemingly, they have autumn colour, they have a long flowering period, a delicious fragrance and foliage of marked distinction—crisp, glossy, rich green and turning bright yellow in the autumn. I often ask what more can one want, but unfortunately *Rosa rugosa* has proved very difficult to bring into the general scheme of rose hybridisation.

Here is a slide of the largest of the Rugosas, the variety 'Scabrosa'. I think it must be one of the tetraploids with extra-large leaves, extra-large flowers and again the beauty of the stamens. For great bushes, standing alone on the lawn, the true Rugosas and the famous hybrid 'Nevada' are ideal specimen shrubs.

R. gallica complicata or 'Complicata' is another of these big rounded bushes but needing a certain amount of support unless you like to see it trailing right down to the ground. It can be left as a large isolated bush or it can be trained into an apple tree as this one is in my garden in shade, only getting a little evening sunlight and clambering over the apple tree. The lovely wide bloom of 'Complicata' brings us once more back to the beauty of the single rose.

Turning now to the lax-growing roses —which embrace ramblers and climbers— I am sure you will all agree that the greatest beauty is revealed by the falling spray. A rose trained up an arch or on to a wall is a colour giver, but is only half revealing the beauty of the plant. This great graceful mound is *Rosa brunonii*; a Musk rose from the Himalayas, it is here growing at Kiftsgate Court; it is 25 feet across and something like 15 to 18 feet in height, supported by an outbuilding. I challenge any other shrub to produce more bloom than that during its flowering period. It is often called *R. moschata*, quite erroneously. *R. moschata* has no floral value whatever and is a comparatively small plant, but as I expressed briefly yesterday afternoon, it is the ancestor of the most perpetual-flowering climbers.

The best form of *R. brunonii* has been put into commerce with the name 'La Mortola' tacked on to it, because it was obtained from the famous garden on the Riviera, La Mortola, and is apt to be spoiled in severe winters. *R. brunonii*, like all other species of roses, varies and hence it is important to buy *R. brunonii* 'La Mortola', and likewise 'Kiftsgate', the finest form of *Rosa filipes*. Probably if you buy them under Brunonii or Filipes you will get perfectly good plants but those just mentioned are recognised ideal garden forms, vegetatively propagated. The 'Kiftsgate' *R. filipes* shown on my slide has grown 40 feet into a copper beech and covers 50 feet in width and some 30 feet in depth of border. It is a giant amongst roses, but it is not so easily cultivated as some of the others in this great group of Synstylae which extend in their various species from Madeira right away across to Japan and also in America. Their special characters are that they have their stigmas united into one column in the centre of the flower, and that they bear their fragrance in their stamens and not in their petals. This is most interesting, because they are the roses which allow their scent to be carried on the air more than any others. Rugosas do it a bit, but the Synstylae have this extraordinary character and that is why every now and again you get a rose which you can smell from afar; you can usually trace back to Synstylae in their ancestry. *R. filipes* 'Kiftsgate' is a wonderful rose where it will grow well. The soil at Kiftsgate is remarkably good for almost any plant, and I have never achieved anything like the majesty of the plant in that garden. So I would suggest that those of you who want something really big and easy should choose *R. longicuspis*, a very close relative, equally fragrant, nearly as vigorous, and it will thrive in a variety of positions and soils. This *R. longicuspis* is growing in my neighbour's pear tree. I didn't realise how clever I was when I gave a neighbour, who was a keen budding gardener, a 'Kiftsgate' and a plant of *R. longicuspis* to plant in his very large pear trees; he lived on the south side of me, and as luck would have it the wind has blown all the trails through to my side. So there is a point for you, be generous with your Synstylae roses, give them to your neighbours as Christmas presents providing they live on the south side! This plant is, I think, 7 years old and it has reached 18 feet. I have one growing into an oak which has achieved 25 feet already; it is a highly satisfactory rose amongst these types and here is a close-up of the single creamy-white flowers; they have unforgettable fragrance and shiny red heps later on.

This is 'Wedding Day', a similar rose raised by Sir Frederick Stern, a picture of whose garden I shall show you in a moment. It is a very good hybrid of equal vigour, but has the slight disadvantage of developing pink spotting after rain when the flowers are going over.

'Kew Rambler' is seldom seen, but it is still grown at Kew. It is one of a few hybrids of *Rosa soulieana* which again is a Synstylae, and it brings light pink into this big group of creamy-white roses, together with the same fragrance and the greyish foliage of *Rosa soulieana* itself. It is not quite so vigorous as the others I have shown you and is just a strong growing rambler, suitable for climbing into your old apple trees. I so often get letters saying, "I want a Kiftsgate Filipes and a Longicuspis to grow into my old apple trees", and I have to write back and say, "Well, it would be quite useless, because in five years you wouldn't see an apple tree at all". But the strong-growing rambling varieties like 'Albéric Barbier', 'Kew Rambler', 'Francis E. Lester' and so on are all very suitable for small garden trees.

'Bobbie James' comes between the two in size. This is, as you see, semi-double, with the same fragrance from the enormous crop of bloom, and superb foliage.

This next picture is of my own pear tree with a rose that we call 'Paul's Himalayan Musk Rambler'; I'm not at all sure about the nomenclature—I found the name in one of Paul's catalogues once, but have never been able to find it again, although I am convinced it is there. But this was a rose given to me some years ago; it is an excessively strong rambler with blush pink double flowers on thread-like stalks, and may well be a hybrid of *R. filipes*. I had a disaster with this rose. I have been in my present garden for twenty years and for the first ten years this pear tree produced no fruit at all. So I decided to plant this rose to grow into the tree. The rose grew rampantly, creating a superb display and at once the pear tree started fruiting. The irony of it is that the pear turned out to be 'Doyenne du Comice', which in my estimation is the only pear worth eating, but now it is impossible to gather them! Here is a close-up of a spray; this is in its full beauty or just going over at the moment, whereas *R. longicuspis* is still in bud. *R. longicuspis* is the last to flower of these and you can have quite a succession of these very vigorous roses in trees.

Here is the late Sir Frederick Stern's garden at Worthing, made in a chalk pit, and I thought it would interest you to know that the Synstylae roses seed themselves and grow in the pure chalk wonderfully well. There is no name for this plant; it is probably a hybrid of *R. longicuspis*, but it is an example of a Synstylae rose growing in absolutely pure chalk. So don't despair, those of you who have to garden in such untoward conditions.

Now we come to just a few of the prostrate roses suitable for ground cover. *Rosa wichuraiana* is a well-known rose, from the hybridising point of view; also in America it is used a great deal to cover graves as a ground cover and is known as the Memorial Rose. It is practically evergreen, completely prostrate, practically thornless, it doesn't flower until August and is a sweetly scented Synstylae rose like the others we have been looking at. I think it is one of the ideal ground-cover plants. For the foreground of a broad shrub border, or on the outskirts of a woodland garden or wild garden, it is ideal. It has been used a great deal to produce hybrids like 'Dorothy Perkins' and all the rest of the ramblers. Those I'm not going to concern myself with today, but I want to show you two of its hybrids which are ideal ground-covering shrubs. 'Max Graf', which has achieved fame in other directions, is one of the best; it is the only good pink among the true ground-covers. It will root and colonise as it grows, mounding itself up to about 4 or 5 feet, and will extend as far as you let it. Impenetrable, prickly of course, and with these lovely single flowers.

The other one is *Rosa paulii*. This is a hybrid with one of the old-fashioned roses, and has this white original form and also a pink sport called *R. paulii rosea*. The sport doesn't grow quite so densely, but it is nevertheless a good ground-cover, and I have no weeds under either of them. *R. paulii* will get up to 5 or 6 feet and very often has a large second crop in August and September. I remember reading that *Rosa multiflora* in the United States was described for roadside planting as "goat-tight, bull-strong and horse-high". I would say that *R. paulii* was proof against intrusion from anything less than an elephant. It is excessively prickly and dense, and is a wonderful plant for covering those big slopes which are so difficult to mow.

My last slide shows you *Rosa chinensis mutabilis*, the one that we looked at before in our borders at Sunningdale. This is an extraordinary rose in every way. Nobody knows its exact origin; it is traced back to Italy. Its buds are flame-orange, it opens to chamois-yellow flowers, and on the second day they turn to coppery pink, and the third or fourth day they turn to coppery crimson. They are single, and are produced in an endless succession. On our nursery, which is pretty cold, it doesn't often achieve more than 4 feet, and in a severe winter gets rather severely spoilt,

but like a floribunda it comes up from the ground with ever increasing numbers of shoots, flowering on the old wood and on the new. This plant has never been pruned, and you can see what it does. At Kiftsgate Court on good soil, five or six hundred feet up in the Cotswolds, in nevertheless a sheltered garden, it achieves something like 8 feet across and 8 feet in height, and is the most superb rose for almost any colour scheme. The general effect is something like that of the old Roman terracotta, which blends with almost anything that you put with it. It is a perpetual-flowering shrub rose of ageless charm and much garden value, and fittingly ends this review of their many assets.

Rose Viruses

Chairman: Professor L. Broadbent, Bath University of Technology

PROFESSOR J. COLHOUN
University of Manchester
Rose Viruses—The Present State of Knowledge

Evidence of the existence of a graft transmissible chlorosis of the rose was provided in France as long ago as 1863. Little further progress was made in the study of rose viruses until about 40 years ago. As a result of the information accumulated up to the present it may be suggested that about eight different viruses cause diseases of roses.

A considerable amount of the information which has become available has been based on symptoms. We have learned, however, that symptoms may vary greatly during the growing season of the rose, and they may not be the same on different varieties and species of ROSA. Symptoms may appear on young leaves and disappear as the leaves become older. Plants which show symptoms at certain times may show no symptoms at other times. It is clear that environmental conditions have a substantial effect on the symptoms of at least certain virus diseases of the rose. Added to this is the fact that roses infected with viruses may show symptoms which are not very far removed from diseases caused

by non-infectious agents. For example, we have the group of diseases caused by deficiencies and toxicities of various elements. Moreover, such symptoms may also be associated with soil conditions, for example, soil moisture and no doubt also with other causes. It follows then that diagnosis of virus diseases on the basis of symptom expression alone is difficult and dangerous in practice. Indeed, exact diagnosis must depend on the identification of the causal virus. This may be done by studying the characteristic reactions of a range of herbaceous plants when inoculated with the virus, or by applying serological techniques. The electron microscope may be employed in the examination of the virus particles.

Very considerable difficulties have arisen in trying to identify rose viruses, for they have proved very difficult to transmit from roses to other plants by mechanical means. These difficulties have now been overcome to a considerable extent so that some viruses can be transmitted mechanically to a number of herbaceous plants; they can be purified so that their properties can be studied and they can be examined in the electron microscope. These advances also permit serological techniques to be employed in identification, and indeed serology offers a most useful tool in determining the virus entity which causes a disease. At this point it may be mentioned that serology has its basis on the fact that when a virus is injected into an animal such as a rabbit, an antibody to that particular virus is produced in the blood of the rabbit so that an antiserum can be prepared and this will then react with the virus initially injected into the rabbit.

Rose Mosaic

This is the name now given to the disease originally described as infectious chlorosis. The symptoms as first described in North America by White (1932) relate to those appearing on a selection of hybrid tea varieties where the plants were dwarfed, but the degree of dwarfing depended on the variety, the severity of infection and the environment. Buds were often imperfect on short stems and bleached. On 'Madame Butterfly' the petals were almost white instead of the normal light pink, tinted with gold at the base. Leaves were variously distorted with the midrib often bent and twisted. Leaflets showed chlorotic areas, especially along the midrib, which causes the leaflets to pucker and ruffle. Usually all leaflets of a leaf showed symptoms, but sometimes one leaflet was free from symptoms.

Workers following White have divided mosaic into different types of disease. For example, Thomas & Massey (1939) distinguished rose mosaics 1, 2 and 3.

Mosaic 1. This is regarded as the typical mosaic of White, with symptoms largely as described above. Some varieties in the field showed pale bands and lines on the leaves, but in general the disease symptoms were more prominent under glass.

Mosaic 2. More conspicuous chlorotic bands and blotches were present on leaves of var. 'Hollywood' than caused by Mosaic 1, and occasionally leaf distortion occurred.

Mosaic 3. Symptoms were more severe than those caused by Mosaic 2, but there was a tendency towards the formation of broad chlorotic blotches on the leaves with a decrease in the occurrence of lines and rings. Sometimes a conspicuous "oak leaf" pattern was produced with not infrequently part, or the whole of the leaf exhibiting a pronounced clearing of the veins.

Some workers grouped Mosaics 2 and 3 together as Rose Yellow Mosaic.

Recently in New Zealand, Fry (1967) has referred to the following three types of symptoms belonging to the rose mosaic group:

Vein banding with creamy-white or yellow bands bordering the leaf veins, both primary and secondary or sometimes only on the fine veins near the leaf margin. Symptoms are only found on leaves formed in spring and autumn. No reduction in plant vigour was noted.

Line pattern with symptoms produced throughout the season. These appear on leaves as pale green, creamy white or yellowish wavy lines, broad bands, spots, ringspots or blotches. Reduction of plant vigour was associated with these symptoms. When symptoms of this type were recorded in England in the Lea Valley by Fletcher & Kingham (1962), they reported stem necrosis occurring directly beneath the developing flower bud and causing death of the bud before the flower opened. Prolific development of the lateral buds accompanied bud death so that affected bushes could readily be picked out by this excessive growth.

Chlorotic mottle appearing throughout the growing season. The mottle is formed by creamy-white areas varying in size from small spots to large blotches, with puckering of the centre of the leaf blades and crinkling of the margins. It may be suggested that chlorotic mottle may correspond to Mosaic 1 of Thomas & Massey.

In recent years suggestions have been put forward that rose mosaic is related to viruses infecting fruit trees, for example, *Prunus* necrotic ringspot virus and also other ringspot viruses. It has been shown that when buds from roses exhibiting symptoms of mosaic are placed in certain varieties of flowering cherry the same necrotic reaction occurs as with *Prunus* necrotic ringspot. It cannot be accepted, however, from evidence such as this that the virus in the rose is the same as *Prunus* necrotic ringspot virus.

Recently it has been found possible to transmit viruses of the mosaic type from the rose to herbaceous hosts and then to purify the virus and carry out serological tests. The results of such work makes us even more cautious about accepting the relationship between the rose mosaic virus (or viruses) and *Prunus* necrotic ringspot virus, but they should help us to understand better the relationships between viruses occurring in the rose and in fruit trees as well as other ringspot viruses.

It has been stated by Halliwell & Milbrath (1962) that, as a result of their work in North America, they identified a virus from roses showing mosaic which by serological methods was established to be Tomato ringspot virus. Indeed they differentiated by serological methods four strains of the rose mosaic virus related to Tomato ringspot virus. Moreover, by examination in the electron microscope they showed that the particles of the rose mosaic virus were of the same size as those of the Tomato ringspot virus.

Against this evidence of the relationship between the rose mosaic virus and Tomato ringspot virus we have to place the results of a very critical study published by Fulton (1967) also working in the U.S.A. Fulton was successful in isolating in pure form a virus from roses showing symptoms which Thomas and Massey perhaps would have related to Mosaic 2 and 3. By serology he showed very clearly that this virus was *not* related to Tomato ringspot virus.

Fulton also showed that, in California, roses infected with *Prunus* necrotic ringspot virus show symptoms which do not differ from those shown by roses infected with his isolate of rose mosaic virus. He distinguishes the *Prunus* necrotic ringspot very clearly from the rose mosaic virus in serological tests. He considered that these two viruses have a small proportion of

common antigens, but since they have similar host ranges and symptom expression on herbaceous indicators it will be necessary to check all isolates serologically, and to do this in a very critical manner. In view of the evidence presented we cannot conclude that rose mosaic is uniformly caused by the *Prunus* necrotic ringspot or Tomato ringspot viruses, and we shall have to await the outcome of more work before this relationship is resolved. There is no doubt, however, that *Prunus* necrotic ringspot virus and Tomato ringspot virus do occur naturally in roses and cause symptoms which would be included under rose mosaic.

Arabis mosaic virus

This virus has recently been shown to be present in England on the varieties 'Masquerade' and 'Jiminy Cricket'. The infected plants of 'Masquerade' showed chlorotic ring spots and vein mottling on the foliage and a reduction in plant vigour. On 'Jiminy Cricket' symptoms were confined to a faint vein mottling on the young foliage which disappeared as the leaves matured.

Strawberry latent ringspot virus

At the same time as he reported the occurrence of *Arabis* mosaic virus in roses, Cammack (1966) also reported that Strawberry latent ringspot virus occurred naturally in roses in England on the varieties 'Ena Harkness', 'Sultane', 'Super Star' and 'Peace'. Symptom expression varied considerably with variety but, in the plants tested, infection was associated with a distinct yellow vein mottle on the young foliage, strapping and reduction in size of the leaflets and loss of vigour.

Both Strawberry latent ringspot virus and *Arabis* mosaic virus are soil-borne viruses transmitted by an eelworm. This must not, of course, lead us to imagine that they cannot be transmitted also by the use of infected rootstocks or infected buds.

Streak

This disease was reported as occurring in the U.S.A. in 1933 on a wide variety of roses.

The following three types of symptoms are reported:

1. Brownish rings and brown vein banding in fully expanded leaves, usually accompanied by brownish or greenish, often water-soaked, ring patterns on stems.

2. Green senescence designs similar to the brown patterns which often appear on leaves prior to their being prematurely abscissed.

3. A yellowish-green vein banding in certain hybrid multiflora roses, usually accompanied by greenish water-soaked rings or dull-brownish rings in the canes.

Dark colourations may, according to Schmelzer (1967) occur on the rachis, on the main veins of leaflets and on the stipules.

When streak-infected buds were set in canes of 'Madame Butterfly' and certain other varieties, the stock turned black and necrotic above the inserted bud soon after union had been established, and the distal parts of the stock died. As with rose mosaic, field diagnosis of streak is difficult because symptoms may be masked in some varieties. Like rose mosaic virus, Streak can be transmitted by budding or grafting.

Wilt or Dieback

This disease was reported as being epidemic in Australia when first recorded there by Grieve (1931). Affected plants had brittle leaves which appeared incurved and crowded together on the petiole. Defoliation began at the tips of the stem and progressed steadily downwards, leaves turning pale yellow and then brown before dropping off. The remaining stem decayed, becoming translucent yellowish green with the base turning brownish-black within a few hours of the leaves abscissing. Temporary recovery sometimes occurred but eventually the plant withered and died.

This disease is not believed to occur in Europe or the United States.

Rose colour break

Although there are many instances of colour break in flowers caused by virus infection, that in tulips being well known in the 17th century, there are few references to colour breaking in roses. There appear

to be only two records of transmission of colour break to a rose variety which normally has self-coloured flowers. One of these records refers to the light red flowered var. 'Maria Enriqueta' which produced only variegated red and pink flowers when grafted with buds from a plant which produced variegated flowers. The other record came from New Zealand in 1966 where colour breaking occurred on 'Queen Elizabeth' and 'Super Star'. On infected 'Queen Elizabeth' bushes the flowers failed to open normally and the petals were crimped at their outer margins. The petals showed areas of white, pink and deep rose with a distinct tinge of green on the outer petals. This condition has been successfully transmitted by budding.

This brief and general review shows how unsatisfactory is our present state of knowledge of rose virus diseases. With substantial advances in the techniques used in such studies, considerable advances should now be possible.

REFERENCES

CAMMACK, R. H. (1966). Soil-borne viruses in roses. *Pl. Path.* **15**, 46–48.

FLETCHER, J. T. and KINGHAM, H. G. (1962). Rose line pattern virus. *Pl. Path.* **11**, 92.

FRY, P. R. (1967). Virus diseases of roses. *New Zealand Gardener*, **24**, 267–268.

FULTON, R. W. (1967). Purification and serology of rose mosaic virus. *Phytopathology*, **57**, 1197–1201.

GRIEVE, B. J. (1931). Rose wilt and dieback. A virus disease of roses occurring in Australia. *Australian J. exptl. Biol. Med. Sci.*, **8**, 107–121.

HALLIWELL, R. S. and MILBRATH, J. H. (1962). Isolation and identification of Tomato ringspot virus associated with rose plants and rose mosaic virus. *Pl. Dis. Reptr.*, **46**, 555–557.

SCHMELZER, K. (1967). Die Strickelkrankheit der Rose (Rose streak) in Europa. *Phytopath. Z*, **58**, 92–95.

THOMAS, H. E. and MASSEY, L. M. (1939). Mosaic disease of the rose in California. *Hilgardia*, **12**, 647–663.

WHITE, R. P. (1932). Chloroses of the rose. *Phytopathology*, **22**, 53–69.

R. R. FROST
University of Manchester
Methods Used in the Study of Rose Viruses

Professor Colhoun has summarised the present day state of our knowledge about viruses in roses. As he has pointed out, really we know very little about the viruses that are present in roses in this country, and we know even less about their effects on the growth and development of rose bushes.

We have just begun a programme of research at Manchester University into the virus diseases of roses, and we thought it would be interesting for you to hear of what is involved in the investigation of virus diseases.

We have to start off, of course, by catching our viruses, so for the past year we have been collecting plants from all over the country which we thought from their symptoms might be virus-infected. We have collected whole plants and cuttings; the bushes we plant in our experimental grounds at Jodrell Bank in Cheshire, while the cuttings have been rooted and grown in an insect-proof glasshouse under extremely clean conditions to prevent spread of the viruses from plant to plant.

The first step with each of these diseased plants is to prove that the disease is caused by a virus, and that it is not due to any other physiological disturbance caused by unfavourable soil conditions, or chemical herbicides, fungicides, etc. To prove this we must be able to transmit the virus from the diseased plant to a healthy plant and get the same symptoms in the experimentally infected plant as in the original naturally diseased plant.

The type of symptoms in roses that we know or believe to be caused by viruses are varied. Some are obvious; one can hardly miss seeing bright yellow vein bandings which some plants show on the older leaves (as shown in the 1967 *Rose Annual*, p. 105). In the early stages of infection, however, even this may be less conspicuous. We frequently find what we call "line pattern" symptoms. These may vary from bright yellow zig-zag lines a

short distance in from the edge of the leaf, to much fainter green lines barely discernible. There may be regular yellow stripes across the leaf, or there may be diffuse yellow blotches on the leaves. Most of the plants showing these symptoms often do not seem to be obviously suffering any loss in vigour—they grow and flower quite well—but only detailed comparison will tell us whether there are subtle effects on growth.

Marked reductions in growth are caused by some viruses, the infected plants being stunted with small misshapen leaves, sometimes with faint green or yellow flecks.

Even this first step of transmitting the virus to a healthy plant and getting reproducible symptoms may be difficult, because viruses differ in their infectiousness. Some can be easily sap-transmitted; that is, by taking an infected leaf, grinding it up, and rubbing the infected sap onto healthy leaves we can infect the healthy plants through the minute wounds made while rubbing the leaves. Other viruses are much more difficult; they may be unstable, fragile and become damaged when the infected leaf is ground up, releasing the virus from its sheltered environment within the plant cells. We can often add various protective chemicals to the leaves during the grinding process to minimise these effects. With yet other viruses it may be impossible to transmit them by these methods, and we may have to either graft infected buds or stems onto healthy plants and watch for the spread of the disease into the healthy stems and leaves, or use the animal vectors, insects, nematodes, etc. which may be responsible for spreading the virus in nature.

There are roughly 3–400 different types of plant virus known. When I say types, some people would call each type a species of virus. Each type or species exists in many different strains or varieties, as do most other organisms. Related strains possess certain characters in common by which they are grouped together into one type, but in other ways they differ, and frequently the difference is in the type of symptoms they produce in an infected plant.

Some viruses will infect only the genus of plants in which they are found, but many will infect all sorts of other plants besides the one from which they were originally isolated. At least one virus will infect over 400 species of plant in widely differing families. The symptoms that a virus causes in these different plants will, of course, vary from virus to virus and with environmental conditions such as temperature and light, but over the years the symptoms caused by the known viruses in certain 'indicator' or 'test' plants have been recorded, enabling us to compare the symptoms caused by our unknown virus with those recorded by previous workers for known viruses. The plants which have become popular as "indicator" plants are such things as tobaccos, cucumber, dwarf french bean, and species of *Chenopodium*.

So we attempt to transmit each virus from the diseased rose plant to a range of indicator plants—we use about 25 different species—and from these results we may be able to say that our virus appears similar to such and such a virus. On the other hand, it may be totally different from anything previously recorded, and then we do not know whether it is a completely new type of virus or simply a new strain of a known type of virus.

To identify viruses conclusively, we cannot rely simply on the symptoms they give on these herbaceous plants; we have to use other techniques. Most plant viruses that have been discovered so far are of one of two basic shapes; they are either spherical or rod-shaped, and different viruses may vary from one another in their length or diameter. I said *may* vary in shape and size, because two different types of virus may be exactly the same shape and size! These virus particles consist simply of a filament of nucleic acid which carries the genetic characters of the virus, similar to the chromosomes of plants and animals, surrounded by a protective coat of protein. Spherical viruses

have the nucleic acid coiled up inside a protein shell; rod-shaped viruses have their nucleic acid in a spiral up the centre of a tube of protein. When a virus particle enters a cell through a wound, the protective protein coat is removed and the nucleic acid takes over the command of part of the cell's physiological processes and instructs the infected cell to make more virus. These new virus particles then move to neighbouring cells and repeat the process, and so on. It is this disturbance of the cell's normal processes that causes the symptoms of disease.

The virus particles are very small, from 20–1,000 millimicrons in size (1 millimicron = 1 millionth of a millimetre), so one can see them only in an electron microscope which magnifies them up to one quarter of a million times, using a beam of electrons to produce an image of the virus on a fluorescent screen. So by looking at the sap of infected plants in the electron microscope and measuring the size of the virus particles we may get a further clue to the identity of the virus.

The ultimate technique in identification is that of serology, where we inject the virus into a rabbit and, as with all foreign proteins injected into an animal, antibodies are produced which react with and precipitate the foreign protein, in this case our virus. If the antibodies from the blood of an injected rabbit are mixed in a test tube with the same type of virus as was injected into the rabbit, then a specific white precipitate is formed which can be readily observed, and which tells us that our virus is of the same type. Antibodies against one type of virus will not react with other types of virus, therefore, once we have built up a collection of antisera to different known viruses, we have an excellent method of identifying viruses. The rabbits, I might add, suffer only the discomfort of being inoculated with the virus, and of donating small quantities of blood at intervals; no disease is caused in the rabbit by plant viruses.

Now assuming we have identified our virus, and as you can see this can be quite a lengthy process in itself, what do we do next? Well, we now want to find out more about the disease itself; we want to know what the effects of environment, temperature, light, etc., are on the expression of the symptoms. We know that symptoms vary during the growing season—which viruses produce what symptoms at what time of the year? How do the symptoms produced by any one virus differ in different varieties of rose? Are some varieties more resistant or more susceptible than others? What are the effects of having two different viruses in the same plant?

We also want to know the effects of each virus on the vigour, life, and flowering ability of the plants, and the effects of infection early in a plant's life compared to infection late in the life of the plant. So we have to set up trials of healthy and infected plants; initially we do this in the glasshouse where we can control the environmental conditions; later we shall do this in the field.

Finally we come to the problem of studying how these viruses are spread in nature. If a virus we isolate is a known virus, then somebody else may have found out already how it is spread. If it is a new virus then we may have to start from scratch and look for whatever is spreading the virus. It may be insects—aphids, leaf hoppers or beetles; it may be soil nematodes or soil fungi; or it may be man himself grafting infected buds onto healthy stocks or *vice-versa*. Having found a vector that will spread the virus in the laboratory we have to assess its importance in the field.

When we have finally amassed all this knowledge, we shall then be in a very strong position to control these diseases effectively, about which Dr Cadman is to say more later. This preliminary work may take months or years, but eventually we hope that the results of our studies will find their way back to you, the rose growers, so that we may all enjoy healthier roses.

DR C. H. CADMAN
Scottish Horticultural Research Institute
Control of Rose Viruses

The main reason I felt able to accept your secretary's invitation is the fact that no one really knows anything very much about rose viruses, far less how to control them. Whilst this is not exactly the best of reasons for occupying your time it compels me to restrict myself to generalities based largely on experience with viruses of other crops and which may, I hope, have some relevance to the problems one can anticipate with roses.

It would be surprising if roses—having been cultivated and propagated for so long —were not riddled with viruses. For a parallel one has only to turn to fruit trees and compare the ignorance and complacency of 20 years ago with the extent of modern knowledge and the elaborate apparatus now needed to secure and maintain virus-free material. It has always seemed to me that much of the folk-lore of rose-growing—the superior performance of maidens and the decline and eventual disappearance of once popular and vigorous varieties, for example—must find its explanation in virus infection. Very likely the major problems lie in the detection of viruses that produce no obvious symptoms rather than with the few, about which a little is known and which cause conspicuous effects on the growth and performance of plants.

Horticulturally roses are somewhat comparable to fruit trees in so far as the plants are dual entities—a combination of stock and scion. But there are important differences. Rose stocks are, for the most part, raised from seed and not vegetatively propagated like fruit tree rootstocks. Also there is a much more rapid turnover in varieties. I would not care to guess at the rate of introduction of novelties to the rose trade, but it far exceeds that of fruit trees. Leaving aside preferences for old and well-tried varieties, the flood of new seedlings year by year tends to oust the old so that few varieties, unless they remain vigorous, persist for very long. This has two important implications for control. First, we must be sure that our rootstocks are virus free. Secondly, we need to work towards the ideal objective of virus-free scion material. Most viruses are not seed-borne so that seedlings from infected plants start life virus free. It so happens that two of the groups of viruses known to infect rose—viruses of the necrotic ringspot type and viruses transmitted by nematodes—are very commonly transmitted through seeds of infected plants. Whilst I know of no efforts that have been made to find out, it would be reasonable to assume that these viruses are seed-borne in rose because they are so in other rosaceous plants. Thus, seed sources for rootstock production must be plants selected for freedom from virus and no doubt this specification would tie in well with the need for standardisation of sources of supply. Collections of wild seed, if this is done to any extent, or from old-established hedges will not, in the future, be good enough.

Where stocks are propagated vegetatively, the risks of producing virus-infected material are, of course, greater. Propagation from indexed and virus-free material will be the ideal, but this depends on progress in the techniques of identifying virus infection and the development of something akin to the programme of virus-free rootstock production which has been developed for tree fruits.

Stocks may contract infection through being planted in soil containing nematode-transmitted viruses. Roses are good hosts for *Xiphinema diversicaudatum*, the nematode that transmits arabis mosaic and strawberry latent ringspot viruses. The second of these seems particularly common in roses and has been found infecting rugosa stocks. These viruses have wide host ranges and are quite likely to occur in land that has never grown roses before. In the U.S.A. *Xiphinema americanum* is a virus vector of some consequence because of its wide distribution and ability to transmit tomato ringspot, a virus also known to infect rose. Whilst the best

remedy is to avoid planting rose stocks in areas where the viruses and vector nematodes occur—and this demands a pre-planting check on samples of soil—soil fumigants, in particular D.D., are reasonably effective means of freeing soils from contamination. Roses may possibly be subject to other nematode-transmitted viruses and, of course, to other viruses of whose mode of spread we are ignorant.

The known hazards of rose stock production apply with equal force to the production of seedlings and the propagation of scion material. It would, I think, be a counsel of perfection to expect breeders to take the meagre facts into account. But the fact remains that both necrotic ringspot viruses, of the type which causes rose mosaic, and the nematode-borne viruses, arabis mosaic and strawberry latent ringspot, are carried in the pollen of plants, so that a proportion of seedlings raised from crosses may in fact be virus infected from the start. If and how frequently this occurs one just does not know. It is, however, a possibility of which breeders may not be aware.

Assuming that a seedling starts life virus free and is budded on a virus-free rootstock, is there anything we can do to prevent it becoming infected? At the moment virtually nothing; for, with the exception of the nematode-borne viruses, we do not know how any of the viruses infecting roses are transmitted and until this essential information is provided we do not know what it is we have to control. What is certain is that once plants become virus-infected, all plants propagated from them are themselves infected and there may be no easy means of ridding plants of infection. Some kinds of plants can be freed from some kinds of viruses by heat treatment and this may well be true of roses. A more sophisticated means of obtaining virus-free plants is by excising a minute portion of the stem tip and inducing this to grow into a plant by culturing it on a synthetic medium. Plants produced in this way are often free from virus although the meristem tips were taken from a virus-infected plant. However, neither of these techniques is foolproof; it is still necessary to find out whether the plants contain virus and success here depends on progress both in the knowledge of rose viruses and the techniques of detecting them. Ultimately, however, one looks towards a mother tree scheme, such as has been developed for fruit trees, where virus-free plants of standard varieties are maintained in a state of virus freedom and serve as sources of clean bud wood.

This, however, is an expensive exercise and the problem with an ornamental crop like the rose is that of striking a balance between what is desirable and what is feasible. With the vast number and comparatively rapid turnover of varieties, it would obviously be a herculean and impracticable task to produce and maintain virus-free stocks of all but a handful of prominent and well-tried varieties. When the time comes it will be very much up to the industry to make the choice of varieties which seem worth perpetuating.

This is perhaps taking the gloomiest prospect. Roses may be subject to fewer viruses and these may be easier to control than I would predict, but if this proves to be so I for one shall be surprised. At the outset of this talk I promised little in the way of constructive thought and I can only reiterate that the factual basis for a logical approach to control of viruses in rose simply does not exist as yet. The commonsense precautions one *can* recommend are three: choice of healthy stocks for rootstock production, avoidance of planting in virus-infected soil, and careful selection of symptom-free plants as sources of bud wood.

Informal Gardening with Roses
Chairman: Dr A. Dick

D. RUSTON
Woodbridge, South Australia
Roses in Borders

I think before I get on to the subject of roses in borders, I should say a little bit about my local growing conditions. I live in a hot, dry part of Australia. The average rainfall is about 9 inches per annum; we get no black spot, no rust, very little mildew and six flushes of blooms per year. I gather that John Van Barnveld from California has seven flushes per year and I am wondering just how he gets that extra flush in on me. As far as growing roses is concerned I grow all mine in borders and not in beds. I find in our growing conditions the hard thing is to keep the bush low. I have never seen roses pruned so low as they are in England and on the Continent; I think the effect of the bedding roses is absolutely superb, but I just find that for a bedding rose you must look down on them, mustn't you? And I have trouble. You really need a step-ladder to look down on them because they are so much higher than you are!

Now as far as roses in borders in England are concerned I have seen several magnificent borders of roses, first at Regent' Park and secondly at St Albans. I thought both were magnificent for colour blending and general layout. I haven't been fortunate enough to go to Sunningdale as yet, but I'll be there as quickly as I can after seeing Mr Thomas' magnificent slides this morning.

I think there are probably four types of rose borders. Firstly, a border entirely of roses; secondly a border of roses mixed with herbaceous plants; thirdly a border of roses with shrubs mixed with them, and fourthly a border of old-fashioned roses. I think it is better to keep your old-fashioned types in one border and your moderns in another. Now to me a rose border must have a foreground; I think the most suitable foreground is a lawn. A rose border, to be a border, must have a background also. That is where trees, shrubs, climbers and species come in so handy. I think a border should be several rows deep to get that massed effect, and I think almost all borders are viewed more from one side than another, as opposed to beds, where of course you walk right round.

I think if you have a border, too, it should lead somewhere, either to an archway or to a beautiful view in the distance or to a fountain or a garden seat. I think that you must have some interest at the end of the border.

Now dealing with roses in borders by themselves, I think the most important thing of all is grading for height. This is quite a complicated business because roses will grow far more vigorously in one part of the country than in another, but I think heights are always comparative; a low-growing bush will always be low in any part of the world, and a tall grower like 'Queen Elizabeth' or 'Buccaneer' may grow 14 feet high in some parts of the world and 4 in another, but it will still be taller than any other variety. As far as roses in borders are concerned, I do not like them too regimented; I think if you have the front row very even, followed by another row behind a little bit higher and grade up, it looks rather like a row of soldiers, but if you have some of your tall ones coming slightly forward and some of your low ones slightly back into the border, you get much more depth to your border and you get a much more interesting scheme. We find in pruning you can help this a great deal; if you have three of four rows of—say 'Circus', well you prune the front row lower than the second row, and then the second row a bit lower than the third, and so we get that tiered effect which is so important in the rose border.

We have a lot more varieties of roses we can use in the rose border than for bedding. The gaunt growers like 'Burnaby', 'Virgo', 'Vienna Charm', 'Spek's Yellow', which are always bare at the base, can be suitably hidden by the other cultivars in front and this helps enormously. For background work, of course, we can have things like Rosa moyesii, which are very very gaunt and bare to

about 6 or 7 feet, but they can be screened by the other cultivars in front. The foreground planting is quite easy; we have varieties like 'Pinky', 'China Doll', 'Meteor', and Mr Harkness' wonderful 'Little Lady', which I saw for the first time the other day and was most excited about. We can use miniatures for the front row, but I do not know whether they always associate so well; they look a little small compared with the background, but of course, it all depends on the amount of room you have to play with.

I think the middle of the border is quite easy, as there are so many varieties that are suitable. The background, I think, is quite easy too; you have tall varieties like 'Queen Elizabeth', 'Golden Giant', and 'Diamant' and you have all the pillars and all the species as well.

Now I think the next most important thing in the rose border is colour blending, which I feel is absolutely superbly done in Regent's Park. You go through pink to mauve, to soft creamy-yellow, to white, to red, to orange, to yellow and then back to red; it is a superb piece of colour blending, and I think that is very important. I think perhaps, if you have plenty of room, the most satisfactory way of blending roses in the border is to keep all your bright hot colours in one border, and your pinks, your mauves, your purples and your whites in another, and use them with grey and white foliage and you get a pleasing effect that is very subtle. All the bright colours are lovely together, but if you are going to mix them together, if you are going to mix—say—bright purple with 'Super Star' and some of the deep magenta pinks you can have a clashing colour scheme, which might look very nice in Mexico, but I don't think it looks quite right with us. But of course, if you want to do things like that you can, for after all your border is your own, and you should plant it as you want it.

Well that is all I have to say about roses alone in borders. I think when we come to roses planted with other things, such as herbaceous perennials, we have wonderful scope. The roses here have to stand by themselves, and I think they should be far more lightly pruned than they would be for bedding. You get great big arching shrubs of varieties like 'Queen Elizabeth' and 'Madame A. Meilland' ('Peace'). Any of the tall growers are marvellous, and just about all the Kordesii hybrids and all the big bushes of floribundas are absolutely wonderful in the herbaceous border. Be careful that you can spray them quite easily. I think if you are going to have a very dense border it is very important that you can get your spraying material at the back of the border as well as the front. You have such wonderful foliage material in England—all the hostas and the various thistles, the grey foliage and the white foliage—you have wonderful material for a stunning mixed border with roses as your most important feature.

Now we come to roses amongst shrubs. I think if the shrubs are fairly vigorous the roses must be very vigorous, or they will have too much competition from the shrubs. Roses and shrubs grow very well with me, but I have good growing conditions and very fertile clay loam soil, and

they seem to associate very well together. If you have very big trees in your shrub border you could be in trouble with root competition, but we find that if you plant your trees and your roses together and they grow up together it will be far more satisfactory as far as the roses are concerned, than trying to plant a rose near a well-established tree; that can be very difficult.

As far as old-fashioned roses in borders are concerned, we saw those magnificent slides of Mr Thomas' this morning and I don't think I can say very much about them. They were some of the finest slides I have ever seen. That subtle blending of colour, that blending of shapes and forms and sizes was superbly done, and I think probably the less I say about that the better. Mr Thomas is, of course, the great authority in the world on the old roses, and the pictures of the old roses in borders were so good. What can be of great help in the border of old roses are some of the lovely autumn tints on some of the rugosas and the wonderful showy heps on a lot of varieties.

BRIGADIER C. E. LUCAS PHILLIPS
Roses with Other Plants

My gardening background, I am sure, is pretty much the same as that of the more ordinary mortals. I didn't start gardening until, due to a rapidly rising family, I had acquired a house. I then *had* to garden. I started off, however, and have remained ever since, what you might call a catholic gardener. I love nearly all flowers and I had a garden of about 1¼ acres, in which I could grow a great many things that I liked, including quite a lot of roses.

I started off by reading all the books and all the authorities and I followed what my masters told me to do. I grew my hybrid tea roses, and indeed most other roses, in a very formalistic manner, bed by bed, spaced out according to what the authorities told me, and I grew some very nice roses. I used to take great care in producing beautiful blooms. That was forty-odd years ago, when we used to grow roses

such as 'Général Jacqueminot', 'Mrs Wemyss Quin', 'General MacArthur' and 'Emma Wright', that lovely little dwarf orange rose, one of the very first orange bedding roses there ever was. This was a time when the hybrid tea had not yet asserted its ascendancy over the hybrid perpetual, and we were still growing a lot of hybrid perpetuals and pernetianas produced by Pernet-Ducher.

As the years went by things changed and there was a war, and one came back to very different social conditions. To cut a long story short, about ten years ago my wife and I decanted ourselves into a cottage, with the smallest garden we have ever had; it extends only to about a third of an acre. I may say my wife chose the house; I wanted another one which had about one acre of woodland and a little stream running through it. I rubbed my hands and said: "Ah! Asiatic primulas, rhododendrons, camellias and all that". But it was the feminine choice of house that decided the issue, and being, as I say, a very catholic gardener, I had to ask myself: How on earth am I going to grow in this very small space all the things that I want? Also, how am I, with the years increasing as they do, going to create a garden where I shall not only break my back, but perhaps my heart as well? So I thought out a plot very carefully of how I could cram everything into this little garden, and give myself no more work than was necessary when I was eighty; that was the basis of my planning. I tried several experiments, some of which failed.

Obviously for me roses had to predominate and anything else that I wanted to grow had to make a suitable marriage with roses. And so I conceived the idea of mixing roses with other plants all through the garden, or nearly all through, but I could not find a satisfactory answer to marrying the hybrid teas with anything else. This was purely due to the preconceived notion that I had had from way back in 1927: that you must grow hybrid teas in a formalised kind of way, that it was a sin to mix them with anything else. That was the teaching, and it still is the teaching of a great many people.

So I have never solved that problem, except that round the edges of my hybrid tea beds I do grow things like Alpine pinks, prostrate thymes and *Gentiana acaulis*, where I can grow it. You will find that it will grow at this end of the bed, but not at that end, so I keep on experimenting until I find a place where it will grow and then I leave it. And, of course, violas, especially blue violas. You can grow these, I find, amongst hybrid teas without offending any kind of aesthetic sense at all—in fact, I believe they improve the aesthetics of the garden, because you have a dainty shape, and you have in your true blues colours that roses don't provide.

With floribundas, the problem solves itself fairly easily. The basis of my planting with floribundas is to mix them with dwarf azaleas. I rather questioned my own wisdom when I started on this, but it has

in fact proved very successful. When you start mixing roses with other plants, you have got to be sure that they are plants that like the same conditions and the same treatment. Anything that you grow with roses must be capable of being mulched and fed with the same things that you apply to roses, and they must also be capable of standing the same sprays. Dwarf azaleas are ideal from this point of view, because you mulch them all, roses and azaleas alike, with manure and with peat; that is the basis of my treatment. I don't give them manure every year; I give it to them every two or three years, and in other years they have a dressing of peat with a little stimulant, plus a midsummer tonic. Together with the azaleas I include a few dwarf rhododendrons, of which 'Carmen', *impeditum* and *keleticum* have proved ideal.

My notion in this azalea–rose marriage was to have, first of all, something nice to look out upon from the house windows in winter and early spring, when to my eye a forest of naked sticks is no object of beauty at all. In a small property it is important to be able to look on a scene that pleases the eye in winter, and a lot of rose sticks do not pass the test. So the foliage of the evergreen azaleas hides all that, and you get your flush of azaleas from April until the end of May, even going on into early June, what time the taller deciduous azaleas in the background continue the theme until the roses take over. As the foliage of the roses grows, they give to the azaleas in their turn the light shade the azaleas like. So to me there seemed to be a perfect marriage, and it has worked out very well. Of course, some of these azaleas grow quite big, so you have to have strong-growing varieties or cultivars to go with them, and I find that some that grow very well indeed with the big azaleas are varieties like 'Red Dandy', which is a superb success, 'Iceberg', which grows to about five or six feet high and wide with me, 'Pink Parfait' and 'Golden Wings', a wonderful rose to grow among azaleas; it reaches five or six feet high and about six feet broad, with a constant succession of bloom.

Holland

THE INTERNATIONAL ROSE STAND at The Summer Show, 1968

England

'GALLANT' (floribunda—H.T. type)
'Super Star' × *'Barbecue'*
Raised by Alex. Dickson & Sons Ltd, N. Ireland
TRIAL GROUND CERTIFICATE 1967

Other plants that I grow among floribundas are lilies. They fill a very useful
gap, and of course, they are very diverse
in their habits and desires and you have
got to find out the spots that they like.
Some of them you can "put your shirt on"
straight away, like the mid-century hybrids. They will grow anywhere where a
daffodil will grow, and such clones as
'Enchantment' and 'Destiny' are very easy,
very beautiful and, with other lilies such
as 'Limelight', 'Thunderbolt', 'Golden
Clarion' and so on, they scent the whole
garden when you come out on a summer
evening in July. The slightly more difficult ones, like *L. auratum* and *speciosum*,
grow in the shade away from the roses,
but you can see them beyond the rose
beds; these grow among camellias and
dwarf rhododendrons.

I grow a little ground cover in these
rose–azalea beds, but rather towards the
back, with the twin objects of suppressing
weeds and providing a leafy background.
I don't know if anybody would be horri-
fied if I said that one of my favourites for
this job is the Labrador violet, *Viola
labradorica*, a little plant, four inches high,
with greeny-purple foliage and the sweetest of violet-coloured violets in spring; it
spreads like mad if it likes you, and I
suppose the purists would say that it
spreads too much, but it is one of those
things that you can easily pull out and
scrap, give to your neighbour or transplant somewhere else. It creeps about
mainly below the azaleas and we don't
let it invade the roses too much. Consequently we have very little work to do.
But if you grow that sort of thing, or any
other carpeting plant, you cannot mulch,
and you have to face that fact.

When one comes to other types of
roses, of course there is not much problem.
The old roses and the species roses can
with perfect propriety be consorted with
something else, in fact they have got to be
in a small garden. Many and diverse plants
can be used. For a ground-cover, one of
the most effective is *Gaultheria procumbens*,
only two inches high, spreading around by
underground runners. You see white
flowers, like little lily of the valley, in

spring and little red berries in the autumn.
It is evergreen and dense. If it starts to
shoot under your roses you can pull it
out, but it is a wonderful saver of labour.
G. miqueliana is choicer but not so
easy.

Things like the true geraniums, (I don't
mean pelargoniums, of course) are the
obvious answer that comes to your mind
at once for planting at the feet of tall
species or other old roses. Campanulas are
also excellent to grow with almost any
kind of rose, and almost any kind of
campanula will do, providing it is not
one of the rampant ones. *Campanula persicifolia*, the peach-leaved campanula, seeds
itself all over the garden with me in forms
of blue and white, and I let it grow
wherever it seeds itself; it grows up in the
middle of thujas; it puts itself right at the
very base of 'Paprika' and a blue spire of
Campanula persicifolia with a rose like
'Paprika' is really wonderful. You couldn't
think of it yourself, but Nature thinks of
it for you. Another kind of plant that
grows well among the old-fashioned roses
is the artemesia, particularly the beautiful
'Landbrook Silver', which is a fountain of
fine silver foliage. *Stachys olympica (lanata)*,
the old "lamb's-ear", is very acceptable, if
you keep it within bounds. Hostas always
look lovely, but their roots are terrific,
very tough and very choking, and so you
must keep them away from anything
precious, but if you can plant them a few
feet away from an old rose, they do a
very good job as weed barriers as well as
being beautiful.

Climbers haven't been mentioned so far.
There is infinite scope for growing climbers with other plants, some of which have
been covered already, not only by Mr
Ruston, but also by Mr Graham Thomas.
The little garden is just the ideal place, if
you have any trees at all, to make use of
another art of Nature. I grow *R. longicuspis*, but it doesn't behave like Mr
Thomas'; it grows on a birch tree, but,
having climbed over the lower branches,
it flops down the other side going away
from me into a horrible transformer shed
belonging to the electricity people. I have
tried several of these species. I have a

beautiful specimen of *R. gentiliana* which I may have to scrap because it is too vigorous; we now can't get by unless we almost crawl on our hands and knees, but at the present moment it is a magnificent spectacle, absolutely showered with those beautiful white blossoms which you can smell twenty yards away.

In my very small experience, the most effective of these wild climbing roses is *R. noisettiana*. That doesn't flop over other branches, it grows straight up; we had it growing up old crab trees and crab apples look pretty dowdy in summer, I think. They want a little freshening up, so I grew *R. noisettiana* up them, and again what a magnificent spectacle! You would be walking along one day towards the end of June, and you would say: "What's that white thing up there?". For there would be enormous sprays of the rose on the topmost boughs of crab apples. People going along not only stopped and looked, they used to stop and sniff; it was very pleasing. I regret to say that I had to throw it out because I had to get rid of its host and it then became a nuisance to my neighbour.

Another way of associating roses with other plants is to plant them in adjacent beds, not the same beds. There we find a terrific success in the dwarf heathers and the dwarf conifers. We have on one side of a three-foot path our rather formal hybrid teas, and on the other side a bed of mixed heathers and dwarf golden conifers, which are lovely all the year. When, from our sitting-room or dining-room, we look out in winter, we don't see the naked roses, but we do see the golden conifers and the dwarf heathers and especially we see them when the heathers are flowering from December right through until April. They are a very comforting and warming sight. We do the same thing in the front, specialising with heathers like *Erica carnea* and *mediterranea*; and, as I have an open garden in front, I'm afraid people do "stop and stare".

One or two roses that we grow and which have not been mentioned hitherto, are particularly good for mixed plantings. One is the delightful 'Réveil Dijonnais'. Many of you will know it, I am sure. It is an orange rose with a lot of red in it, and its habit is rather spreading—at least it always has been so with me—and it will bend gracefully over low herbaceous or other plants, diversifying the scene and extending one's scope for the use of roses. Some people grow it as a pillar rose, but I prefer to grow it in its natural form, and it is one of the very few roses that associate well with heathers.

JACK HARKNESS
R. Harkness & Co. Ltd
Climbing Roses

I am very glad to have the chance of speaking about climbers, because they are plants that I am extremely fond of and I think, from the gardener's point of view, there is no way in which you can spend a few shillings and get a longer and more generous reward. At the same time, although I do recognise and appreciate the advances that are being made in climbers, I think that in many respects we are still some way from what I would consider my ideal.

To me, a climber is a plant which must first of all satisfy the plantsman's desire to have beauty of growth, attractive foliage and pleasant appearance as a plant. I seem to observe nowadays that there is a tendency to say, "Well, any old angular scraggy thing with no leaves at the bottom, as long as it's got a few large flowers on it in the summer, and a few more in the autumn—can be described as an ever-blooming new miracle climber." I am dead against this.

Climbers really need selecting quite carefully according to the way that you choose to grow them. To my mind the most beautiful—those I really love myself—are the old-fashioned ones which I am for ever budding too many of at the nursery and getting ticked off by the foreman next spring when we still have about 250 'Félicité et Perpétue' left on our hands. But still, you are so fond of them that you do these silly things.

The most beautiful types to my own mind—and I am not asking anyone else to go along with me in this, just putting my own ideas—are the old Wichuraianas, and the most beautiful way of growing them is so that the whole of the plant can be seen most of the way down. And this really means, for those which are not too vigorous in growth, a pillar.

Now pillars are a glorious way to grow roses, and I would much rather myself grow pillar roses than standards. The method is merely to knock in a fairly sturdy post, and then just tie the plant to it. When you want to prune the plant, you can just shave the side shoots back close to the pillar if you are in a hurry; or if you are going to give it a thorough pruning, you can cut the whole plant from the post, thin it out and then re-tie. It is really only necessary to do this every two or three years.

I think a lot of mistakes are made in pruning these old types of climbing roses. Where there are good strong shoots, even if they are a few years old but still producing nice side shoots, I can never see the sense in taking them all out and reducing the poor plant to a few rather bare growths of the current year. If the wood is going to produce more flowers, why not leave it in?

And again with a pillar, you know where the post goes down, and sooner or later it rots or is blown over. But there is no great difficulty in knocking another one into the same place. The more particular may make more permanent arrangements.

Another way we have of growing these Wichuraiana types is in beds; this may sound rather improbable, but it has been done to provide something tall in our rose garden. We bought a cheap lot of old metal piping and second hand copper wire. I won't pretend that these are ideal materials to use, but they certainly work like a dream. We make something the

shape of a wigwam, as high as we have got a reasonable length of piping; we drill holes in the top of the piping and fix pegs at the side of the bed, running the copper wire down from the top of the pipe to the side of the bed. In this way you make a bed of rambler roses looking like a tent. This is very beautiful because there is an outward and downward slope from the top to the ground at your feet, and the flowers tend to come out absolutely looking at you.

Regarding the varieties we grow on these pillars and wigwams, I think my favourite of all, or one of them anyway, is 'François Juranville', an old rambler which came from Barbier of France in the early 1900s. It has lovely dark shiny foliage, right from the top of the plant to the base; the flowers are a clear glistening light pink, shaded yellow at the base of the petals, absolutely perfect in conjunction with the foliage, the whole thing a-shine and a-glitter and a beauty from the time that it starts growing in the spring until the foliage goes off in the winter.

And of course another thing about the Wichuraianas is that many of them have very persistent foliage. One of the very best is 'Sanders' White', which is the most marvellous plant for covering itself with flowers. Here again we have this choice, either to have something which is one mass of beauty for a few weeks, or something which is so-so for a few months. I go for the short life and the merry one, and 'Sander's White' certainly lives it; you do, incidentally, get quite a nice bonus of occasional later blooms. Again there is beautiful burnished foliage, quite small in the case of that variety, and a very pleasant scent.

Another one which is very well-known is 'Albéric Barbier', the variety we always recommend to all those people who say, "I can't grow any roses here". I have seen it flourishing in the most unlikely places, and I think it the very best rose to plant where you have a difficult position, either in shade or even on north walls.

'Dr W. Van Fleet' is very easy to manage. Handsome in foliage, and with the most glorious scent, it bears lovely light pink flowers, beautiful as cut flower material. My cousin Ena is very good on flower arrangement, and what she can do with some sprays of 'Dr W. Van Fleet' or 'New Dawn' and some perennial flowers is just "out of this world".

Then we have a variety which was mentioned yesterday, 'Crimson Shower', raised by Albert Norman. This is a good red, a very nice pillar rose because it is not too rampant, and it usually comes out with us about 20-25 July and is flowering most of the time up to the end of August.

Another old one which we still love is 'Emily Gray'. Here again, there is absolutely first-rate foliage and a very pretty shade of yellow, just slightly off yellow, almost a hint of coppery yellow in it, with very elegant buds.

And to go back to something which may seem an absolutely crazy choice, there is a little rambler rose called 'Jersey Beauty', one of the parents of 'Emily Gray'. This has very small single creamy-yellow flowers, which spangle the plant and show against the dark shiny foliage to perfection. It is very transient but beautiful.

One more in this genre is 'May Queen', a variety I never met until I saw it in the Tillotson catalogue which we have from America, and I wrote and got some budwood from them. 'May Queen' again has the attractive Wichuraiana foliage; it has a double flower, in a clear pink, a nice satisfying colour, with nothing pale about it. It has the most charming quartered form and I consider it a great variety.

I do not think that one can go wrong with this Wichuraiana strain as long as one keeps away from those mildew addicts like 'Dorothy Perkins' and 'Excelsa'. Most of them do not give you a lot of trouble from disease.

While we are discussing this sort of rose, there are a few of the old types which are not so pleasing in foliage as the Wichuraianas, but which have such beautiful flower form that one would not be without them. One of my favourites is 'Félicité et Perpétue', again with beautiful, quite small white flowers, the formation absolutely symmetrical and lovely. This has rather duller foliage, a little greyer than the dark shiny green of the Wichuraianas, but it is a very beautiful and rewarding rose to grow. It has quite a nice long flowering period and I have seen it used most effectively in our district as a wall plant.

Another one that I love, and we grow this one on pillars ourselves, is 'Zéphirine Drouhin'. This is celebrating its hundredth anniversary this year, and I do not think I need stop and tell such a distinguished audience very much about this almost thornless rose, except that its bold carmine pink colour and its lovely scent please nearly everybody who comes to our home. We have got about six or seven pillars of it, and we love it.

One more which I like to have about the place is 'Climbing Cécile Brunner'. I do not think anybody would regret planting it, not necessarily in the showplace of the garden, but where you will be passing by. It is hard to resist whipping off a finger-nail-sized buttonhole, a perfectly formed miniature of a shapely hybrid tea. It is a wonderful climbing rose to grow, and one which I think would never pall, with rather handsome foliage.

When we come to look at other sorts of climbing roses, for growing on walls, we may well want something which is a little bit stiffer, somewhat more upright and with larger flowers. I am not a great lover of climbing hybrid teas, as I think they are very often disappointing, but you do see some very lovely plants on walls flowering quite early in the summer, as you go about the country. I rarely see anything better than 'Climbing Etoile de Hollande' in established plants; 'Climbing Mrs Sam McGredy' can be very nice; 'Climbing Golden Dawn' is I think a good one, which perhaps has faded out of popularity rather sooner than it deserved. Of the newer climbing sports I think the two best I have seen are 'Climbing Sutter's Gold' and 'Climbing Isobel Harkness'. The latter is not very well known and we have never grown many of it; it sported in America, and came back to us from Armstrong's, and it certainly is quite a nice yellow hybrid tea sport.

Of the other large-flowered types

'Elegance' takes a lot of beating. The only thing that makes it an embarrassment to a nurseryman is that the customers think it is about as yellow as 'Spek's Yellow', whereas actually it is only creamy yellow, but in such a satisfying flower, so good in form, and with that nice yellow at the base. It really looks very handsome, but is difficult to train and keep under control. It makes a forest of thorns, is a terrifically strong grower and, to my mind, is the ideal rose to grow on an open post and rail fence.

We are not really terribly well off for large-flowered dark red climbers. After mentioning 'Climbing Etoile de Hollande' and 'Climbing Ena Harkness', you are soon coming down to 'Guinée'. Of course, 'Guinée' is a climbing rose which can be a great delight to people who really long for this dark blackish-crimson flower, but as a climbing plant I must say it is rather scraggy.

Then one of the roses which I should never want to be parted from is 'Mermaid' —that beautiful primrose-yellow hybrid, which does not get established very easily; we plant it on a west or south wall round our place and we now have some very nice plants.

One more of these large-flowered types that I would like to mention, because it is surprising how often it is sent to us to be identified, is 'Madame Grégoire Staechelin'. This is a large, rather floppy pink rose with frilled petals, a most delicious scent and a climber which just covers itself with bloom in the early part of the summer and gives nothing else later. But if there is a spare wall that can accommodate a 'Madame Grégoire Staechelin', well, for two or three weeks in June you are certainly going to be very thrilled with it.

Just in passing, there is another little section of climbing roses which I think is absolutely beautiful, and that is the two or three climbing miniatures that we have. Unfortunately, these are neither very well-known nor are they very popular as far as I can see, but we have been growing 'Pink Cameo' and 'Perla Rosa' in the climbing form, and these actually can be grown just on a stout bamboo cane, to make plants about 4 or 5 feet high. They flower right down to the ground; they have quite a long flowering season and are exceptionally pretty. When we were all listening to the 75 requirements of the users last night at the breeders' Symposium, I do not think anybody said anything about climbing miniatures, but this is certainly one of the objectives that we have in our breeding programme. I think a range of plants like that, which would grow up in a lovely column of flowers to about 5 feet and flower over a long period, would be absolutely marvellous. To my mind you could then throw all the standards on the fire—I would rather have climbing miniatures in the garden any day.

Of the more modern climbers we have great successes in the Kordesii types, 'Maigold', 'Parkdirektor Riggers', 'Leverkusen' and so forth. These are what I consider nice strong durable plants which are going to give the average person a lot of satisfaction. I must confess that, apart from 'Maigold' (because its scent, colour, foliage and thorny stems are so attractive) they seem utilitarian to me; not quite so beautiful as a plant as some of the older ones which have been mentioned. Perhaps I am just a little prejudiced on this subject, but I have not come to love the modern climbers as well as I love the older ones.

But among them, one of the best is 'Danse des Sylphes', and the signs of an advance to something even better in larger flowered repeating climbers are coming, I think, largely from Sam McGredy in the form of 'Handel', 'Bantry Bay' and 'Schoolgirl'. Here he is getting the sort of purity of colour and the attractiveness in the form of flower which we want to make this type of rose a success. Alex. Cocker's 'Rosy Mantle' is another good example.

It is very difficult to recommend a really good orange climber. In fact I don't think there is a large flowered bright orange climber, in the 'Réveil Dijonnais' colour that the Brigadier was talking about. 'Ruth Alexander' is perhaps the nearest and is a wonderful colour. It is not an attractive plant and has only a short flowering season, but whilst in bloom it is marvellous.

Another beautiful variety to have is 'Sweet Sultan'. You have probably seen this at the shows and at the Trial Ground, but it is not widely grown yet. It has very large, wide, practically single, very deep blackish-crimson flowers with conspicuous yellow stamens in the middle.

Finally, another little favourite which will not do well everywhere, but is very nice where it will grow, is 'Wedding Day'. It bears glorious huge sprays of tiny single flowers, with a flush of yellow in them, changing, alas, to a rather motley red at the end, but most lovable at several stages of its development.

I am afraid that this has been rather a jumble of ideas and prejudices about climbers. I do trust that it has been of some interest to you and of help to the discussion.

WHY DOES THE ROSE?

Why does the Rose its scented favours bring
When I stalk through my garden in a rage
And round my garments send its thorns to cling
As if to hold me as a serving page?

Is there soft sentiment about this flower
That likes its world subservient, at rest,
And goads itself to regulate the hour
With that regality its buds attest?

For I have known when tired and out of joint
With dull routine and penance of my days
A 'Crimson Glory' in its pride anoint
My head with odours and my path with praise.

So I would have the peonies in their place
Hard by the Rose to hold the balance fair;
In puce and purple to proclaim my pace
And Hollyhocks aloof to stand and stare.

Yet shall the Rose still hold us all in fee
Right till the end when rage has spent its lease;
Bringing my garden in tranquillity
After the storm to heaven scented peace.

ROBERT ARMSTRONG

Obituary

WILLIAM C. THORN

With the death of William C. Thorn the R.N.R.S. has lost a friend of forty-eight years' standing. He was one of its honoured Vice-Presidents and, with his knowledge of printing and photography, he was a valued member of the Editorial Board and previously of the Publications Committee. Throughout his long life he was a keen rosarian and won trophies at the Royal Windsor Rose Show in competition with the late W. E. Moore, Gilbert Burch and A. E. Griffith.

He settled in Colchester in 1946 and was largely instrumental in reviving its once-famous Rose Society of which he was Chairman for fifteen years. He was interested in the local Flower Arrangement Society and in the East of England Division, being in great demand as a lecturer in support of those and other organisations, using his own excellent colour slides and films.

He attended Dedham's grand Church and was respected by all who knew him and loved by a wide circle of friends to whom he was just "Bill". He would wish to have recorded his debt to his devoted wife Doreen, whose sense of loss is comforted by the memories of thirty-nine years of happy married life.

A.M.A.

HERBERT OPPENHEIMER, D.H.M.

On several occasions I have visited Herbert Oppenheimer at his home at Maidenhead when his large greenhouses, containing a collection of roses, were in full bloom. I have never seen a finer collection by an amateur and his exhibitions at the Spring Shows, alas no longer held, were always most noteworthy. He died on 25 September 1968 in his ninety-third year.

He was a great supporter of the late Courtney Page, who was Secretary of the Society for many years, and on one occasion, I remember, when the Council was criticising Page, he came back specially from Switzerland during his holidays, to take the chair as President.

Oppenheimer was born in Frankfort in 1875 and joined the Society in 1912; he was elected to the Council in 1921 and became President in 1931–1932. He was President on two other occasions, in 1937–1938 and in 1943–1944, unique in the history of the Society.

He started in practice in 1899 when he founded the firm of Herbert Oppenheimer, Nathan and Vandyke and remained in practice about 60 years. Apart from his profession and his roses he was also a musician of distinction—indeed, in his youth there was talk of him becoming a professional pianist, but fortunately for us this was decided against and he came to England to become a solicitor. During his later years he devoted more time to his music and wrote a number of short pieces for the piano, which were highly regarded and played by Myra Hess at her concerts.

BERTRAM PARK

The Decorative Classes

JULIA CLEMENTS

The occasion of the International Rose Conference might have been the reason behind the bigger and brighter look of the decorative classes at the Summer Show, but whatever the cause, the effect was appraised by all who saw the exhibits.

The Queen Alexandra Memorial Trophy for a table decoration, a most coveted prize, was won this year by Mrs M. Brooker of Swindon. The class was for a Buffet table for a special occasion and she chose to use pink and mauve old fashioned roses, with some of 'Queen Elizabeth', in a tall Meissen china compote container, with two similar plates on the left and a small arrangement to the right, all on a lime green cloth, which she entitled "For Grandmother". It was very lovely.

Mrs Brooker also won the Royal National Rose Society Challenge Trophy for the best exhibit in Classes 84-91, which are restricted to amateurs who grow and arrange their own roses.

Close on her heels in the Buffet table class came Mrs B. Green, an experienced exhibitor from Chelmsford, who staged a table called "Graduation Day". She used a celadon green cloth on which was a low triangular arrangement of red roses, flanked with green goblets on one side, and a graduate's cap and scroll on the other.

Mrs Green also took a first in the "Frontal Arrangement of Roses" class, using red and flame-coloured roses in a bronze container on a brown velvet base. This was expertly staged with no back drape, a welcome change from the pointed piece of material placed at the back of so many exhibits.

Class 94 called for a past period arrangement, using appropriate roses and accessories to interpret the period, which had to be stated. Mrs K. Wells, of Dover, was deservedly first in this class, staging a beautiful exhibit in the Regency manner, using old roses with maidenhair fern and quaking grasses in a period vase, staged against green velvet with a side drape of red and silver Regency striped material, simulating a curtain. Many queried the use of grasses, since the class called for "appropriate roses and foliage and accessories", but, in the front of the schedule it stated that "*Grasses*, sedges, rushes, succulents and bulrushes are classed as *foliage*"; so the lesson to be learned was that the schedule should be read and studied before judging and passing comment. Mrs B. Green came second here with a Victorian exhibit, staged on red plush with tea-pot and strainer.

Mrs E. M. Woodcock took first prize with her 4 ft high large pedestal group, and I know she will not mind my stating that I felt the roses were all too tightly in bud and similar in size. I liked Mrs B. Green's pedestal group in this class much better, as I felt it was more loose and flowing. Another exciting exhibit in this class was staged by David Ruston of South Australia, who made a huge display of lovely copper-coloured roses brought from Australia, set in a copper tea urn that he bought in London. This was much admired, although we in England could not appreciate the fact that Australians do not seem to make their roses flow out at the back for a pedestal group, theirs being flat. Mrs Woodcock took first prize in Class 87 for an arrangement of old fashioned roses, and here she used R. *hugonis* and 'Rosa Mundi' roses, with the green R. *viridiflora* rose and R. *rubrifolia* sprays, all in old china on a moss green velvet base.

In the class for those who have not won a first prize before, Mrs E. Lockton, of Iver, Bucks came first with a very well executed arrangement of old roses in a black metal container on a green base. A point here to remember is that in judging, "suitability of flowers to container" is considered, so another time Mrs Lockton would do well not to use a black metal container (modern) with *old fashioned* roses.

In Class 91, which was for an arrangement of roses on any natural base, i.e. wood, slate, stone, wicker, Mrs M. Brooker was first, and I liked Mrs E. Urquhart's second prize exhibit of 'Wendy Cussons' roses, staged on a cane base against peacock blue silk.

A different note was struck in the class for floribunda roses incorporating a mirror. Some laid the mirror flat and made the arrangement on it; others stood the mirror on end, making a design at the top. However, Mrs K. Wells took first prize with a side design of 'Allgold' and 'Faust' roses, encircling one side of a gold framed mirror stood on a tray.

Miss P. Broadhurst, of Totnes, came first with a lovely arrangement of 'Queen Elizabeth', 'Guinevere' and 'Lady Seton' roses in the class for an arrangement of roses of tints, shades and tones of one colour.

My notes remind me that this was the best Summer Show I had seen for a very long time, and looking back on it, I still agree.

Autumn Show

This show displayed the best exhibit I have seen at a Royal National Rose Society occasion for the past ten years, and it was staged by Mrs W. M. Crabb, of Croydon, in the class for a Christmas Buffet table decoration. Using bright red 'Baccara' roses with variegated holly and pine in a gilt container, with two red candles, on a green, gold-fringed cloth, the off-centre design swerved from left to right, where it met a bowl of fruit. In the centre at the back was a bottle of champagne with glasses, and in front were red crackers with roses tucked in each one. All the containers and bases were sprayed gold to match; in fact, it was perfectly staged and very well designed. Mrs K. Wells came a very close second with a triangular central arrangement of red roses, variegated holly and ivy, with fruit on one side and candles on the other. Mrs

Woodcock took third prize, but all the exhibits in this class were of a very high standard.

The class entitled "By Candlelight" drew a number of very interesting exhibits, Mrs W. M. Crabb again taking first prize with a triangular pattern of yellow roses and pale green nephrolepis ferns, staged on two different yellow chiffon drapes, with three yellow candles in a holder on the right, surrounded with miniature yellow roses. Pink, grey and black were the colours chosen by Mrs K. Wells who took second in this class, using pink roses in a black container on pink silk with black velvet back drape, the foliage being grey *Senecio greyii* and Centaurea, with pinky grey Begonia rex in the centre.

In the class for "An Arrangement in a box or basket with a lid", it is wiser to leave part of the lid showing; otherwise, all is hidden and the container could be a bowl-like item. Bearing this in mind, Mrs E. M. Woodcock came first with a left to right arrangement made in a copper tan basket on brown rep cloth, using tan coloured 'Beauté' and 'Bettina' roses with *R. rubrifolia* sprays. I liked Mrs K. Field's exhibit in this class too, as it was not too full.

Weird-looking twisted and knotted wood was used by Mrs J. A. Rush, of Rayleigh, in the class for rose foliage, heps and driftwood. She used pale green and maroon foliage, dark and light heps, and all was stood on a dark wood base on a brown cloth. Mrs K. Wells came second, using light and dark leaves with wood, in front of a beige hopsack drape.

The "Not more than five roses" class always brings forth some very interesting designs, and this autumn was no exception. 'Super Star' is a good eye catcher, and Mrs Woodcock came first in this class, using five 'Super Star' roses in a vertical design, placed low on two cane bases backed with a brown drape.

Exhibitors and onlookers alike welcomed the fact that in a number of classes "Any other foliage" was allowed. The beginners did well, the main advice being to remember to place some roses "in" and others protruding "out". This gives an uneven effect in the front, creating a third dimension. One beginner also made a lovely frontal display, but completely forgot to flow out at the back, which left a flat and bare back view.

The Decorative Classes were well filled, and well staged by the Committee, who also produced an exciting schedule. This seemed to please all the visitors from overseas and at home, and even if there were controversies, it made this section one of the liveliest parts of the show.

The Summer Show

A. G. L. HELLYER

Only the weather marred the summer show, held in the Alexandra Palace on 28 and 29 June. It had caused some cancellations in the amateur section and on the Friday rain continued to fall pitilessly and no doubt reduced the number of visitors to what was, despite everything, a magnificent display of roses and a splendid opening to the international rose conference, which got into its full stride at the London Hilton Hotel the following week.

R. Harkness & Co. again proved their supremacy as exhibitors by winning both the Championship Trophy for the best exhibit in the show and the Queen Mary Trophy for the best exhibit against a background. It was the familiar well-packed bank of superbly grown blooms against traditional black velvet and it proved just as effective as ever, despite the challenge of more modern methods of staging. The new Harkness varieties, such as 'Merlin', 'Guinevere', 'Sir Galahad' and 'Sir Lancelot' were well displayed and a large semi-double lilac rose named 'Lake Como' attracted a lot of comment. A third award to this very fine exhibit was a Large Gold Medal.

John Mattock Ltd won the Coronation Trophy for the best island exhibit and a Large Gold Medal, again without the assistance of any gimmicks in the way of display stands or background. It was the sheer quality of their roses that did it, nicely arranged in large black bowls and vases on a black and white ground cover. The exhibit was open without being thin, and I particularly admired a new floribunda named 'Shepherdess', with fairly large pale gold and pink flowers very freely produced.

Three further Large Gold Medals were awarded to C. Gregory & Son Ltd, Samuel McGredy & Son Ltd and Cant's of Colchester. All contained roses of the highest quality and many new varieties. The contrasts in styles of display were also most interesting.

C. Gregory & Son divided their double-sided bank into a number of sections with white partitions, which had the merit of displaying individual varieties very well but slightly impeded the overall effect of the exhibit. 'Summer Holiday' was one of the most discussed roses here, a vermilion hybrid tea of great size and substance, which seemed to outvie even 'Super Star' in brilliance. 'Orange Silk', a shapely orange-vermilion floribunda and 'Pamela's Choice', a striking canary yellow sport from 'Piccadilly', were two other good newcomers; and among the slightly older roses the hybrid tea 'Apricot Silk' (no connection with 'Orange Silk') and the large-flowered pink climber 'Etude' were specially notable.

The McGredy exhibit had a gold coloured carpet as a base for an erection of light stainless steel rods bearing varnished wood stands, some covered with white or yellow plastic net mats. It was all very modern and effective and served well to display a magnificent array of roses. 'Timothy Eaton', one of the new pink hybrid teas, proved to be a pleasantly warm shade. 'Heaven Scent', a floribunda which is said to throw its fragrance well, is shapely, free and a pleasant slightly dulled shade of red. 'Brasilia' is a real eye-catcher, a kind of currant red and gold variant of the more purple-crimson and gold 'Kronenbourg', which was also well shown. 'Silver Star' is a clean heliotrope colour and 'Lavendula' a big full mallow-purple rose with an old fashioned look.

Cant's staged their exhibit against one of the walls of the Great Hall, using a grey cloth base and a blue background with curving wood stands to break the line of what must have been one of the largest exhibits in the show. 'Apricot Silk' was again outstandingly good and so was the coppery apricot 'Serenade' and deep scarlet 'Red Dandy'.

There were three awards of the Society's Gold Medal, to the Blaby Rose Gardens, Sunningdale Nurseries and John Waterer, Sons & Crisp, respectively, and here too one was struck by the very different styles of display. Blaby Rose Gardens attempted a rather natural effect with a woven fence background and mottled grey slab base. The deep gold 'Belle Blonde' was exceptionally well shown and 'Pepe', speckled and splashed with crimson on gold, stood out because of its unusual colouring. Sunningdale Nurseries set out to show old fashioned and shrub roses with something of the atmosphere of a cottage garden, using old ironwork arches to support climbing roses and interspersing the more normal vases and bowls with long sprays of 'Cerise Bouquet', 'Constance Spry' and other such informal roses.

The Waterer exhibit, by contrast, was very stylish with gilded metal stands, brass bowls and a wrought iron screen in the centre. There were plenty of good roses too, including 'Green Fire', a floribunda with a marked hint of green in its shapely little yellow flowers, 'Dreamland', a coral pink floribunda with flattish flowers very freely produced, and 'Copper Delight', a floribunda that I would call corn-coloured rather than coppery.

Silver-gilt medals went to Alex Dickson & Sons, E. B. Le Grice, William Lowe & Sons Ltd, Warley Rose Gardens Ltd, Harry Wheatcroft & Sons, Chaplin Bros and Wheatcroft Bros. The Norman Rogers Cup for the best exhibit not exceeding 100 sq. ft was won by R. Murrell with an attractive exhibit which included a pleasant hybrid tea rose named 'Golden Picture'. The fairly full, fragrant blooms are the colour of ripe corn.

There was also a remarkable exhibit of old, species and historic roses, staged by the Royal National Rose Society itself, against a background in the form of an immense chart, showing the botanical affinities of the various races of roses and their chromosome counts. It was most attractive to the eye and of great educational value.

The vagaries of the weather were revealed in the amateur classes, not only by the unusual number of last minute cancellations, but by the rather uneven quality. The best exhibits were as good as ever, either because the growers had been exceptionally skilful in combating the rain or because they had been lucky enough to miss it. But there was evidence, too, of the trials and hazards which many rose growers had had to surmount to get to the show at all.

A little of all this showed in the twelve specimen blooms with which Lady Pilkington won the Edward Mawley Challenge Cup in the "open to all" section. At first sight this was a superlatively good box, and blooms of 'Pink Favourite', 'Ethel Sanday' and 'Christian Dior' stood up to much closer examination. But there was also evidence of weather damage on otherwise very nice blooms of 'Royal Highness', 'Perfecta' and 'Papa Meilland', and 'Paris Match' looked a trifle flat.

The S. W. Burgess Memorial Cup was won by F. Wiltshire with a very nicely balanced set of six vases. Only 'Grandpa Dickson' was not quite up to standard, 'Memoriam', 'Royal Highness', 'Josephine Bruce', 'Wendy Cussons' and 'Montezuma' being all very good indeed.

There was only one entry in Class 24 for the R.N.R.S trophy, but it was a good one. The class calls for three vases of floribunda roses and C. C. Hart chose 'Orange Sensation', 'Iceberg' and 'Firecracker', the last outstanding for quality and brilliance.

L. Poole won the very difficult Class 27 for a box of 24 specimen blooms and with it the Lindsell Cup. Almost every bloom had some slight blemish but as a whole this was quite a good box, certainly the best in the class. All the same he was happier, I fancy, with the imposing set of six vases with which he won the H. R. Darlington Memorial cup in Division B, restricted to amateurs who grow and stage without assistance. Here his varieties were 'Charlie's Aunt', 'Red Devil', 'Gavotte', 'Princess', 'Royal Highness' and 'Norman Hartnell', the last possibly the weakest but still very good. He was also the winner of the Courtney Page Memorial Cup for the highest aggregate of points.

The Nicholson Challenge Cup for a box of twelve specimen blooms comes into this same Division B, and was won by W. Pearl with a rather uneven lot, of which the best was possibly 'Brilliant'.

All were fine roses in the box of six which won J. Jamieson the Brayfort Challenge Cup. 'Princess' was in top form, 'Grandpa Dickson' large, shapely and well coloured, and the other four were 'Red Lion', 'Honey Favourite', 'Fritz Thiedemann' and 'Leonora de March'.

F. Bowen had a very good bowl of twelve hybrid tea roses to win the Alfred Hewlett Memorial Class, with 'Ernest H. Morse' probably his best bloom, well supported by two 'Grandpa Dickson', two 'Perfecta', 'Royal Highness', 'Dame de Coeur', 'Montezuma', 'Rose Gaujard', 'Red Devil', 'Gavotte' and 'Norman Hartnell'.

Division C is restricted to amateurs with not more than 500 rose trees and has two cup classes of its own and one shared with divisions A and B. This last is the Rev. H. Honywood d'Ombrain Memorial Cup, awarded to the best exhibit in Classes 26, 39 or 46, all of which are for a bowl of floribunda roses, not more than twelve stems. It says a lot for the keenness of the smaller growers that it was Mr. H. V. Mitchell's exhibit in Division C that won this award. His varieties were 'Iceberg', 'Circus', 'Evelyn Fison' and 'Lilli Marlene'.

Had there been a similar overall prize for a box of 12 specimen blooms it might well have gone to Division C too, for L. E. J. Wood's entry in Class 40 was outstandingly good. He had a huge, unmarked 'Ena Harkness', excellent blooms of 'Ernest H. Morse' and 'Klaus Störtebeker', a very good 'My Choice', a really lovely specimen of 'Diamond Jubilee' and good blooms of 'Peace', 'Montezuma' and 'Dorothy Goodwin'. Only his 'Anne Letts' was a little small, and 'June Park' had a faulty centre. This fine exhibit won the Sam McGredy Challenge Cup. Moreover he capped this success by winning the other cup class in the division—the Edward J. Holland Memorial Cup for three vases of hybrid tea roses with 'Montezuma', 'Pink Favourite' and 'Memoriam'. Not surprisingly he was awarded the Edward Mawley Memorial Medal for the highest aggregate of points in Division C.

To complete the triumph of Division C exhibitors one of them, M. L. Watts, had the best bloom in the show from an amateur. It was a huge 'Gold Crown' exhibited in a vase of six hybrid tea roses which won Class 44.

Exhibitors in Division D must grow no more than 250 rose trees. The Gilbert Burch Memorial Class for a box of six specimen blooms was won by T. J. Vale with nice clean flowers of medium size. The Slaughter Memorial Cup, for three vases of hybrid tea roses, went to J. S. Jellyman, who staged superb flowers of 'Rose Gaujard', 'Isabel de Ortiz' and 'Silver Lining'.

There is only one cup class in Division E, restricted to amateurs with not more than 150 rose trees and this, carrying the Charles Rigg Cup, is for a box of six specimen blooms. It was won by F. E. Rixon, who may not grow many roses but certainly grows them supremely well. Perhaps some of the larger growers were lucky not to have to face the competition of this fine box with its outstandingly good specimens of 'Gail Borden', 'Perfecta' and 'Grandpa Dickson'.

The corresponding class in Division F for amateurs with no more than 100 rose trees is the Kathleen Louise Mahaffy Class, and it was won by J. H. Kirsop. His roses were all large and well grown, but some of them looked a bit tired.

The really small growers with no more than 50 rose trees have a chance to compete in the Albert E. Griffith Memorial Class for a vase of six hybrid tea roses. This year only two exhibitors had a go and R. Holmes was successful with 'Pink Favourite', 'Isabel de Ortiz', two blooms of 'Piccadilly',

'Peace' and 'Femina', the last a large coppery-salmon rose. **L. J.** Foad won the Gardeners Company Challenge Cup with the highest aggregate of points in Sections 5 and 6 for the novice exhibitor.

Finally there are two cups for the Affiliated Societies, the Hereford Centenary Cup for a display against a background on a table space 5 ft long and 4 ft wide, and the Franklin Dennison Memorial Cup for two bowls, one of floribundas, the other of hybrid teas. The first attracted some fine entries, the cup going to the Worcester Park Horticultural Society for a very professional-looking exhibit in which the various rose colours were well handled against a background of green and black drapes. 'Zambra', 'Evelyn Fison', 'Orange Sensation', 'Masquerade' and 'Dorothy Wheatcroft' made an exciting mixture of red, orange and yellow; 'Daily Sketch', 'Ama' and 'Iceberg' gave red and white, and the pale yellow and pink of 'Peace' was effectively used to intensify the vermilion of 'Super Star'.

The bowl class was won by the East Kent Rose Society with very good blooms of 'Princess', 'Grandpa Dickson', 'Red Lion', 'Anna Wheatcroft' and 'Korona'.

HEART ROSE—A SONG.

Upon the garden of my heart there grows
A radiant rose; nor fades the smell
Of scented dew that all around you flows,
By day the petals gaily tell
Of love that overflows; at dusk they close
With silent sighs into the shell
Of sleep. So like this rose is your repose,
So moist your petalled eyes. How well
Upon your tranquil face the moonshine glows
With mystic grace, and casts its spell
Upon my cell of beating breath. Who knows
When God will transpose her to dwell
In Heaven's Garden dell? But when she goes
Nothing will quell my breath's farewell
Or stem the tears left by my rose.

GILLIES SHIELDS

The Northern Show, 1968

J. CLARKE

The Northern Show was again held at Roundhay Park, Leeds in co-operation with the Roundhay (Leeds) Horticultural Society. Unfortunately, on the opening day of the Show the weather was atrocious, but despite the almost constant downpour of the previous week the roses shown in the trade marquees bore a minimum amount of weathering and the nurserymen should be congratulated on having managed to stage roses of such quality under adverse conditions.

The premier award of the Brotherton Trophy went to Fryers Nurseries of Knutsford for a colourful exhibit; their blooms were probably at their peak of perfection. Outstanding in their exhibit, which also received a Large Gold Medal, was a centrepiece of the new orange-vermilion floribunda 'Fred Loads'. 'Diorama' and 'Duke of Windsor' were also shown in splendid condition. 'Pernille Poulsen,' both here and also in other trade exhibits, gives every indication of being an attractive pink floribunda which will stand up to adverse weather conditions. It is an early variety to flower—a decided advantage for a floribunda—and of compact, bushy habit of growth.

Large Gold Medals were awarded to S. McGredy & Son Ltd and C. Gregory & Son Ltd. McGredy's had massive vases of their new scarlet and gold bicolour hybrid tea, 'Brasilia', and also last year's winner of the President's Trophy—their scarlet floribunda, 'City of Belfast'. 'City of Leeds' too was shown in good form.

Included in Gregory's exhibit was 'Pamela's Choice',—a beautiful self yellow sport from 'Piccadilly', which looked most attractive.

W. Lowe & Sons staged a splendid Gold Medal exhibit on a wall site. 'Miss Ireland' and 'Pink Parfait' were among the many bowls which created much interest.

E. B. Le Grice (Roses) Ltd, showed their new floribunda 'Dimples,' basically creamy-white with a lemon yellow centre and pleasantly scented. Their centrepiece was of 'Goldgleam' which they consider a successor to 'Allgold', in a deep canary yellow which does not fade.

Harry Wheatcroft and Sons Ltd and Geo. De Ruiter (Roses) Ltd also won Silver Gilt Medals. The latter exhibited several varieties of their associated firm's raising, including the orange-salmon floribunda 'My Girl', red and yellow 'Travesti' and the velvety scarlet-crimson 'Scania'.

An attractive display was staged by H. Robinson who was awarded the R.N.R.S. Cup and a Silver Gilt Medal. He showed the coppery reddish salmon 'Fairlight' and yellow, edged flame 'Lucky Charm', both floribundas of his own raising, in good form.

'BLESSINGS' (floribunda—H.T. type)
'Queen Elizabeth' × *unnamed seedling*
Raised by C. Gregory & Son Ltd
CERTIFICATE OF MERIT 1968
See page 184

'MICHELLE' (floribunda)
Seedling × 'Orange Sensation'
Raised by G. De Ruiter, Holland
TRIAL GROUND CERTIFICATE 1968
See page 185

Trade exhibits were also shown by Yorkshire nurserymen including Charles Kershaw Ltd and David E. Lister.

New Seedlings
Many new seedlings were shown. From C. Gregory & Son Ltd, 'Summer Holiday', a vivid dark vermilion hybrid tea, 'Orange Silk', a vermilion-orange floribunda and 'Indian Chief', a currant red, shaded orange hybrid tea gave promise of being popular varieties when better known.

E. B. Le Grice (Roses) Ltd, showed 'Vesper', an unusual floribunda in a unique shade of Mars Orange, likely to be popular for floral arrangements; 'White Spray' is a white floribunda with a cream heart, of hybrid tea shape, and 'News' will undoubtedly make news, being an entirely novel colour break of plum-purple, among the floribundas.

S. McGredy & Son Ltd staged seven new seedlings including splendid bowls of 'City of Belfast', the golden yellow hybrid tea from Kordes 'Peer Gynt' and the rich pink hybrid tea 'Timothy Eaton'; the new climber 'Swan Lake', white with a pink heart, was also very attractive.

Amateurs
Although as might be expected there were missing exhibits in the Amateur Section there were, nevertheless, entries which had overcome the difficulties of the weather to a remarkable extent. T. Thornley of Skelmanthorpe took first prize in Class 204 for a box of twelve specimen blooms and was also successful in Class 205, a box of six blooms.

The award for the Best Bloom went to J. H. Greening of Grange-over-Sands for a magnificent specimen of the bright vermilion 'Princess'. This competitor also had a splendid example of 'Silver Lining' in the same vase. The first prize in Class 206 was awarded to J. M. Robinson of Kendal for six very fine blooms of 'Perfecta'.

In section 5 for Affiliated Societies, magnificent bowls of floribundas and hybrid teas were staged by the Congleton Horticultural Society who deserve the utmost praise for having brought blooms in such splendid condition from so far afield.

An outstanding bowl of floribunda roses was shown by L. Moores of Congleton in Class 220. The variety used was the bright red 'Evelyn Fison' and the same exhibitor took first prize in Class 219.

For any intending exhibitor who may feel some diffidence in journeying to Leeds, it may act as a spur and encouragement to learn that one such enthusiast journeyed from distant Cheshunt and took four firsts out of his five exhibits. An abiding pleasure for him—may many others follow in his footsteps.

The Autumn Rose Show

GORDON FORSYTH

By general consent of exhibitors, competitors and visitors from far and wide who literally streamed in from the moment of opening, the Society's Autumn Rose Show, held in both Horticultural Halls, Westminster, on 10 and 11 September 1968, was a magnificent success. Obviously, in one of the wettest seasons on record, some signs of weather damage were inevitable, but it says much for the sturdy constitution of the pick of the modern varieties of our own, and indeed of the world's most popular flower, that quality in general was superb.

The trade growers supported the show magnificently and filled the new hall with a glorious array of blooms, indeed, those responsible for the lay-out of the show deserve special congratulations, for every exhibit could be viewed quite comfortably.

Most interesting among the new roses on view was E. B. Le Grice's new colour break in floribundas, rather aptly named 'News'. Its comparatively large semi-double blooms, of velvety rose-purple, are in dense clusters and, listening to the comments of visitors, I put the voting for and against at about 50–50. Personally, I rather liked it on first sight, but it will need careful placing to set it off to best effect. I was also enchanted by his ivory-white upstanding floribunda 'White Spray', and richly fragrant, shapely, deep velvety crimson hybrid tea 'Incense'.

De Ruiter's 'Manjana', a floribunda with delicate salmon-pink H.T.-type blooms set off well by rich green foliage, was an eye-catcher certainly worth watching. I was attracted also, in the section for new roses, by Gregory's floribunda 'Gay Maid', with large erect clusters of double blooms, cream in the bud, opening rich pink, and orange-vermilion 'Orange Silk', very shapely in the bud, which may well prove a winner.

Special mention is also deserved by John Sanday's new hybrid tea rose 'Fred Gibson', not only because it pays worthy tribute to the great past president and champion exhibitor whose name it bears, but because, as shown, it is perfect in form and exquisite in its rich apricot-cream colouring. And from the Sanday "stable" I also admired the full-petalled hybrid tea 'Bristol', vivid red with paler reverse.

Unstinted congratulations to John Mattock of Nuneham Courtenay, Oxford, winner of the Society's Autumn Roses Challenge Cup and Large Gold Medal for the best exhibit against a background. It was a really astounding display of no fewer than 110 kinds; hybrid teas and floribundas in a top selection of the best for general garden planting; repeat-flowering climbers; shrub roses including a goodly range of *Rosa rugosa* varieties (or should I say

178

cultivars?) and hybrids, and an interesting selection of fruiting species, notably *R. macrophylla* and *R. moyesii*.

All were arranged in what one might call a functional and instructive display, which certainly "rang the bell". The climbers in particular attracted me, especially large and shapely, fragrant orange-apricot 'Schoolgirl', crimson-red single 'Altissimo'; 'Swan Lake' with hybrid tea-shaped blooms, white with the daintiest tinge of pink, and vigorous cream, pink-flushed 'Handel'.

Never, if memory serves me right, have Bees of Chester put up a better exhibit at any R.N.R.S. show than on this occasion, to win with no question of doubt the D'Escofet Cup, and Large Gold Medal for the best island group, which combined superb quality with artistic arrangement and display of each variety to best advantage. Their representative selection of hybrid teas included especially good "blues" in 'Cologne Carnival' and 'Blue Moon'. 'Gail Borden', 'Piccadilly' in top form, 'Ideal Home', 'Stella', 'Super Star', 'King's Ransom', 'Grandpa Dickson' and new dainty pink 'Marylene' were magnificent, supported by an equally grand selection of floribundas.

Needless to say, good quality was the keynote of the group arranged against a background by R. Harkness & Co., which won the Jubilee Trophy and Gold Medal. I noted particularly their hybrid teas pink 'Guinevere', upstanding cerise-red 'Albion' and pure yellow 'King's Ransom', with floribundas 'Pink Parfait', perfect in its own right and the parent of some of the best Harkness creations, including their new cream, amber-tinged 'Moonraker' and semi-double, rosy magenta, fragrant 'Escapade', both shown in superb condition.

In the island group with which the Warley Rose Gardens won the Society's Autumn Challenge Trophy, hybrid teas of outstanding merit included scarlet 'Red Devil', the large white, pink-tinted 'Memoriam', and fragrant bicolour 'Isabel de Ortiz', rich pink with silvery reverse.

All the best varieties for autumn garden display were shown in massed array by Cants of Colchester. Of the floribundas in this Gold Medal exhibit, a quartet of exceptional quality were 'Elizabeth of Glamis', 'Orange Sensation', orange vermilion 'Irish Mist' and, rather surprisingly, pink 'Dearest', while the pick of their hybrid teas for colour and quality were apricot-coral 'Serenade,' shapely 'Apricot Silk', large pink-tinted 'Carla', 'Ernest H. Morse' in grand form, the superb apricot-yellow 'Beauté' and 'Gail Borden'.

Star hybrid teas in the artistically arranged Gold Medal display by Gregory's of Stapleford that attracted immediate attention included their new brilliant red 'Indian Chief', golden yellow 'Pamela's Choice', a very promising sport from 'Piccadilly'; and 'Duke of Windsor'. Needless to say, they showed 'Wendy Cussons' in fine form, and pink 'Percy Thrower', together with their new floribunda of H.T. type, the very shapely and free blooming 'Blessings', in coral pink.

Gold Medals were awarded to the Waterhouse Nurseries, who incidentally have a very charming new bright pink floribunda in 'Duchess of Kent', and to Gandy's Roses, whose hybrid teas included in my opinion the best in the show blooms of 'Fragrant Cloud', with superb orange-apricot 'Vienna Charm', 'Ernest H. Morse', velvety red 'Christian Dior', long-budded, rich yellow 'Summer Sunshine' and the brilliant orange floribunda 'Princess Michiko'.

In an attractive display by E. B. Le Grice, several of his own recent raising were conspicuous and certainly worth noting, especially the large fragrant hybrid tea 'City of Hereford', and floribundas coppery-orange 'Vesper', H.T.-type 'Goldgleam', glowing red 'Firecrest' and large attractively waved salmon-pink 'Charming Maid'. Noteworthy in the S. McGredy group were their scarlet and gold bicolour hybrid tea 'Brasilia', 'Mischief' in grand form and large, full-petalled red 'Liebestraum', with floribundas yellow 'Jan Spek', rose-red 'Beatrice' and cerise-salmon 'City of Leeds'. Eye-catching floribundas shown by De Ruiter's were superb 'Orange Sensation' and 'Elizabeth of Glamis', and the large fully double orange and biscuit 'Fresco'. The new hybrid tea 'Manuella', with shapely bright pink blooms, looked very promising in the Harry Wheatcroft and Sons collection, together with 'Duke of Windsor', superb 'Chicago Peace' and white, flesh-tinted 'Royal Highness'. Wm. Lowe's group of reliable bedding roses included the yellow hybrid teas 'Grandpa Dickson', 'Summer Sunshine' and 'King's Ransom', a grand trio, and in their attractive exhibit Wheatcroft Bros. displayed their new orange-gold hybrid tea 'Whisky Mac' and salmon pink 'Gypsy Moth' to good advantage.

Competition was keen, with quality high, in the open section for amateurs. In her cup-winning box of twelve blooms Lady Pilkington, St Helens, had exceptionally fine specimens of 'Fragrant Cloud', 'Super Star', 'Peace' and 'Isabel de Ortiz', and I greatly admired the first prize box of two blooms each of 'Super Star', 'Memoriam' and pink 'Gavotte' from R. P. Court, Ramsgate. The classes for bowls of hybrid teas were keenly contested, with Col. W. B. Wright, Instow, again first with eighteen blooms of superb quality, and E. E. Gatward, Cambridge, deservedly the winner in the strong class for twelve stems. Another exceptionally good class was that for a bowl of twelve stems of floribundas, won by Capt. C. A. E. Stanfield, Walmer, with magnificent 'Fred Loads', 'Europeana', 'Evelyn Fison', 'Anna Wheatcroft' and glorious 'Irish Mist'. His first prize bowl of one variety, brilliant orange red 'Dorothy Wheatcroft', was also outstanding.

In my humble opinion, the six specimen blooms which won first prize for L. E. J. Wood, Waddesdon, in Division B, were among the best in the show, really superb examples of 'Gavotte', 'Super Star', 'Pink Favourite', 'Chicago Peace', 'Red Devil' and salmon-pink 'Femina', and he was equally successful in the popular class for three vases of distinct hybrid tea varieties, winning the R.N.R.S. Challenge Cup with grand blooms of 'Super Star', 'Rose Gaujard' and 'Peace'.

A perfect specimen of coral-salmon 'Mischief' was adjudged the best bloom in the amateur's section. It was shown, with 'Fragrant Cloud' and 'June Park', by M. L. Watts, Northampton, in his first prize vase of three blooms.

Division C. produced very keen competition in all the classes for the Society's Challenge Cup, won by Mrs M. Short, Liphook, with 'Gavotte', 'Pink Favourite' and 'Montezuma' in grand form. She also had the best vase of three blooms, light red 'Norman Hartnell', 'Brilliant' and 'Stella', while C. A. Brown, Ashbourne, was a clear winner with 'Gavotte' and two glorious specimens of 'Wendy Cussons'.

Specially noteworthy first prize exhibits in Division D, for growers of not more than 150 rose trees, were F. E. Rixon's box of six blooms, varieties. 'Princess' and 'Show Girl'; the individual blooms of 'Norman Hartnell', 'Paris-Match' and 'Gavotte' shown by G. J. Bushy, Solihull, and superb specimens of 'Fragrant Cloud' shown by K. G. Clarke, Sevenoaks.

In the novices section F. E. Owen, Tamworth, was the most successful exhibitor, but the blooms I admired most were those of 'Gavotte' shown in his first prize box of six blooms by Judge Gage, Widdington.

> Some as they went the blue-eyed violets strew,
> Some spotless lilies in loose order threw,
> Some did the way with full-blown roses spread,
> Their smell divine, and colour strangely red;
> Not such as our dull gardens proudly wear,
> Whom weathers taint, and winds rude kisses tear:
> Such, I believe, was the first Rose's hue,
> Which at God's word in beauteous Eden grew;
> Queen of the flowers that made that orchard gay,
> The morning blushes of the spring's new day.
>
>   COWLEY

The Trial Ground and Display Garden 1968

L. G. TURNER

An article on the development of the gardens will be found elsewhere in *The Rose Annual* and although so much of our interest during the year has been centred on this work I will not refer to it in this report. First, mention must be made of the weather that prevailed in St Albans during the greater part of the summer. Although we had rain before and during the Summer Show the wonderful weather during the Conference week at the beginning of July appeared to herald a great rose season. Unfortunately, this was not to be. The following week it began to rain and from then until the end of August hardly a day passed without at least one shower and sometimes heavy rain. During this period Scotland, North Wales and the North were apparently enjoying continuous sunshine.

The poor weather was reflected in the fall in attendance at St Albans, but those who braved the rain could pick out the varieties that would stand up to such trying conditions.

Was there more Black Spot in evidence during 1968? I do not know, but from correspondence I gather it was very widespread. It was interesting to learn of a number of places where it had appeared for the first time. There seems little doubt that this is a direct result of the Clean Air Act which is depriving the urban rose grower of the sulphur fungicide in the atmosphere.

Fortunately, in the display garden at St Albans no more than three varieties were affected, making this by far the most successful year we have had since adopting preventative spraying. In the Trial Ground, which is of course adjacent to the garden, and where no spraying is done, there was a considerable amount of Black Spot. It cannot be denied that the prevalence of disease in the trials is causing the Management Committee concern; at the same time, to carry out a regular spraying programme throughout the period of the trials would be to defeat one of the main objects, which is to ascertain resistance to disease. As from 1969, however, a regular spraying programme will be carried out for the first year only—this will ensure that all varieties have a fair start and as they are not judged during this first year this should not affect the results.

Having found our spraying programme so successful I offer no apology for repeating it for the benefit of members encountering disease for the first time.

Towards the end of November take off the tops of the bushes to reduce wind-rock. If severe rust has been present clear up the fallen leaves and burn them and then spray with Bordeaux mixture, applying one gallon to 7–10 sq. yds. If a knapsack sprayer is used then fit a coarse nozzle or, alternatively, apply with a plastic watering can.

After pruning many rosarians spray with maneb but there is no evidence that such an early spray application is beneficial. Normally it suffices to give the first maneb spray about mid-June, thereafter spraying every fortnight until the end of October. It is particularly important to spray regularly during August and September.

Many rosarians advocate a winter spray of copper sulphate solution, at 1 oz./gallon of rain water but there is now some evidence that Bordeaux mixture is to be preferred. When such a solution is used it must be prepared in a plastic container.

Unfortunately, our rose nurseries are no more immune to disease than our own gardens and, even though spraying is carried out, it is a wise precaution to dip or spray new arrivals with Bordeaux mixture or Copper Sulphate as recommended.

Although disease seems inevitable in the trial ground, the Management Committee very quickly sanctions the removal of any variety that is particularly susceptible. No fewer than forty-five varieties have already been removed from the 270 sent in 1966/67 and now finishing their second year of trial. Most breeders are conscious of the need to discard highly susceptible varieties and their ready approval to taking out what is possibly one of their cherished varieties is much appreciated.

The Trial Ground perimeter bed, which contains all varieties that have received an award since 1963, has attracted much interest during the summer. Here may be seen the latest novelties growing together and visitors find it easy to compare their relative merits. So far, only bush varieties have been planted, but during the winter shrubs and climbers will be added to the collection.

The awards to New Roses in 1968

*Denotes varieties for which it is understood protection is being sought under the Plant Varieties and Seeds Act 1964.

The President's International Trophy for the Best New Seedling Rose of the year and Gold Medal were awarded to:

MOLLY McGREDY (Flori./H.T. type). 'Paddy McGredy' × ('Mme Léon Cuny' × 'Columbine'). Trial Ground No. 1308. Reg. No. 1214. *Raiser:* S. McGredy IV. *Distributor:* S. McGredy & Son Ltd, N. Ireland. Bloom: cherry red with silver reverse, full, 4½ in., 35 petals, borne several together. Growth: upright and bushy. Foliage: glossy, dark green.

The Henry Edland Memorial Medal awarded to the most fragrant rose on trial, irrespective of country of origin, and Certificate of Merit:

*DUKE OF WINDSOR (H.T.). 'Prima Ballerina' × unnamed seedling. Trial Ground No. 1406. Reg. No. 1143. *Raiser:* M. Tantau, Germany. *Distributor:* Harry Wheatcroft & Sons Ltd, Nottingham. Bloom: orange-vermilion, full, 30 petals, large, borne several together, very fragrant. Growth: upright, bushy. Foliage: large, leathery, dark green.

Certificates of Merit were awarded to:

*BLESSINGS (Flori./H.T. type). 'Queen Elizabeth' × unnamed seedling. Trial Ground No. 1179. Reg. No. 1134. *Raiser and Distributor:* C. Gregory & Son Ltd, Stapleford. Bloom: coral pink, full and flat, 30 petals, 6 in., large, borne several together, fragrant. Growth: vigorous, bushy and branching. Foliage: dull.

*GLENGARRY (Flori./H.T. type). 'Evelyn Fison' × 'Wendy Cussons'. Trial Ground No. 1270. Reg. No. 1203. *Raiser and Distributor:* J. Cocker & Sons Ltd, Aberdeen. Bloom: vermilion, full, 32 petals, 3½–4 in., borne singly and several together, slightly fragrant. Growth: compact and bushy. Foliage: light to mid-green, semi-glossy.

Trial Ground Certificates were awarded to:

ADAIR ROCHE (Flori./H.T. type). 'Paddy McGredy' × 'Femina' seedling. Trial Ground No. 1316. Reg. No. 1218. *Raiser:* S. McGredy IV. *Distributor:* S. McGredy & Son Ltd, N. Ireland. Bloom: medium pink with silver reverse, full, 30 petals, large, 5 in., borne in trusses. Growth: upright, vigorous. Foliage: glossy, medium green.

*BIRMINGHAM POST (H.T.). 'Queen Elizabeth' × 'Wendy Cussons'. Trial Ground No. 1485. Reg. No. 1158. *Raiser and Distributor:* Watkins Roses Ltd, Hampton-in-Arden. Bloom: pale pink with deeper reverse, full, large, 37 petals. Growth: upright, vigorous. Foliage: large, leathery, medium green.

*COPACABANA (Semi-Climber). 'Coup de Foudre' × unnamed seedling. Trial Ground No. C.76. Reg. No. 1061. *Raiser:* F. Dorieux & Fils, France. *Distributor:* Bees Ltd, Chester. Bloom: vermilion, deeper at edge of petals, full and compact, 3½ in., 40 petals, borne in trusses. Growth: vigorous. Foliage: large, glossy, dark green.

*COPPER POT (Flori.). Seedling × 'Spek's Yellow'. Trial Ground No. 1121. Reg. No. 1097. *Raiser and Distributor:* A. Dickson & Sons Ltd, N. Ireland. Bloom: medium orange yellow with deeper reverse. Moderately full, 14–17 petals, medium, 3½–4 in., borne in trusses. Growth: tall, vigorous, upright. Foliage: glossy, bronzy, dark green.

*DR BARNARDO (Flori.). 'Vera Dalton' × 'Red Dandy'. Trial Ground No. 1042. Reg. No. 1178. *Raiser and Distributor:* R. Harkness & Co. Ltd, Hitchin. Bloom: crimson, full, 30 petals, 4½ in., slightly fragrant, borne in trusses. Growth: upright, bushy. Foliage: large, medium green, glossy.

*ELIZABETH HARKNESS (H.T.). 'Red Dandy' × 'Piccadilly'. Trial Ground No. 1257. Reg. No. 1235. *Raiser and Distributor:* R. Harkness & Co. Ltd, Hitchin. Bloom: red in bud opening to buff, tinged pink. Full, 34 petals, large, borne singly and several together. Slightly fragrant. Growth: upright, bushy. Foliage: medium green, semi-glossy.

*FRED GIBSON (H.T.). 'Gavotte' × 'Buccaneer'. Trial Ground No. 1339. Reg. No. 1073. *Raiser and Distributor:* John Sanday (Roses) Ltd, Almondsbury, Bristol. Bloom: amber yellow to apricot, full, 30 petals, borne singly and several together. Growth: tall and vigorous. Foliage: dark green, semi-glossy.

GINGER ROGERS (H.T.) 'Super Star' × 'Miss Ireland'. Trial Ground No. 1065. Reg. No. 1220. *Raiser:* S. McGredy IV. *Distributor:* S. McGredy & Son Ltd, N. Ireland. Bloom: salmon, moderately full, 23 petals, slightly fragrant. Growth: upright and vigorous. Foliage: medium green, coppery. (Trial Ground Certificate 1967.)

*LIEBESTRAUM (H.T.). 'Colour Wonder' × 'Liberty Bell'. Trial Ground No. 1412. Reg. No. 1180. *Raiser:* W. Kordes, Germany. *Distributor:* S. McGredy & Son Ltd, N. Ireland. Bloom: cherry red, very full, 50 petals, large, borne several together. Growth: vigorous and upright. Foliage: medium green.

MICHELLE (Flori.). Seedling × 'Orange Sensation'. Trial Ground No. 1469. Reg. No. 1239. *Raiser:* G. de Ruiter, Holland. *Distributor:* Geo. de Ruiter, Nottingham. Bloom: salmon pink, moderately full, 25 petals, 3 in., fragrant. Growth: upright and vigorous. Foliage: light green.

*SUMMER HOLIDAY (H.T.). 'Super Star' × unknown. Trial Ground No. 1180. Reg. No. 1093. *Raiser and Distributor:* C. Gregory & Son Ltd, Stapleford. Bloom: orange red with paler reverse, very full, 48 petals, fragrant. Borne singly and several together. Growth: vigorous and spreading. Foliage: medium green, semi-glossy.

*SUMMER MEETING (Flori.). 'Allgold' × 'Circus'. Trial Ground No. 1254. Reg. No. 1156. *Raiser and Distributor:* R. Harkness & Co. Ltd, Hitchin. Bloom: yellow, very full, 45 petals, 3½ in. Slightly fragrant. Borne several together and in trusses. Growth: compact, bushy, medium height. Foliage: medium to dark green, glossy.

*SUPER SUN (H.T.). Sport from 'Piccadilly'. Trial Ground No. 1337. Reg. No. 1139. *Distributor:* W. Bentley & Sons Ltd, Wanlip. Bloom: orange with scarlet shadings, paler reverse, full, 34 petals, large, borne singly and several together. Growth: upright and vigorous. Foliage: medium to dark green.

International Awards 1968

ROME

LARGE FLOWERS		
Gold Medal	'Baronne E. de Rothschild'	Louisette Meilland, France
First Certificate	'Marie-Antoinette'	Armstrong Nurseries, U.S.A.
Certificates	'Climbing Maria Callas'	Meilland, France
	Unnamed	Meilland, France
SMALL FLOWERS		
Gold Medal	Unnamed	Meilland, France
First Certificate	Unnamed	Meilland, France
Certificates	'Roman Festival'	J. B. Williams, U.S.A.
	'Starina'	Meilland, France

PARIS—BAGATELLE

Gold Medal	'Parure d'Or' (climber)	Mme. Marie Delbard, France
Silver Medal	'Roman Festival' (Flori.)	J. B. Williams, U.S.A.
Certificates	'Adair Roche' (Flori. H.T. type)	S. McGredy, N. Ireland
	'Varo–Iglo' (H.T.)	G. Verbeek, Holland
	Unnamed	Alain Meilland, France

GENEVA

LARGE FLOWERS

Gold Medal	Unnamed	
Silver Medal	'Baronne E. de Rothschild'	Louisette Meilland, France
Certificate	'Summer Holiday'	C. Gregory & Son Ltd., England

SMALL FLOWERS

Certificates	'Espéranza'	H. Delforge, Belgium
	' Taconis'	G. de Ruiter, Holland

CLIMBERS

Silver Medal	'Parure d'Or'	Delbard, France

THE HAGUE

FLORIBUNDA

Gold Medal	'Espéranza'	H. Delforge, Belgium
First Certificate	'City of Belfast'	S. McGredy, N. Ireland
Second Certificate	'Copper Pot'	A. Dickson & Sons Ltd., N. Ireland

HYBRID TEA

Gold Medal	Unnamed	M. Tantau, Germany
First Certificate	'Brasilia'	S. McGredy, N. Ireland
Second Certificate	'Timothy Eaton'	S. McGredy, N. Ireland

CLIMBER

First Certificate	'Climbing Border Coral'	C. Gregory & Son Ltd., England

In the beds of roses planted out in the Westbroekpark the International Jury awarded the *Golden Rose of The Hague* to 'Orange Sensation' (Flori.) raised by G. de Ruiter, Holland; a *First Class Certificate* to 'Parkdirektor Riggers' (climber) raised by W. Kordes, Germany and a *Second Class Certificate* to 'Tom Pillibi' (Flori.) raised by M. Combe, France. The Crystal Trophy for the most fragrant rose was awarded to 'Chinatown' (Flori.) raised by D. T. Poulsen, Denmark.

ORLÉANS

FLORIBUNDA

Golden Rose of the City of Orléans	'Sangria'	Louisette Meilland, France
First Certificate	'Zorina'	Jackson & Perkins Co., U.S.A.

RECURRENT CLIMBERS

Gold Medal	'Intervilles'	M. Robichon, France
First Certificate	'Natalie'	Hemeray-Aubert, France

U. S. A.

ALL AMERICA ROSE SELECTIONS
'Angel Face' (H.T.) raised by H. C. Swim, U.S.A.; 'Pascali' (H.T.) raised by Louis Lens, Belgium; 'Comanche' (Flori.) raised by Swim & Weeks, U.S.A. and 'Gene Boerner' (Flori.) raised by the late Eugene S. Boerner, U.S.A.

BELFAST

HYBRID TEA

Gold Medal and Prize of The City of Belfast	'Grandpa Dickson'	A. Dickson & Sons Ltd., N. Ireland
Certificates	'Lady Seton'	S. McGredy, N. Ireland
	'Criterion'	G. de Ruiter, Holland
	'Tradition'	R. Kordes, Germany

The "Uladh" Award
for fragrance   'Silver Star'   R. Kordes, Germany

FLORIBUNDA
The "Golden
Thorn" Award   'Jan Spek'   S. McGredy, N. Ireland
Certificates   'City of Leeds'   S. McGredy, N. Ireland
                  'Ice White'   S. McGredy, N. Ireland
                  'Coral Queen Elizabeth'   C. Gregory & Son Ltd., England
                  'Elka Gaarlandt'   G. A. H. Buisman, Holland

LYON

HYBRID TEA
Gold Medal and
title "La Plus Belle
Rose de France"   'Baronne E. de Rothschild'   Louisette Meilland, France
Silver-Gilt Medal 'Tanagra'   P. Gaujard, France
Certificates   Unnamed   P. Croix, France
                     'Jacques Estérel'   P. Croix, France

POLYANTHA/FLORIBUNDA
First Certificate   Unnamed   Alain Meilland, France
Second Certificate   'Prince Tango'   G. Delbard, France
Third Certificate   'Seria'   Louisette Meilland, France

CLIMBER
Certificate   'Guirlande Fleurie'   M. Robichon, France

MINIATURE
Certificate   'Starina'   Meilland, France

BELGIUM—ROEULX

LARGE FLOWERS
Gold Medal   Unnamed   Meilland, France
                'Grand Prix'   G. Delbard, France
Silver Medal Unnamed   Meilland, France
Certificate   'Blessings'   C. Gregory & Son Ltd., England

SMALL FLOWERS
Certificates   Unnamed   Meilland, France
                  'Fred Loads'   R. Holmes, England
                  'Dimples'   E. B. Le Grice, England

CLIMBER
Silver Meda   Unnamed   F. Dorieux, France

JAPAN

HYBRID TEA
Gold Medal   'Lido di Roma'   G. Delbard, France
Silver Medal   'Summer Holiday'   C. Gregory & Son Ltd., England
Bronze Medal   Unnamed   W. Kordes, Germany
Certificates   'Lady X'   A. F. Meilland, France
                 'Grand Prix'   G. Delbard, France
                 'Yu-ai'   Seizo Suzuki, Japan

MASS EFFECT
(other than H.T.)
Gold Medals   'Clg. Sarabande'   A. F. Meilland, France
                 'Starina' (Min.)   A. F. Meilland, France
Silver Medal   'City of Belfast' (Flori.)   Sam McGredy, N. Ireland
Bronze Medal   'Taconis' (Flori.)   G. de Ruiter, Holland
Certificates   'Prince Tango' (Flori.)   G. Delbard
                 Unnamed   Jan Leenders, Holland

The Rose Analysis

L. G. TURNER

It has been obvious from the analysis of the last two or three years that 'Peace' could not continue to hold on to the glory of being the top of at least one table for much longer. At last the inevitable has happened and this outstanding variety is now among the "also rans". Undoubtedly it will work back down the table for a number of years, but we cannot let its supremacy end without reference to the unequalled record it has maintained for so long. Introduced in this country in 1948 it appeared the following year at the bottom of the table for large specimen blooms and garden cultivation combined; by 1951 it was at the top of the table for large specimen blooms and within three years headed all tables for exhibition and general garden cultivation. It was the top rose every year, but for the occasional intervention of 'Ena Harkness' in one table, until 1966 when it was superseded as the premier exhibition variety. A truly outstanding achievement.

Apart from the varieties no longer eligible in the Audit of New Roses, owing to date of introduction, there are few changes in the tables, which is surprising in view of the inconsistent weather of the past summer. Varieties omitted from the hybrid tea audit are 'Gavotte', 'Uncle Walter', 'Vienna Charm', 'Pascali', 'Papa Meilland'. 'Gavotte' has done well to be placed second and eighth in the South and North tables respectively for specimen blooms. This is a popular variety at the shows and I am sure it will remain high in the table for some time. It is, however, not too happy in a wet season and the habit of the plant may not appeal to every gardener, which is possibly the reason it is lower in the tables for general garden cultivation. 'Pascali' has found a place in this table but the other three have been dropped. Newcomers to the hybrid tea audit are 'Red Devil', 'Red Lion', 'Santa Fé', 'Shannon' and 'Brandenburg'. 'Santa Fé' is a typical example of the current aim of the hybridist to produce a plant carrying on each basal stem a symmetrical inflorescence of a number of hybrid tea type blooms.

In the newer floribundas audit, 'Europeana', 'Violet Carson', 'Scarlet Queen Elizabeth', 'Manx Queen' and 'Charleston' are no longer eligible, but with the exception of the last-named all have found a place in the ordinary Floribunda table. 'Europeana' in tenth place is the most popular, but what a pity that, like its parent 'Rosemary Rose', it can be such a slave to Mildew. 'Irish Mist', 'Sir Lancelot', 'Redgold', 'Apricot Nectar' and 'Escapade' appear in the Floribunda audit for the first time.

The tables were prepared from questionnaires returned by 90 members and 6 affiliated societies to whom the Editorial Board wishes to record its thanks for the time and trouble given in making returns.

AUDIT OF NEWER ROSES—FLORIBUNDAS

This table includes only varieties introduced in this country since 1 January 1964

Position	Number of points	NAME	Introduced	COLOUR
1	737	*Elizabeth of Glamis	1964	Light salmon
2	606	City of Leeds	1966	Rich salmon
3	501	Sea Pearl	1964	Pale pink with yellow
4	376	*Arthur Bell	1965	Golden yellow, pales with age
5	342	*Scented Air	1965	Salmon pink
6	290	*Pernille Poulsen	1965	Salmon pink fading lighter
7	255	Princess Michiko	1966	Coppery orange
8	215	Irish Mist	1967	Orange salmon
9	209	*Goldgleam	1966	Deep yellow
10	196	Charlotte Elizabeth	1965	Deep rose pink tinged red
11	185	Sir Lancelot	1967	Apricot yellow
12	184	Redgold	1967	Golden yellow edged cherry red
13	172	Golden Treasure	1965	Deep yellow
14	138	Apricot Nectar	1965	Pale apricot with golden base
15	88	Escapade	1967	Magenta with white centre

FLORIBUNDA ROSES

This table includes only varieties introduced in this country before 1 January 1964

Position	Number of points	NAME	Introduced	COLOUR
1	1387	Iceberg	1958	Pure white tinged pink in bud
2	1118	Evelyn Fison	1962	Vivid red with scarlet shading
3	1091	Queen Elizabeth	1955	Clear self pink
4	796	*Orange Sensation	1961	Light vermilion
5	761	Orangeade	1959	Bright orange vermilion
6	732	Allgold	1956	Unfading golden yellow
7	723	Lilli Marlene	1959	Scarlet red
8	687	*Dearest	1960	Rosy salmon
9	652	Paddy McGredy	1962	Carmine, lighter reverse
10	647	Europeana	1963	Deep crimson
11	616	Pink Parfait	1962	Medium pink, yellow base
12	603	Anna Wheatcroft	1959	Light vermilion
13	465	Violet Carson	1963	Soft pink, silvery reverse
14	445	Circus	1955	Yellow, pink and salmon
15	387	Dorothy Wheatcroft	1960	Bright orient red
16	383	Scarlet Queen Elizabeth	1963	Orange scarlet
17	371	Paprika	1958	Bright turkey red
18	367	Woburn Abbey	1962	Orange with yellow
19	321	Masquerade	1950	Yellow, pink and red
20	319	Korona	1954	Bright orange scarlet
21	314	Manx Queen	1963	Gold, orange tipped
22	298	Frensham	1946	Deep scarlet crimson
23	267	Vera Dalton	1961	Pale camellia rose
24	235	Chanelle	1958	Cream, overlaid peach pink

* Most fragrant

THE ROSE ANALYSIS

AUDIT OF NEWER ROSES—HYBRID TEAS

This table includes only varieties introduced in this country since 1 January 1964

Posi-tion	Number of points	NAME	Intro-duced	COLOUR
1	785	*Fragrant Cloud	1964	Geranium lake
2	766	*Ernest H. Morse	1965	Rich turkey red
3	711	Grandpa Dickson	1966	Yellow fading to creamy yellow
4	530	*Diorama	1965	Apricot yellow, flushed pink
5	428	*Blue Moon	1964	Silvery lilac
6	385	Princess	1964	Vermilion
7	374	*Red Devil	1967	Scarlet with lighter reverse
8	352	*Lady Seton	1966	Deep rose pink
9	296	Norman Hartnell	1964	Deep cerise
10	241	*Red Lion	1966	Deep cerise pink
11	219	Colour Wonder	1964	Orange salmon, reverse buttercup yellow
12	186	*Mister Lincoln	1965	Dark red
13	108	Santa Fé	1967	Pink, lighter reverse
14	91	Shannon	1965	Bright pink
15	90	Brandenburg	1965	Deep salmon, lighter reverse

HYBRID TEA ROSES PRODUCING LARGE SPECIMEN BLOOMS SUITABLE FOR EXHIBITION

This table includes only varieties introduced in this country before 1 January 1964

Northern Counties

Posi-tion	Number of points	NAME	Intro-duced	COLOUR
1	253	Pink Favourite	1956	Deep rose pink
2	226	Perfecta	1957	Cream, shaded rose red
3	215	Peace	1942	Light yellow edged pink
4	183	Stella	1958	Carmine shading to cream
5	164	*Wendy Cussons	1959	Cerise flushed scarlet
6	163	Memoriam	1960	White tinted pale pink
7	158	Royal Highness	1962	Soft light pink
8	152	Gavotte	1963	Light pink with silvery reverse
9	149	*Silver Lining	1958	Pale rose with silver reverse
10	148	Isabel de Ortiz	1962	Deep pink with silver reverse
11	145	*Super Star	1960	Pure light vermilion without shading
12	111	Brilliant	1952	Rich scarlet
13	107	Chicago Peace	1962	Phlox pink, base canary yellow
14	88	Gail Borden	1956	Deep rose pink, reverse shaded creamy yellow
15	87	Margaret	1954	Pink with lighter reverse
16	86	Christian Dior	1959	Velvety scarlet
17	85	Dorothy Peach	1956	Yellow edged buff
18	78	Liberty Bell	1963	Claret rose, reverse light cream
19	77	*My Choice	1958	Pink, reverse pale yellow
20	75	Rose Gaujard	1958	White, flushed rich carmine
21	73	*Ena Harkness	1946	Bright crimson scarlet
22	72	Montezuma	1956	Deep salmon red
23	53	*Eden Rose	1950	Deep pink, lighter reverse
24	47	Anne Letts	1953	Pale pink with paler reverse

★ Most fragrant

HYBRID TEA ROSES PRODUCING LARGE SPECIMEN BLOOMS SUITABLE FOR EXHIBITION

This table includes only varieties introduced in this country before 1 January 1964

Southern Counties

Posi-tion	Number of points	NAME	Intro-duced	COLOUR
1	386	Pink Favourite	1956	Deep rose pink
2	371	Gavotte	1963	Light pink with silvery reverse
3	368	Stella	1958	Carmine shading to cream
4	350	Perfecta	1957	Cream, shaded rose red
5	335	*Wendy Cussons	1959	Cerise flushed scarlet
6	325	Isabel de Ortiz	1962	Deep pink with silver reverse
7	314	Royal Highness	1962	Soft light pink
8	310	Peace	1942	Light yellow edged pink
9	299	Memoriam	1960	White tinted pale pink
10	272	Rose Gaujard	1958	White, flushed rich carmine
11	267	Brilliant	1952	Rich scarlet
12	230	*Super Star	1960	Pure light vermilion without shading
13	211	Gail Borden	1956	Deep rose pink, reverse shaded creamy yellow
14	205	Montezuma	1956	Deep salmon red
15	199	*My Choice	1958	Pink, reverse pale yellow
16	197	*Silver Lining	1958	Pale rose with silver reverse
17	162	Chicago Peace	1962	Phlox pink, base canary yellow
18	160	Anne Letts	1953	Pale pink with paler reverse
19	136	Gold Crown	1960	Very deep yellow
20	134	Margaret	1954	Pink with lighter reverse
21	126	Karl Herbst	1950	Deep red with lighter reverse
22	111	Dorothy Peach	1956	Yellow edged buff
23	105	*Josephine Bruce	1952	Deep velvety crimson scarlet
24	78	Piccadilly	1960	Scarlet, yellow reverse

SOME HYBRID TEA ROSES FOR INDOOR DECORATION

NAME	Intro-duced	COLOUR
*Super Star	1960	Pure light vermilion without shading
*Wendy Cussons	1959	Cerise flushed scarlet
Mischief	1960	Coral salmon
Queen Elizabeth	1955	Clear self pink
*Blue Moon	1964	Silvery lilac
*Sutter's Gold	1950	Light orange shaded red
Peace	1942	Light yellow edged pink
Mojave	1954	Deep orange and reddish flame
Virgo	1947	White
Pascali	1963	White
*Lady Sylvia	1927	Light pink with yellow base
*Ernest H. Morse	1965	Rich turkey red

* Most fragrant

HYBRID TEA ROSES FOR GENERAL GARDEN CULTIVATION

This table includes only varieties introduced in this country before 1 January 1964

Northern Counties

Posi-tion	Number of points	NAME	Intro-duced	COLOUR
1	458	★Super Star	1960	Pure light vermilion without shading
2	433	★Wendy Cussons	1959	Cerise flushed scarlet
3	423	Peace	1942	Light yellow edged pink
4	366	Pink Favourite	1956	Deep rose pink
5	339	Stella	1958	Carmine shading to cream
6	334	Piccadilly	1960	Scarlet, yellow reverse
7	319	Mischief	1960	Coral salmon
8	311	★Prima Ballerina	1958	Deep pink
9	276	Rose Gaujard	1958	White flushed rich carmine
10	256	Chicago Peace	1962	Phlox pink, base yellow
11	247	Gail Borden	1956	Deep rose pink, reverse shaded creamy yellow
12	193	Perfecta	1957	Cream shaded rose red
13	181	King's Ransom	1961	Rich pure yellow
14	171	★Silver Lining	1958	Pale rose with silver reverse
15	145	★My Choice	1958	Pink, reverse pale yellow
16	125	★Ena Harkness	1946	Bright crimson scarlet
17	112	Pascali	1963	White
18	111	Margaret	1954	Pink with lighter reverse
19	106	Gold Crown	1960	Very deep yellow
20	99	Memoriam	1960	White tinted pale pink
21	97	★Eden Rose	1950	Deep pink, lighter reverse
22	96	★Josephine Bruce	1952	Deep velvety crimson scarlet
23	87	Isabel de Ortiz	1962	Deep pink with silver reverse
24	84	Gavotte	1963	Light pink with silvery reverse

REPEAT FLOWERING CLIMBERS

Posi-tion	Number of points	NAME	Intro-duced	COLOUR
1	641	Danse du Feu	1954	Orange scarlet
2	567	Golden Showers	1957	Golden yellow
3	509	★Zéphirine Drouhin	1868	Bright carmine pink
4	434	★New Dawn	1930	Pale flesh pink
5	409	Pink Perpetue	1965	Clear pink with carmine pink reverse
6	405	Mermaid	1917	Primrose yellow
7	388	Handel	1965	Cream edged rose pink
8	378	Parkdirektor Riggers	1957	Blood red
9	335	Casino	1963	Soft yellow, deeper in bud
10	317	Royal Gold	1957	Deep yellow
11	238	★Maigold	1953	Bronze yellow
12	201	Meg	1954	Pink with apricot

The following varieties may also be recommended: ★ 'Aloha', 'Bantry Bay', 'Dortmund', 'Hamburger Phoenix', 'Parade' and 'Schoolgirl'.

★ Most fragrant

HYBRID TEA ROSES FOR GENERAL GARDEN CULTIVATION

This table includes only varieties introduced in this country before 1 January 1964

Southern Counties

Posi-tion	Number of points	NAME	Intro-duced	COLOUR
1	827	*Super Star	1960	Pure light vermilion without shading
2	763	*Wendy Cussons	1959	Cerise flushed scarlet
3	736	Peace	1942	Light yellow edged pink
4	616	Rose Gaujard	1958	White flushed rich carmine
5	585	Pink Favourite	1956	Deep rose pink
6	552	Piccadilly	1960	Scarlet, yellow reverse
7	536	Mischief	1960	Coral salmon
8	529	Stella	1958	Carmine shading to cream
9	409	*Silver Lining	1958	Pale rose with silver reverse
10	401	*Prima Ballerina	1958	Deep pink
11	369	*Ena Harkness	1946	Bright crimson scarlet
12	348	*Josephine Bruce	1952	Deep velvety crimson scarlet
13	342	*My Choice	1958	Pink, reverse pale yellow
14	330	Perfecta	1957	Cream shaded rose red
15	316	Isabel de Ortiz	1962	Deep pink with silver reverse
16	300	Chicago Peace	1962	Phlox pink, base yellow
17	241	Gavotte	1963	Light pink with silvery reverse
18	236	*Eden Rose	1950	Deep pink, lighter reverse
19	200	*Sutter's Gold	1950	Light orange shaded red
20	199	Margaret	1954	Pink with lighter reverse
21	193	Pascali	1963	White
22	178	Montezuma	1956	Deep salmon red
23	160	King's Ransom	1961	Rich pure yellow
24	142	Summer Sunshine	1962	Rich yellow

WICHURAIANA CLIMBING AND RAMBLING ROSES—SUMMER FLOWERING

Suitable for pergolas and fences

Posi-tion	Number of points	NAME	Intro-duced	COLOUR
1	614	*Albertine	1921	Salmon opening to copper pink
2	494	Paul's Scarlet Climber	1915	Bright scarlet crimson
3	415	American Pillar	1902	Bright rose with white eye
4	370	Emily Gray	1916	Rich golden buff
5	333	Excelsa	1909	Bright rosy crimson
6	307	Chaplin's Pink Climber	1928	Bright pink
7	304	Dorothy Perkins	1901	Rose pink
8	265	Sanders' White	1915	White
9	264	*Albéric Barbier	1900	Yellow to creamy white
10	236	Crimson Shower	1951	Crimson
11	218	*Dr W. van Fleet	1910	Pale flesh pink
12	146	Crimson Conquest	1931	Deep scarlet, white base

* Most fragrant

CLIMBING AND RAMBLING ROSES FOR SPECIAL PURPOSES

Posi-tion	NAME	Intro-duced	COLOUR
	Suitable for walls or closeboard fencing		
1	Danse du Feu	1954	Orange scarlet
2	Mermaid	1917	Primrose yellow
3	★Albertine	1921	Salmon opening pink
4	Cl. Mrs Sam McGredy	1937	Bright orange copper
5	Royal Gold	1957	Deep yellow
6	★Maigold	1953	Bronze yellow
7	★Cl. Shot Silk	1937	Light carmine shaded orange
8	★Cl. Ena Harkness	1954	Bright crimson scarlet
9	★Cl. Etoile de Hollande	1931	Deep red
	Suitable for open fences		
1	★Albertine	1921	Salmon opening pink
2	Danse du Feu	1954	Orange scarlet
3	★New Dawn	1930	Pale flesh pink
4	Parkdirektor Riggers	1957	Blood red
5	Paul's Scarlet Climber	1915	Bright scarlet crimson
6	American Pillar	1902	Bright rose with white eye
7	Emily Gray	1916	Rich golden buff
8	★Albéric Barbier	1900	Yellow to creamy white
9	★Maigold	1953	Bronze yellow
	Suitable for pillars		
1	Golden Showers	1957	Golden yellow
2	Danse du Feu	1954	Orange scarlet
3	Handel	1965	Cream edged rose pink
4	Casino	1963	Soft yellow, deeper in bud
5	★Zéphirine Drouhin	1868	Bright carmine pink
6	Royal Gold	1957	Deep yellow
7	★Albertine	1921	Salmon opening pink
8	Paul's Scarlet Climber	1915	Bright scarlet crimson
9	Pink Perpetue	1965	Clear pink with carmine pink reverse

SHRUB ROSES—REPEAT FLOWERING

NAME	COLOUR	Height in feet
★Chinatown	Yellow sometimes tinted pink	6
★Penelope	Creamy salmon	5
Nevada	Pale creamy white sometimes with pink	6
Bonn	Orange scarlet	6
Joseph's Coat	Yellow, orange and red	5–6
★Cornelia	Pink with yellow base	5–6
Heidelberg	Bright red	5–6
Kassel	Scarlet red	6
★Felicia	Salmon pink, shaded yellow	6
Elmshorn	Light crimson	5
★Fred Loads	Vermilion orange	6–7
★Blanc Double de Coubert	Pure white	6

★ Most fragrant

SHRUB ROSES—SUMMER FLOWERING ONLY

NAME	COLOUR	Height in feet
R. moyesii	Deep red	8–10
Frühlingsgold	Clear light yellow	6
Canary Bird	Rich yellow	6
R. rubrifolia	Pink, foliage tinted mauve and grey	6
Frühlingsmorgen	Deep pink to yellow, maroon stamens	6
R. hugonis	Yellow	5
*Celestial (Alba)	Pure pink	5
R. gallica versicolor	Crimson striped pink and white	4
*Mme Hardy	White	6
*Maiden's Blush (Alba)	Warm pink shading to cream pink	5
R. cantabrigiensis	Yellow	8
R. highdownensis	Light red	8–10

REPEAT FLOWERING ROSES FOR HEDGES
Up to 5 ft

Position	NAME	Introduced	COLOUR
1	Queen Elizabeth	1955	Clear self pink
2	Iceberg	1958	Pure white
3	Peace	1942	Light yellow edged pink
4	Frensham	1946	Deep scarlet crimson
5	*Super Star	1960	Pure light vermilion without shading
6	*Chinatown	1963	Yellow sometimes tinted pink
7	Dorothy Wheatcroft	1960	Orient red with deeper shades
8	Scarlet Queen Elizabeth	1963	Orange scarlet
9	Masquerade	1950	Yellow pink and red
10	*Penelope	1924	Creamy salmon
11	Shepherd's Delight	1958	Flame, orange and yellow
12	*Fred Loads	1967	Vermilion orange

REPEAT FLOWERING ROSES FOR HEDGES
Over 5 ft

Position	NAME	Introduced	COLOUR
1	Queen Elizabeth	1955	Clear self pink
2	*Chinatown	1963	Yellow sometimes tinted pink
3	Nevada	1927	Pale creamy white, sometimes with pink
4	Bonn	1949	Orange scarlet
5	Golden Showers	1957	Golden yellow
6	Uncle Walter	1963	Scarlet with crimson shadings
7	Joseph's Coat	1963	Yellow, orange and red
8	*Zéphirine Drouhin	1868	Bright carmine pink
9	Frensham	1946	Deep scarlet crimson
10	Heidelberg	1958	Bright red
11	Kassel	1958	Scarlet red
12	*Cornelia	1925	Pink with yellow base

* Most fragrant

WEATHER RESISTANT ROSES—HYBRID TEAS

NAME	Intro-duced	COLOUR
Peace	1942	Light yellow edged pink
*Super Star	1960	Light vermilion without shading
*Wendy Cussons	1959	Cerise flushed scarlet
Stella	1958	Carmine shading to cream
*Ernest H. Morse	1965	Rich turkey red
Mischief	1960	Coral salmon
Rose Gaujard	1958	White flushed rich carmine
Piccadilly	1960	Scarlet, yellow reverse
*Fragrant Cloud	1964	Geranium lake
Pink Favourite	1956	Deep rose pink
Gail Borden	1956	Deep rose pink, reverse shaded creamy yellow
Grandpa Dickson	1966	Yellow fading to creamy yellow

WEATHER RESISTANT ROSES—FLORIBUNDAS

NAME	Intro-duced	COLOUR
Iceberg	1958	Pure white tinged pink in bud
Evelyn Fison	1962	Vivid red with scarlet shading
Queen Elizabeth	1955	Clear self pink
Orangeade	1959	Bright orange vermilion
Allgold	1956	Unfading golden yellow
Lilli Marlene	1959	Scarlet red
*Elizabeth of Glamis	1964	Light salmon
*Orange Sensation	1961	Orange vermilion
Paprika	1958	Bright turkey red
Korona	1954	Bright orange scarlet
Frensham	1946	Deep scarlet crimson
Europeana	1963	Deep crimson

MINIATURE ROSES
Mostly of about 6 to 9 in. in height, rarely more

Position	NAME	COLOUR
1	Baby Masquerade	Yellow and red
2	Rosina	Sunflower yellow
3	Coralin	Coral red to orange red
4	Pour Toi	White tinted yellow at base
5	Cinderella	White tinted carmine
6	Baby Gold Star	Golden yellow
7	Perla de Montserrat	Clear pink with deeper shadings
8	New Penny	Salmon turning pink with age
9	Colibri	Bright orange-yellow

* Most fragrant

TO A ROSE

In a world from which beauty has gone like a bell-note
   That quivered and died in the long, long ago;
A mad world, where music is changed into swingtime,
   Where speed less than sixty, is voted too slow.
Where dancing is jive, and where love seldom lingers,
   Where sentiment's "corn," and its advocates "green",
You still hold the colour and form and the scent of
   The roses I knew, back in nineteen thirteen.

You Symbol of Sanity; stand you unchanging
   Like ranges of mountains when seen from the sea?
You promise the past will return with its plenty
   And laughter and leisure again there will be.
I almost gave up all my hope for the future— —
   For people who'll live in this garden of mine . . .
Then I saw your beauty unchanged so serenely,
   And felt that the future of Man is sublime.

Admitted—I know it—the past was not perfect—
   Injustice and poverty muddied the stream;
But in vision splendid, we planned for improvement,
   For peace in the future—we followed a gleam.
But somewhere and somehow, we followed a false star
   That led us to bogs and to terrible woes . . .
My hope for amendment's now steadily growing
   For right is still right—and a rose still a rose.

                                        C. V. GODDARD

Articles for *The Rose Annual* should be submitted to the Hon. Editor by the end of August, addressed to him at The Royal National Rose Society's Offices, Bone Hill, Chiswell Green Lane, St Albans, Herts. They should be the author's own work, should not have been accepted by any other publication and should be typed in double spacing or, if hand-written, the lines should be well spaced. Black and white photographs of good definition, featuring items of general interest to members, are also welcomed.

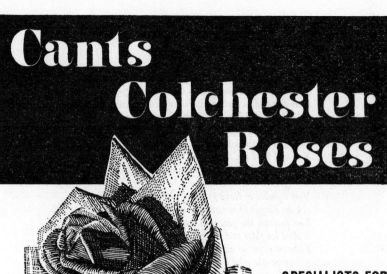

198

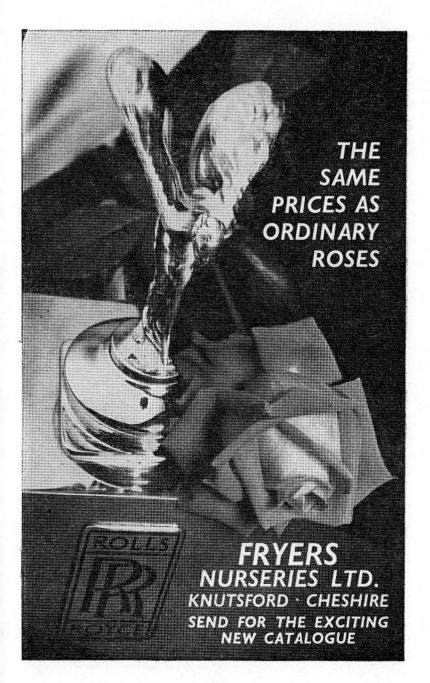

200

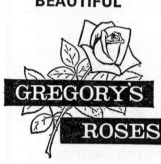

202

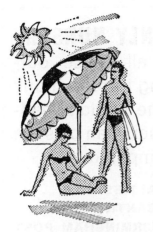

203

204

I have been working on our 1969 Catalogue, and put it aside for a few moments to write this advertisement. As my mind is full of Catalogue, I will use this space to announce that it is in many respects an entirely new and original production.

For years we have tried to make our Catalogue an honest and reliable guide. For instance, it may be perfectly true that Josephine Bruce is a glorious dark red Rose. But how many Catalogues add that it often gets mildew, and even, in some places, rust? I believe that it is only fair to tell the truth about Josephine Bruce, and about other Roses too, not excepting our own introductions.

Therefore the six vital features of each Rose are bluntly described according to our own observations— *colour: form: freedom of flower: growth: health: scent:* if known we add the Raiser, year of introduction, parentage and RNRS awards. The above qualities are boiled down to facts, none consciously avoided; none obscured by fancy fal-la-lals.

An idea occurred to me (I have not seen it done exactly in this way before) which ought to present the Roses and the information very helpfully. I shall not tell you what it is, in case some of my distinguished competitors should read this page, and start 'phoning' their printers. But I hope you will send for a copy, and believe you will want to keep it among your special things.

Jack Harkness

P.S. Send to R. Harkness & Co. Ltd. The Rose Gardens, Hitchin, Herts., for your free copy. Write now, while you think of it. We start mailing in June.

Our 1969 Introductions

Dr. Barnardo

Deep red Floribunda; flowers large, double, well formed, very free flowering; growth strong, fairly tall, bushy; appears very healthy; little scent. Harkness 1969. Ann Elizabeth × Red Dandy. RNRS Trial Ground Certificate. 10/6

Elizabeth Harkness

Pastel Hybrid Tea, off-white by creamy buff, pretty markings at centre from rose to rosy amber; flowers large, double, of very beautiful form; extremely free flowering; growth strong, forming excellent well-covered bush, medium height; appears very healthy; honey scent. Harkness 1969. Red Dandy × Piccadilly. RNRS Trial Ground Certificate. 12/6

Fairy Dancers

Pastel Floribunda, or perhaps more truly a small flowered Hybrid Tea; most unusual variety, the colours creamy buff and light rose; flowers small, borne in pretty sprays, extremely neat in formation, with very powerful appeal for floral arrangement. Very free flowering, continuity is good, growth also unusual, rather short and wide, flowers borne straight upwards; appears of good average health; sharp, if sometimes elusive fragrance. Cocker 1969. Wendy Cussons × Diamond Jubilee. 10/6

Gay Gordons

Brilliant red and yellow Hybrid Tea, after the style of Piccadilly, a deeper more satisfying yellow making it livelier still. Excellent form of flowers, they are medium HT size with far more petals than normal in this colour, giving long lasting bloom. Very free flowering; growth is bushy, on the short side. Healthy in Aberdeen, took a little black spot in Hitchin (see what an advantage immediate trial so far apart gives us). Little scent. Cocker 1969. Belle Blonde × Karl Herbst. 10/6

Glengarry

Extremely brilliant pure scarlet Floribunda; large flowers of superb high centred form; free flowering; vigorous growth, forming a handsome bush of medium height or more; appears very healthy, slight scent. Cocker 1969. Evelyn Fison × Wendy Cussons. RNRS Certificate of Merit. 10/6

Lively Lady

Brilliant vermilion Floribunda; the flowers when set beside Duke of Windsor look very similar in colour. They are large, double, of beautiful regular form; free flowering, with excellent continuity. Vigorous growth, about medium height; appears very

healthy; pleasantly, but not strongly
fragrant. Cocker 1969. Elizabeth of
Glamis × Super Star.   12/6

Marjorie Proops

Deep red Hybrid Tea with medium
HT size flowers of high centred form,
lasting well. Very free flowering; makes
a good bush of medium height.
Appears very healthy. Sweet scent.
Harkness 1969. Red Dandy × Ena
Harkness.   10/6

Tam O'Shanter

Floribunda, with corn yellow to cream
flower centres, surrounded by red. The
flowers are somewhat similar to
Orange Sensation in size, opening to
show the colour effect very clearly.
Free flowering. Growth is short,
compact. Appears healthy; slight
scent. Cocker 1969. Orange
Sensation × Circus.   10/6

White Cockade

White Climber, or could be grown as
a Shrub. The flowers are of medium

Floribunda size, and truly beautiful
HT form, with good petallage, lasting
well. Very free flowering, can compare
with Golden Showers and Rosy Mantle
in that respect. Growth is vigorous,
rather thorny, suitable as short climber.
Appears very healthy. Fragrance
pleasant, not strong. Cocker 1969.
New Dawn × Circus (Will be hard to
get this year, as we do not have many).

So few seasons have passed since we
entered the field as Rose Breeders, yet
look at the awards our Roses have already
won from the RNRS Trials.

3 Certificates of Merit

Escapade, Glengarry, King Arthur.

9 Trial Ground Certificates

Dr. Barnardo, Elizabeth Harkness,
Guinevere, Merlin, Moonraker, Sir
Lancelot, Summer Meeting, and two
un-named seedlings.

10 award-winning varieties in three
years.

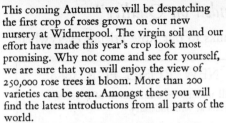

R.A.—14

210

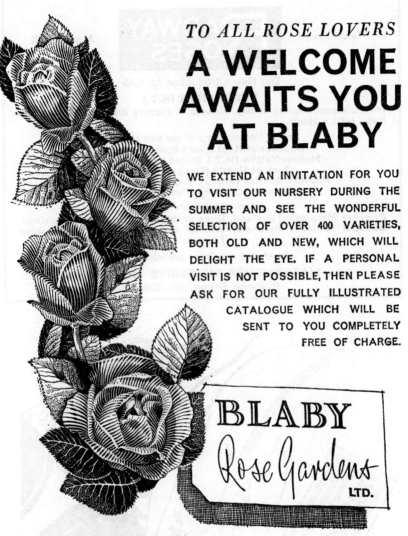

213

214

OUR OWN NEW INTRODUCTIONS FOR 1969

PATIENCE STRONG (H.T.)
Medium sized, well shaped, weather resistant, crimson scarlet flowers together with abundant, healthy, grey green foliage and attractive slightly spreading growth. This rose, we feel sure will give immense pleasure as do the verses of the charming lady in whose honour we have named it.

15/-d. each.

TIPSY (H.T.)
A very free-flowering rose of light coral-salmon; moderately vigorous and healthy. A neat plant that gives plenty of bloom. 9/6d. each.

FLIGHTY (Flori.)
We offer this rose because of its particular attraction to so many visitors to our Nurseries who have seen it growing on trial. Cherry red in bud, as the flower opens it changes to a light mauve, giving a most unusual colour effect.

9/6d. each.

TAXI (Flori.)
Medium sized double blooms of a striking vermilion; strong bushy growth with deep green, healthy foliage; a nice bedding rose. 9/6d. each.

During the summer months visit our showgrounds and see these, together with many other new and recent introductions, in full bloom.

Open Seven Days a Week   **Large Car Parks Available**

If you cannot visit us, send for our beautifully illustrated colour catalogue which will be sent to you *FREE*, as soon as it is published

BASILDON ROSE GARDENS LTD., (Dept. R.A.) BURNT MILLS ROAD, BASILDON, ESSEX

215

From THE great rose grower

3 great new roses

Manuela

I believe this will set a new standard in pinks. The deep rich rose colour gradually suffuses throughout the exquisitely formed bloom as it matures. These blooms are borne singly on stout upright stems and are extremely fragrant.

Battle of Britain

We are proud to introduce this rose in the same year as the premiere of the new epic film "The Battle of Britain". The colour is golden yellow with carmine on the outer petal edges gradually increasing in intensity as the flower grows; the form is delicate, of the traditional buttonhole type. An exceptionally vigorous rose, it flowers continuously and is amazingly resistant to rain. Very fragrant and most suitable for cutting.

Coral Star

The rich coral pink blooms of this highly recommended variety are all of exhibition quality and beautifully scented. Vigorous and healthy.

See these and many others in my free full colour catalogue available late spring 1969.

Also in my new catalogue I am offering a selection of magnificent reproductions of rose paintings by the great Pierre Joseph REDOUTÉ, imported direct from France.

Harry Wheatcroft & Sons Ltd.

Edwalton, Nottingham 17.

This year Sam McGredy has bred a new bicolour rose. Molly McGredy. Latest in a long line of award-winning roses from the world's leading hybridist. McGredy roses have taken the top international awards year after year. Many like Molly McGredy have won the President's Trophy.

For full colour catalogue write to Samuel McGredy and Son Ltd. Dept. RA, Royal Nurseries, Portadown, N. Ireland

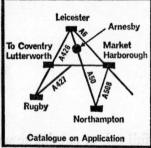
220

223

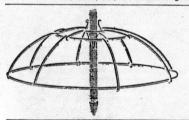

David Austin Roses

Roses for the Connoisseur

The country's most complete selection of roses, Hybrid Tea and Floribunda, including the pick of the new introductions, shrub,

old fashioned, climbing roses and many other rare and unusual roses.

New 1969

This year we are introducing for the first time a set of new hybrids, which we have developed from crosses between old fashioned varieties (mainly gallicas), and modern hybrid tea and floribunda roses. We have taken names for these charming little roses from Chaucer's Canterbury Tales, CANTERBURY, THE KNIGHT, THE WIFE OF BATH, THE PRIORESS, THE YEOMAN, THE FRIAR, DAME PRUDENCE. These have the character, charm and fragrance of the old roses, while at the same time possessing the perpetual free flowering character of the modern rose. These roses will be available only in very limited quantities this season.

New Hybrid Tea Selwyn Bird

Our hybrid tea introduction for 1969. Fragrant Cloud X Stella. This rose produces large pink and cream blooms in quantity. We believe that its continuity of flower and resistance to damp and disease and generally robust constitution mark it out as a distinct advance on Stella. Fragrant.

David Austin Limited,
Dept. A. Albrighton,
Wolverhampton, Staffs.

Fifty years ago Wheatcroft Brothers offered their first
rose trees for sale.   For fifty years gardens everywhere
have been made beautiful with Wheatcroft Roses.
Today, fifty years on, the new generation of Wheatcroft
Brothers pay tribute to the old, by continuing to grow,
for the discerning, the finest trees of the world's best varieties. These are the qualities that for fifty years have made

Wheatcroft **THE NAME IN ROSES**

227

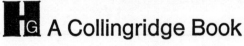

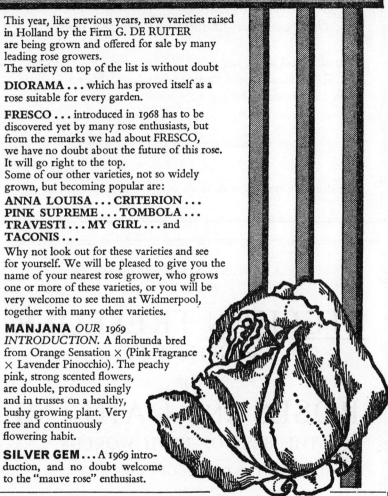
231

232

234

235

236

237

238

wholesale
growers of
quality roses
and
specialists in
the production
of budding-eyes
of new and old
varieties

wisbech plant co ltd
Lynn Road, Wisbech, Cambs.
Telephone: 2588 & 2589

239

240